de Romanis

BOOK 2:
homines

ALSO AVAILABLE FROM BLOOMSBURY

de Romanis Book 1: dei et deae, Katharine Radice, Angela Cheetham,
Sonya Kirk and George Lord

Latin to GCSE Part 1, Henry Cullen and John Taylor

Latin to GCSE Part 2, Henry Cullen and John Taylor

Latin Stories, Henry Cullen, Michael Dormandy and John Taylor

Aeneas: Virgil's Epic Retold for Younger Readers, Emily Frenkel

Essential GCSE Latin, John Taylor

Supplementary resources for *de Romanis* Books 1 and 2 can be found at
www.bloomsbury.com/de-romanis-resources

Please type the URL into your web browser and follow the instructions to
access the Companion Website. If you experience any problems, please
contact Bloomsbury at academicwebsite@bloomsbury.com

de Romanis

BOOK 2:
homines

KATHARINE RADICE,
ANGELA CHEETHAM,
SONYA KIRK AND
GEORGE LORD

BLOOMSBURY ACADEMIC
LONDON • NEW YORK • OXFORD • NEW DELHI • SYDNEY

BLOOMSBURY ACADEMIC
Bloomsbury Publishing Plc
50 Bedford Square, London, WC1B 3DP, UK
1385 Broadway, New York, NY 10018, USA

BLOOMSBURY, BLOOMSBURY ACADEMIC and the Diana logo
are trademarks of Bloomsbury Publishing Plc

First published in Great Britain 2020

Cover design: Terry Woodley
Cover image © graphixel/Getty

A catalogue record for this book is available from the British Library.

A catalog record for this book is available from the Library of Congress.

ISBN: PB: 978-1-3501-0007-7
       ePDF: 978-1-3501-0009-1
       eBook: 978-1-3501-0008-4

Typeset by RefineCatch Limited, Bungay, Suffolk
Printed and bound in India

To find out more about our authors and books visit www.bloomsbury.com and sign up for our newsletters.

CONTENTS

Latin stories are printed in **blue** in the chapter lists below.

Contents

PREFACE TO BOOK 2

THE STRUCTURE OF *DE ROMANIS*

de Romanis has two volumes. Book 1: *dei et deae* focuses on stories about the gods and aspects of Roman religion. Book 2: *homines* discusses Rome's major political revolutions and the impact Rome's growing power had on its own community and the countries it conquered.

There are six chapters in each book, and each of these chapters contains five different sections.

1. **Introduction**: this will introduce you to the theme of each chapter, and give you the knowledge of Roman culture and context that will help you make sense of the Latin stories.

2. **Sources to Study**: each chapter includes four different sources that offer you the chance to understand something about the Romans from a direct engagement with the evidence we have.

3. **Questions for Discussion**: these are wide-reaching questions that encourage you to reflect upon the cultural and historical content of each chapter in an analytical and imaginative way.

4. **Core Language**: this contains all the new Latin material for the chapter. In the Core Language section you will find 30 new words to be learned, and the explanations of new grammar. There are sentences to translate from Latin to English, and stories written in Latin which will help you learn more about the world of the Romans. The exercises within a chapter make use of the new words for that chapter, and so it is important to learn the new vocabulary at the start. Each chapter also uses words from previous chapters; if you forget any of these, you can look them up in the Vocabulary List at the back of the book.

5. **Additional Language**: these exercises offer further practice for the grammar and vocabulary introduced in each chapter and can be tackled as you work through the Core Language to supplement the exercises there. There are many different types of Additional Language exercises, and they will help you strengthen your understanding by practising material in different ways. The Additional Language exercises also provide the opportunity to translate from English into Latin.

It is unlikely that you will complete all the material in each chapter: there is a wide range so that it is possible for you and your teacher to pick and choose the material which is most helpful for reinforcing or extending the content of each Core Language section.

REFERENCE MATERIAL

At the back of the book are three reference sections:

1. **Reference Grammar**: this section contains a summary of all the grammar for the book and explanations about how the different forms of Latin are used. It is a very useful section for revision, or for checking the form of a word.

2. **Glossary of Names**: the names of people, gods or places which are important for each chapter are listed at the start of the Core Language section. Unlike the other names that appear in the Latin stories, these names do not appear in the vocabulary lists underneath each story. If you forget a name, you can look it up in the Glossary of Names.

3. **Vocabulary List**: this contains all the core vocabulary which you will meet in this book. If you forget a word, you can look it up here, either from Latin into English, or from English into Latin. Sometimes the Latin stories use words that are not part of the chapter vocabulary lists: the meanings for these are given at the end of each story and they do not appear in the vocabulary list at the back.

SUPPLEMENTARY MATERIALS ONLINE

de Romanis is supplemented by a range of materials available online via the Bloomsbury companion website:

www.bloomsbury.com/de-romanis-resources

Among these materials are the following.

Teacher's Guide containing:

- a detailed explanation of the course's structure and design
- guidance for teaching the new content within each chapter.

Culture and context materials:

- Power Point presentations to introduce the background material for each chapter
- worksheets for students to complete based on the introductory material for each chapter
- suggested links to relevant videos
- multiple choice interactive quizzes.

Language materials:

- malleable copies of the Latin text for each Latin story
- comprehension questions for two of the Latin stories within each chapter
- PDF worksheets for each of the Additional Language exercises
- a spreadsheet of all the words from the chapter vocabulary lists so that words can be sorted by part of speech or by chapter
- links to interactive exercises such as vocabulary testing.

Some materials will only be accessible to teachers. These are:

- end of chapter tests for all 12 chapters
- answers for all Core Language and Additional Language exercises

Where online materials correspond to particular exercises in the book, you will see a
icon in the margin.

TIMELINE

This timeline will help you understand how some of the important events and the people you
will meet in Chapters 7–12 of *de Romanis* fit into the broader span of Rome's history.

the very beginnings of time		The mythical origin of the world, and the rise of the Olympian gods.
pre-9th century BC		The age of heroes, many of whom fought in the great war between Troy and Greece. The founding father of the Romans, Aeneas, was believed to have fought in the Trojan War. When Troy lost, he travelled to Italy to start a new community there.
8th–7th centuries BC		Greek myths and legends began to be written down. Over time, many of these stories were adopted by the Romans and absorbed into Roman culture.
mid-8th century BC	Roman kings	Romulus and Remus, the twin sons of the god Mars, were believed to have founded a small city in central Italy. Romulus killed his brother and the city was named Rome.
late 6th century BC		In 509 BC, the Romans expelled Tarquinius Superbus, their seventh and last king and became a Republic. Brutus, the leader of the rebellion, became one of Rome's first consuls.
5th century BC		The city-states of Greece at this time led the western world in art, architecture, literature and philosophy. In time, their achievements in these fields would all influence Roman culture heavily.
4th century BC	The Roman Republic	Tribes from modern-day France, known as the Gauls, attacked the city of Rome and nearly won. The Romans were able to repel their stealth attack because of a warning from Juno's sacred geese.
3rd century BC		The Romans fought a series of wars against Carthage, a powerful city in north Africa. Hannibal, Carthage's most successful general, brought the Romans to the brink of defeat, but the tide turned when the daring general Scipio defeated the Carthaginians on their own turf. After this, Rome became the dominant power in the Mediterranean.

2nd century BC		Rome defeated Greece and absorbed much of Greek culture. The Roman army underwent a series of reforms, initiated by Marius' tactical and logistical brilliance.
		Roman society struggled to handle the imbalance in power its growing wealth and success brought. This led to widespread civil wars. In 88 BC, Sulla marched his soldiers into Rome itself. As the years rolled on, there was frequent violence on the streets of Rome as nobles started to use force to achieve their aims. The leader of one such attempted coup, Catiline, was controversially condemned to death in 63 BC by the famous orator Cicero, one of Rome's consuls at the time.
1st century BC		Julius Caesar, arguably Rome's best-known general, won significant areas of new territory for Rome and established Roman rule in Gaul. He then led his army in a civil war against Pompey and the Roman senate. Caesar defeated his opponents and was appointed dictator for life. Many Romans believed that he wanted to be king, and on this basis he was assassinated in 44 BC. His death triggered another civil war between his opponents (the Liberators), and those who wished to defend his name.
		Julius Caesar's nephew and adopted son, Octavian, established himself as one of Rome's most wealthy and powerful nobles. He formed an alliance with Mark Antony and Lepidus, but over time this alliance crumbled. Octavian held power in Rome and the west of Rome's empire; Antony ruled in the east, where he fell in love with the Egyptian queen, Cleopatra. By 30 BC Rome was in the grip of a major civil war, from which Octavian emerged as the winner. He was renamed Augustus and became the first Roman emperor. He declared peace across the Roman empire.
1st century AD	Roman emperors	In AD 14 Tiberius, Augustus' heir, became emperor after Augustus' death. This established the position as a hereditary role. He was followed by Caligula, Claudius and Nero.
		In AD 43 the emperor Claudius won territory in Britain and established the Roman province of Britannia.
		Under the reign of Nero, Boudicca led the Iceni in a major rebellion against Roman rule in Britain in the 60s AD.
2nd century AD		In AD 117 The Roman empire reached its greatest size under the emperor Trajan.
		The emperor Hadrian rebuilt the Pantheon, Rome's most well-known temple. In AD 122 he gave orders for a wall to be built across the northern border of Britannia.

CHAPTER 7
THE HISTORY OF
ROME – KINGS AND
THE REPUBLIC

CW Chapter 7: Introduction

The story of Rome: history or myth?

The Romans were very interested in their own identity and much of the Latin we read today comes from the history books written by authors such as Livy, Sallust and Tacitus. By the time these were written, the city of Rome was already over 700 years old. As Livy himself acknowledges, the stories which make up the beginning of Rome's history are more like myth than fact. For the Romans, these stories were interesting nonetheless because they offered an insight into Rome's character and values. As discussed in Book 1, many of these

FIGURE 7.1 *Intervention of the Sabine Women* **by Jacques-Louis David**

This painting was created in 1799 and it is now part of the collection in the Louvre in Paris, France. It shows the Romans fighting the Sabines after the theft of the Sabine women, and the dramatic moment when the women ran onto the battlefield to stop the fighting. The central figure is Hersilia, the new wife of Romulus and the daughter of the Sabine leader. Romulus is positioned on the right hand side; on his shield is an image of the she-wolf who saved him. Hersilia's young children are at her feet: she reminds the two sides that they are now related by marriage, and that the men at war are fathers and grandfathers to the same children.

stories show us the characteristics which the Romans admired, qualities such as courage, hard work, and a readiness to put one's community first.

Many of these stories, however, also have a darker flavour to them. As you read in Book 1, Rome's first king, Romulus, killed his own brother and the Romans' first wives were stolen from the families of their Sabine neighbours. This abduction caused war between the Romans and the Sabines, and men now related by marriage killed each other on the battlefield. In this chapter you will read a story from later in Rome's history: Exercise 7.5 tells the story of Publius Horatius, who won an outstanding victory, but then murdered his sister in a fit of rage when he returned to Rome. Horatius' sister had been engaged to one of the men he had killed, and he was furious when she wept at his death. Stories like these show us that there are often tensions within communities, and the need to avenge a crime can cause further harm. Loyalties to the different people within one's community can often pull in different directions; this too can bring betrayal and hurt. The Romans were proud of their city's glorious rise to power, but they understood that their community had not grown by good deeds alone.

From roughly the 3rd century BC onwards, our understanding of Roman history is built more on facts than myth. Buildings, inscriptions, sculpture and coins provide information about who held power and why. In addition, the Romans kept careful records of their decisions, their rulers and their practices. Roman writers often made use of these records when they wrote their own history. It is important to understand, however, that creative storytelling continued to lie at the heart of the way the Romans described their past. The work of Roman historians is rich in vibrant character descriptions, imaginative speeches and powerful emotions. As Livy notes in the preface to his extensive history of Rome, his interest is not so much in the dry facts of the past as in the lives, the customs, the people and the skills through which Rome's power grew so great.

Rome ruled by kings

According to myth, Romulus was the first king of Rome. Six kings followed Romulus, and the reign of the kings lasted for over 200 years. The kings, however, were not the only people to hold power in Rome. Romulus was said to have created Rome's two most important political institutions: the people's assemblies and the senate.

The people's assemblies were a vital part of the Roman kingdom. Their original role was to vote on the proposals put before them by the king. The number and structure of assemblies changed over time, but it is thought that the oldest one, known as the comitia curiata, was created by Romulus. Romulus had divided the people of Rome into three tribes, each managed by an official known as a tribune. Each tribe was then divided into ten groups, called curiae. These divisions helped the king to arrange taxes and raise armies from the

FIGURE 7.2 The Roman forum

The forum was the centre of public life in the city, where one could witness criminal trials, political speeches, religious ceremonies and ordinary people conducting business. The details of the buildings which still remain provide an excellent insight into the history of Rome.

citizens. When representatives from all thirty curiae met together, they formed an assembly. Whenever the king wanted to pass a new law, he would gather this assembly to seek the approval of the people.

The Roman senate was originally an advisory council, chosen by Romulus to help him rule. Romulus picked one hundred men to join the senate, each one the head of a leading Roman family. The members of the original senate were known as the *patres*, and their families became known as patricians. These patrician families formed Rome's aristocracy. Romans who were not part of these distinguished families were known as plebeians and their social status was lower.

As you will read in Exercise 7.2, when Romulus died, it fell to the senate to decide who should replace him as Rome's king. After some debate, the senate decided that the king should be elected by the people. The assembly now had two main powers: the power to vote on the passing of laws, and the power to elect the men who would rule them.

Each of the kings was believed to have left his mark on Roman society, either by conquering new territory or by creating new buildings and institutions. For example, Rome's second king, Numa, was renowned for developing many of Rome's early religious practices and laws. As mentioned in Chapter 3, Numa built the Temple of Janus which served as a visible sign of whether Rome was at war or not. The fifth king, Tarquinius Priscus, established the Circus Maximus and the annual chariot races during the Ludi Romani, as you read in Chapter 5.

As Rome's political institutions developed, power became increasingly linked to wealth. The sixth king, Servius Tullius, created a new assembly, known as the comitia centuriata, which was attended by all the citizens of Rome. The wealth of a citizen, however, now determined the order in which they voted and the votes of the wealthy carried more weight than those of the poor. The wealthy minority could easily outvote the poorer majority. The rich held power and not every vote was equal at Rome.

FIGURE 7.3 **Cloaca Maxima**

Tarquinius Priscus, the fifth king of Rome, was thought to have begun the construction of the *Cloaca Maxima* in the late 7th century BC. It started as an open-air canal that ran through the Roman forum and it was used to drain the local marshes. Eventually it was covered over and turned into a sewer, carrying waste to the River Tiber. As you can see, some of the ancient structure is still visible in Rome today.

The last king: Tarquin the Proud

The seventh and final king, Lucius Tarquinius, was a notorious character. Livy writes that the sixth king, Servius, had married his two daughters to the two sons of the fifth king, Tarquinius Priscus. Servius' elder daughter, Tullia, believed her husband to be cowardly and unambitious; Lucius Tarquinius, the husband of her sister, however, was rather different. Tullia and Lucius Tarquinius plotted, murdered their spouses and married each other. As you will read in Source 7.1, Tullia then urged her new husband to seize power. He criticised Servius in front of the senators and, when the king arrived to defend himself, he forced him from the senate and had him killed. To add insult to injury, Tullia drove over her dead father's body in a chariot. Lucius Tarquinius refused to bury the former king, earning for himself the title *Superbus*, an adjective which refers to the characteristic of arrogance, or a readiness to think oneself above others or the law.

Lucius Tarquinius Superbus is known in English as Tarquin the Proud. He ruled through violence and intimidation, killing senators who did not agree with him and handing out death sentences without listening to advisors. As you will read in Exercise 7.7, the final straw came in 509 BC when Tarquin's son raped a Roman noblewoman named Lucretia in her own home. After this horrendous deed had taken place, Lucretia summoned her father and husband to tell them what had happened before killing herself out of shame. Her relatives quickly gathered a group of followers who marched to Rome and drove the king and his family into exile.

The crimes of Tarquin the Proud and his family were seen as the result of a system that allowed one man to hold too much power. Never again would kings rule in Rome. Even the word *rex* became toxic, used as an insult against Romans whose power became too great. A new system of government was set up to avoid men like Tarquin ever ruling Rome again. The senate continued to discuss laws and make recommendations, but the people now elected their rulers on a yearly basis. Under the new system, power lay firmly in the hands of the people. The Latin label for this – *res publica* – became the name for the new form of government: the Roman Republic.

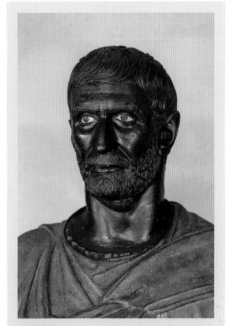

FIGURE 7.4 **Brutus, one of the founders of the Roman Republic**

Brutus was the nephew of Tarquin the Proud, but he helped to lead the rebellion against the royal family. This bronze bust was made several hundred years after his death. It is currently held in the Capitoline Museums in Rome.

The Roman Republic

The kings had ruled for life, but now elected officials known as magistrates governed the Republic, all holding office for just one year at a time. The magistrates' role was to conduct the business of government and to discuss which decisions would be best for the Roman state. The most senior position within the Republic was the consulship. The consuls had the power to chair meetings of the senate, to propose laws for the assembly to vote on, and to lead armies in war. Every year, the Romans elected two consuls. This was because if they were to elect only one, he might start to behave like a king. At the heart of this system were the principles that power should be shared and that decisions were made best by discussion and agreement.

The senate continued to be the most important institution within the Republic: the size of the senate changed over time, but it averaged 300–500 members. Originally, the kings had decided who could join the senate, but in the Republic, membership was open to people who were wealthy enough and had held one of the elected offices of the Republic. This meant that, even in the Republic, wealth and political power continued to be linked.

FIGURE 7.5 **Fasti Capitolini for 264–172 BC**

During the Republic, new consuls were elected each year, and the names of these consuls were used as a way to record dates. For example, instead of 264 BC, the Romans would say 'during the consulship of Appius Claudius and Marcus Fulvius'. The Romans kept records of these names on marble tablets, called the *Fasti Capitolini* or *Fasti Consulares*, and it is thought that these records ran from 483 BC to AD 13. Originally the *Fasti* would have been on display in the forum, but the reconstructed fragments shown here are now in the Capitoline Museums in Rome.

Dictators

There was, however, an exception to the principles that power should be shared and decisions should be made through discussion and agreement. In times of emergency, such as foreign invasion, decisive action was required instead of debate and discussion. It was feared that two consuls might not agree on what to do and that this disagreement might endanger the Republic. To avoid this problem, the two consuls could be replaced by a temporary, higher magistrate known as a dictator. A dictator was empowered to make all necessary decisions to protect the Republic. As soon as the crisis had been resolved, or after a period of six months, the dictator was expected to resign his office and allow the Republic to return to its annual elections. This was to avoid the dictator behaving like a king.

Some dictators, such as Cincinnatus, whom you will meet in Exercise 7.9, obeyed this rule, but a few did not and remained in office for longer. Most famously, Julius Caesar, as you will read in Chapter 9, was made dictator on four separate occasions. On the last of these he was declared dictator for life. It was no surprise that some Romans thought things had come full circle and that they were ruled by a king again, just with a different title. It is for this reason that Caesar was assassinated in 44 BC.

Different forms of power: *imperium, auctoritas*, wealth, patronage and corruption

So far we have discussed the structure of political power in Rome, but it is important to note that an individual's power could have more than one form. The power to command, *imperium,* was the power held by the higher elected magistrates: the more senior the magistrate, the greater his *imperium*. It was an official power and it was limited to the magistrates' time in office. *auctoritas*, however, was the influence a Roman held as a result of his own past deeds and the deeds of his family. The senate was full of people who had once held *imperium* as magistrates and then relied on their *auctoritas* to have their opinions taken seriously. Exercise 7.11 tells the story of a disagreement between Quintus Fabius Maximus and the new consul Publius Cornelius Scipio. Fabius was at the time the most senior man in the senate, the *princeps senatus:* Scipio, as consul, held greater *imperium*, but Fabius relied on his great *auctoritas* to try to persuade the senators to agree with him instead of the young consul Scipio.

In addition to *imperium* and *auctoritas*, wealth was very clearly linked to power in Rome and continued to be a huge dividing factor in society. As we have seen, membership of the senate depended partly on a citizen's wealth, and within the assemblies the votes of the rich continued to be counted first and were worth more than the votes of the poor. Furthermore, Roman society was interconnected by a system known as patronage. Poorer Romans would seek to become clients of wealthier citizens, who were known as patrons. In most cases these relationships acted as a sort of welfare safety net. A patron could offer support to his clients in the form of money, favours or the promise to help in legal matters. In return, it was not unreasonable for a patron to expect his clients to support him and his family, particularly during elections. The wealthier the patron, the more clients he was likely to have; this meant that wealthy citizens who had a large number of clients had an advantage when it came to securing votes.

It is important to note that wealth also brought with it a very raw form of power. Wealthy and ruthless Romans could bribe voters to support certain candidates or even pay thugs to intimidate their opponents with threats and acts of violence. In Source 7.4 you can read an account of corruption in the assembly. Throughout the history of the Republic, laws were passed which tried to prevent this: for example, one law sought to narrow the passageways used by people queueing up to vote so that men could not move up and down the line offering bribes. Strict penalties could be imposed for those who were found guilty of disobeying these laws: the penalties included being banned from standing in elections, exile or even death.

FIGURE 7.6 **Modern-day SPQR fire hydrant cover**

SPQR is the abbreviation of *senatus populusque Romanus* or 'the senate and the people of Rome'. By the 1st century BC, the Republic was often referred to in this way and the abbreviation regularly appeared on coins, documents and monuments. The title has continued to be used and it is one of the official emblems of the modern-day city of Rome.

The strengths and weaknesses of the Roman Republic

At its core, the Roman Republic was a system of shared power. It placed emphasis on debate, discussion and consensus. There were clear strengths to it and it was a relatively stable form of government. The famous democracy of ancient Athens survived for just under two hundred years, but the Roman Republic lasted for almost five hundred. Crucially, during this time, the city of Rome became the dominant force in Italy, then the Mediterranean and finally the world.

There were, however, several weaknesses too. The Republic had put power more directly into the hands of the people, but there was still significant inequality in Roman society. As noted above, citizens were divided by wealth and ancestry and, when it came to political rights, there were stark differences by gender: male citizens could vote in elections and stand for office, but women could not. In addition, citizens had greater rights than freedmen and slaves. Freedmen could vote, but they were not allowed to stand for office. Slaves had no political rights whatsoever.

Moreover, there was tension between the principles of shared power and the role of wealth and individual ambition. Wealth was unevenly distributed and had too much influence on important matters. As Rome's territory expanded, so too did its wealth and the power-gap between rich and poor grew wider. Individual ambition meant that Rome's elite competed for success in a way that was increasingly aggressive. By the 1st century BC, power struggles between individual Romans were on such a large scale that they resulted in repeated civil wars. The focus of Chapters 8–11 is on the historical figures who led these power struggles during the final days of the Roman Republic and the ways and means in which they built their own power and destroyed the power of their enemies.

FIGURE 7.7 **Four slaves attend their *domina***

Slavery was one of the clearest signs of inequality in Roman society. This carved scene dates from the 1st century BC: it shows a wealthy lady sitting in a finely made chair. Around her, four slaves help her with her hair and appearance. It is hard to know how many slaves there were in Rome at any one time, but it is estimated that by the end of the 1st century BC the ratio of slave to free citizens may have been as high as 1:3.

CHAPTER 7: SOURCES TO STUDY

Source 7.1: Tullia and Tarquin

In the late 1st century BC *and early 1st century* AD, *the historian Livy wrote a long history of Rome, stretching from its earliest beginnings right up to Livy's own time. In Book 1 of his history, Livy relates some of the horrific crimes which marred the end of the Roman kingdom. One of these is told in the extract below.*

The sixth king of Rome, Servius, had married his two daughters to the two sons of the fifth king of Rome. The elder of these two daughters, Tullia, was ruthless and ambitious in character, and she found her equal in Tarquin, her sister's husband. Tullia and Tarquin conspired: they murdered their spouses and married each other. According to Livy, at Tullia's request, Tarquin tried to seize the throne from his father-in-law and, when he met opposition from Servius, used violence to take power. Tullia responded to the murder with savage contempt.

Young and vigorous as he was, Tarquin seized the aged Servius round the waist, picked him up and threw him out from the senate, down the steps and into the street below. Then he went back into the building to get control of the senators. The king's attendants and retinue fled. While Servius himself was making his way half-stunned and unattended to the palace, he was caught and killed by Tarquin's assassins.

It is thought that the deed was done at Tullia's suggestion; and such a crime was not, at least, inconsistent with her character. All agree that she drove into the forum in an open carriage in a most brazen manner, and, calling her husband from the senate, was the first to hail him as king. Tarquin told her to go home, as the crowd might be dangerous; so she started off, and at the top of Cyprus street, where the shrine of Diana stood until recently, her driver was turning to the right to climb the Urban hill on the way to the **Esquiline**, when he pulled up short in sudden terror and pointed to Servius' body lying mutilated on the road. Then there was a foul and inhuman crime – history preserved the memory of it in the name of the street, the Street of Crime. The story goes that the crazed woman, driven to frenzy by the terrifying ghosts of her dead sister and husband, drove the carriage over her father's body. Blood from the corpse stained her clothes and spattered the carriage, so that a grim relic of the murdered man was brought by those gory wheels to the house where she and her husband lived. The household gods of that family did not forget it; they were to see to it, in their anger at the beginning of a bad reign, that as bad an end should follow.

> The **Esquiline** was the name given to the largest of the seven hills of Rome.

Livy, *The Early History of Rome* Book 1.48 (trans. adapted)

Source 7.1: Questions

1 Describe in detail how Tarquin removed Servius from the senate.
2 Who killed Servius?
3 What did Tullia do in the forum to help establish her husband as the new king?
4 Why did Tarquin tell Tullia to go home? What does this show about some of the Romans' reaction to Tarquin's attempt to seize power?
5 Livy then describes a 'foul and inhuman crime': what was this?
6 List as many details as you can from this story which highlight the brutal characters of Tullia and Tarquin.

Source 7.2: Good morals of the early Republic

Sallust lived through the final years of the Roman Republic and he wrote several works of history. He is famous for his interest in Roman morals, and his writing often suggests that the Romans of his day had fallen a long way from the good behaviour that characterized the start of the Roman Republic.

Then, when the rule of the kings had turned into lawlessness and tyranny, they changed their form of government and established for themselves yearly terms of office and two rulers. In this way they thought that the human spirit would be least likely to grow arrogant through unlimited power. Once they had gained freedom from the kings, it is incredible how quickly the Roman state grew, since such great desire for glory had come over them.

The young Roman men, as soon as they were old enough for war, learned – through hard work in the military camps – a soldier's duties, and they had a greater passion for gleaming armour and war horses than for prostitutes and parties. Therefore, for such men, hard work was not unfamiliar, no terrain was hard-going or steep, no armed enemy was terrifying. Their greatest contests were between each other and for glory: each man hurried to strike the enemy, to climb a wall, to be seen while doing such a deed. They believed this to be wealth, this to be a fine reputation and a great nobility.

Good customs were practised at home and while serving in the army. There was the greatest harmony, the least greed, and fair play thrived among them because of their own nature just as much as because of their laws. In their offerings to the gods they were lavish, at home they were thrifty, towards their friends they were loyal. They protected themselves and their community by these two qualities: boldness in war, and, when there was peace, fairness.

Sallust, *Bellum Catilinae,* 6.7–9.3 (with omissions)

Source 7.2: Questions

1 In your own words, explain the reason Sallust gives for the Romans' decision to replace the rule of kings with two consuls who would rule for one year at a time only.
2 How did military training benefit the character of the young men at the start of the Roman Republic?
3 Sallust writes that 'their greatest contests were between each other and for glory'. What sorts of actions does Sallust claim the Romans thought glorious?
4 What does Sallust tell us about the way the Romans treated the gods, their friends and their money at the start of the Roman Republic?
5 What do you think about early Roman society as described by Sallust? Was it a community in which you would like to have lived? Explain your answer.

Source 7.3: *Imperium* and *auctoritas* in the Roman Republic

As explained in the introduction to this chapter, the Romans distinguished between auctoritas, *which was the personal influence someone might have, and* imperium, *which was the power that came with holding office.*

*The source below was written in the 2nd century AD, but it tells a story from the 3rd century BC. In this anecdote, the son of the illustrious Roman noble **Quintus Fabius Maximus** was elected consul the year after his father. When the two men met on horseback, there was a moment of confusion. The elder Fabius deserved respect both because he was the younger Maximus' father and because he was a famous and influential Roman with great* auctoritas. *The younger Fabius, however, surrounded by his bodyguards, wielded the* imperium *of a consul.*

> You can read more about **Quintus Fabius Maximus** in Exercise 7.11.

The father, while riding a horse, met his son the consul, and did not wish to dismount because he was his father. The bodyguards, because they knew that there was the greatest harmony between father and son, did not dare to order him to dismount. When the son drew close, he then – as consul – said, 'What next?' The bodyguard who was there quickly understood what he meant, and ordered the elder Fabius to dismount. The father obeyed the command and praised his son, since he was upholding the power which he had as the gift of the people.

Aulus Gellius, *Attic Nights* 2.2.13 (with omissions)

Source 7.3: Questions

1 Explain in your own words why the elder Fabius did not dismount when he met his son on horseback.
2 Why do you think the consul's bodyguards did not at first order the elder Fabius to dismount?
3 When did the elder Fabius dismount and how did he respond to his son?
4 In the context of what you have read in this chapter, what does the elder Fabius mean when he describes his son's power as 'the gift of the people'?
5 What do you think this story shows about the power of the consuls and the relative importance of *imperium* and *auctoritas*?

Source 7.4: Corruption in the Republic

This source dates from the turbulent end of the Roman Republic. It is from a letter written by the statesman Cicero to his friend Atticus in 61 BC. A proposal had been discussed and agreed in the senate and it was due to be put before the assembly for a vote. In the extract below Cicero conveys his shock that Piso, the consul responsible for the proposal, made a U-turn and spoke against it before the assembly. In addition, thugs hired by an unscrupulous noble, Clodius, disrupted the voting process. After a powerful speech by a noble called Cato, the senate was gathered once again, this time to vote on the decision that both consuls – including Piso – should urge the Roman people to support the proposal.

> **Optimates** was the label Cicero gave to (what he viewed as) the better class of politicians who acted in accordance with Republican principles.

When the day came for the proposal to be put to the assembly under the terms of the senatorial decree, there was a flocking together of our young upstarts to plead for its rejection. What's more, the very man who had made the proposal in the senate, Piso, our consul, spoke against it. Clodius' hired thugs had taken possession of the voting gangways. The voting tablets were distributed to the voters without any 'yes' votes among them. Suddenly, up springs Cato to the platform and gives Piso the consul a spectacular battering, if one can apply such a term to a most impressive, powerful, in fact wholesome speech. He was joined by our friend Hortensius and many honest men besides, Favonius' contribution being especially notable. At this rally of **optimates** the assembly was dismissed, and the senate summoned. A full house voted a decree instructing the consuls to urge the people to accept the proposal. Piso fought against it, and Clodius went on his knees to every member individually, but Curio, who proposed the rejection of the decree, only got about 15 votes against a good 400 on the other side. So that was that.

Cicero, *Letters to Atticus* A.14 (I.14) (with omissions, trans. adapted)

Source 7.4: Questions

1 How does Cicero make it clear that he disapproves of the young men who turned up to the assembly to speak against the bill?
2 What did Clodius do to disrupt the voting process?
3 How does Cicero make it clear that he approves of Cato?
4 The proposal was taken back to the senate for further discussion. Cicero tells us that three men opposed the proposal. Who were they?
5 Cicero tells us that Clodius 'went on his knees to every member individually': what does this suggest about Clodius' character?
6 What was the result of the vote in the senate? Does this affect your opinion of Clodius?
7 Based on this extract, what is your impression of the Republic: do you think it presents the political process as a failure or a success?

CHAPTER 7: QUESTIONS FOR DISCUSSION

1 How useful are the stories of Rome as a way of learning about early Roman history?

You might like to consider

- the values and characteristics they present
- the role of an author's imagination
- the impact upon the reader
- the differences between a story and, for example, an inscription

2 Do you think the Roman Republic was an improvement on rule by kings or not?

You might like to consider

- the stories which survive about the kings
- the political principles of the Republic
- the weaknesses within the Republic

3 Would you like to have lived during the Roman Republic?

You might like to consider

- the rights of men, women, freedmen and slaves
- the principles of government
- the system of patronage
- the role of wealth

ⓒⓦ Chapter 7: Core Language Vocabulary List

ambulō	ambulāre, ambulāvī	walk
habitō	habitāre, habitāvī	live
līberō	līberāre, līberāvī	set free
salūtō	salūtāre, salūtāvī	greet
dīcō	dīcere, dīxī	say; speak; tell
domina	dominae, f	mistress
Rōma	Rōmae, f	Rome
via	viae, f	street; road; way
dominus	dominī, m	master
hortus	hortī, m	garden
lībertus	lībertī, m	freedman; ex-slave
mūrus	mūrī, m	wall
nūntius	nūntiī, m	messenger
forum	forī, n	forum; market place
cīvis	cīvis, m / f	citizen
senātor	senātōris, m	senator
clārus	clāra, clārum	famous; clear
paucī	paucae, pauca	few; a few
omnis	omne	all; every
hic	haec, hoc	this, these
ille	illa, illud	that, those; he, she, it
is	ea, id	he, she, it; that, those
quī	quae, quod	who, which
quis?	quis? quid?	who? what? which?
ubi		when; where
antequam		before
postquam		after; when
quamquam		although
et ... et		both . . . and
quoque		also; too

People and places

Rōmulus, Rōmulī, m
mid–late 8th century BC

As you read in Chapter 2, **Romulus** was the semi-mythical founder and first king of Rome.

Numa, Numae, m
mid 8th century BC
–early 7th century BC

Numa was from the nearby Sabine community and became the second king of Rome.

Horātius, Horātiī, m
mid–late 7th century BC

Publius Horatius was a Roman soldier from the early history of Rome. He ended a war by winning a duel almost single-handedly, but shamefully killed his sister in a fit of rage after he returned home.

Sextus Tarquinius,
  Sextī Tarquiniī, m
Lucrētia, Lucrētiae, f
late 6th century BC

Sextus Tarquinius was the son of the seventh and final king of Rome. His wicked deeds unintentionally brought an end to the monarchy. The most outrageous of these deeds was the rape of the noblewoman **Lucretia**.

Cincinnātus, Cincinnātī, m
late 6th century BC
–mid 5th century BC

Cincinnatus was a Roman hero who was brought out of retirement to act as dictator and save the early Roman Republic in a time of crisis.

Carthāgo, Carthāginis, f
Hannibal, Hannibalis, m

Carthage was a city in modern-day Tunisia and one of Rome's main rivals. **Hannibal** was Carthage's most successful general: he invaded Italy by marching his army over the Alps and waged a campaign there which lasted for 16 years. During these years there was frequent debate and disagreement in the Roman senate about how best to handle the threat: **Quintus Fabius Maximus** urged a cautious campaign, whereas the ambitious and daring **Scipio** proposed the aggressive plan of a counter-attack on Hannibal's homeland.

Quīntus Fabius Maximus,
  Quīntī Fabiī Maximī, m
Scīpiō, Scīpiōnis, m
3rd–2nd century BC

Subordinate clauses: *quod, quamquam, postquam, antequam, ubi*

Sentences often contain more than one section; if a section contains a **finite** verb (i.e. a verb with a person ending and a tense), then it is known as a **clause**.

The sentence below has two finite verbs, and so it has two clauses: we call the more important of these clauses the **main clause**, and the less important clause the **subordinate clause**.

Because the kings were cruel, the Romans were often afraid.

subordinate clause   main clause

Subordinate clauses always have a word or phrase at the start which shows how they connect to the main clause. This word is called a **conjunction**. Subordinate clauses can connect in different ways: for example, some subordinate clauses show the time of the main clause, while other subordinate clauses show the cause of the main clause.

After Romulus killed Remus, he was the first king of Rome.

Romulus killed Remus **because** he was angry.

Latin often uses **subordinate clauses**. Here are some of the Latin **conjunctions** which are used at the start of a subordinate clause.

quod	because
quamquam	although
postquam	after
antequam	before
ubi	when; where

> **Watch out!** You have also met *ubi* at the start of a question; in questions *ubi* means **where. . .?**

EXERCISE 7.1

1. antequam cīvēs senātōrem in forō salūtāvērunt, per viās ambulābant.

2. quamquam rēgēs saepe crūdēlēs erant, multōs annōs regēbant.

3. postquam domina servōs pūnīvit, omnēs ancillae cēnam celeriter parāvērunt.

4. laeta sum quod amīcus adest!

5. ubi per hortum ambulābāmus, nōn miserī erāmus.

6. antequam senātor verba nūntiī audīvit, perterritus erat.

7. quamquam et domina et dominus saevī erant, servus audāx nōn timēbat.

8. senātōrēs salūtāvī quod clārī erant.

9. quamquam hortus tuus magnus est, hīc nōn manēbō.

10. ubi per viās cīvēs ambulābant, templa et magna et sacra vidēbant.

EXERCISE 7.2: ROME ELECTS ITS SECOND KING

After Romulus died, it was unclear who should be the next king. The Roman community was a mixture of men who had joined Romulus at the city's foundation, and men from the Sabine community who had joined later. There was disagreement between these two factions as to who should be king. At first the senators proposed that the senators should share power in rotation; after the other citizens were angry at this plan, the senators proposed that the new king should be elected by the citizens.

omnēs cīvēs trīstēs erant quod Rōmulus mortuus erat. cīvēs rēgem novum habēre volēbant. quamquam omnēs cīvēs rēgem novum habēre volēbant, mox erat dissensiō magna: 'volumus rēgem Sabīnum,' clāmāvērunt Sabīnī, 'quod sumus Sabīnī!' 'volumus rēgem Rōmānum,' clāmāvērunt Rōmānī, 'quod sumus Rōmānī!'

5 senātōrēs tamen, ubi verba cīvium audīvērunt, cōnsilium novum cēpērunt: 'quīnque diēs erō rēx,' inquit senātor clārus. 'tum quīnque diēs senātor secundus erit rēx, tum senātor tertius, omnēs senātōrēs in vicem rēgēs erunt!' postquam cōnsilium audīvērunt, senātōrēs laetī erant quod potestātem magnam habēre volēbant. cīvēs tamen īrātī erant: 'nunc centum dominōs habēmus,' inquiunt,
10 'nōn rēgem ūnum. nunc sumus servī multōrum dominōrum. nōlumus centum dominōs habēre: ūnum rēgem habēre volumus.'

senātōrēs ānxiī erant: perīculum timēbant quod cīvēs īrātī erant. 'fortasse cīvēs contrā senātōrēs pugnāre volent quod īrātī sunt,' inquiunt
15 senātōrēs. 'necesse est rēgem ēligere: et cīvēs et senātōrēs rēgem nostrum ēligent.'

tum et cīvēs et senātōrēs cīvem clārum, Numam nōmine, ēlēgērunt quod Numa erat cīvis bonus et sapiēns. multōs annōs Numa Rōmānōs regēbat.

dissensiō, dissensiōnis, f	disagreement
Sabīnus, Sabīna, Sabīnum	Sabine
cōnsilium, cōnsiliī, n	plan
diēs (accusative pl)	days
in vicem	'in turn'
potestās, potestātis, f	power
ānxius, ānxia, ānxium	anxious
fortasse	perhaps
necesse	'necessary'
ēligō, ēligere, ēlēgī	choose; elect
sapiēns, sapientis	wise

Pronouns: *is, ea, id*

Pronouns are words that can be used to represent nouns. For example:

The king was cruel. The Romans killed **him**.

One of Latin's most common pronouns is the word for **he, she, it, they**. Here are its different forms:

	masculine	feminine	neuter
nominative sg	is – he	ea – she	id – it
accusative sg	eum	eam	id
genitive sg	eius	eius	eius
dative sg	eī	eī	eī
ablative sg	eō	eā	eō
nominative pl	eī – they	eae – they	ea – they
accusative pl	eōs	eās	ea
genitive pl	eōrum	eārum	eōrum
dative pl	eīs	eīs	eīs
ablative pl	eīs	eīs	eīs

- This pronoun has to match the noun it represents in **gender** and **number**. If it represents a feminine plural noun, it will need a feminine plural form, and so on.
- The **case** of the pronoun, however, depends on its role in the sentence.

rēx **eum** laudāvit.	The king praised **him**.
fēminae adsunt; **eās** timēmus.	The women are here; we fear **them**.
eum rēgem timēbam.	I feared **that king**.

Note that sometimes *is, ea, id* is used together with a noun; in this use it means *that, those*.

EXERCISE 7.3

1. quod senātōrēs clārī erant, omnēs cīvēs eōs laudābant.
2. līberī meī equum bonum ēmērunt; nunc eīs pecūniam dabō.
3. ancillae cēnam malam parāvērunt: eās pūniam!
4. paucī nūntiī in forō adsunt et eōs audīre volō.
5. in eā vīllā domina et multae ancillae habitābant.
6. cīvis clārus in forō ambulābat. vīdistīne eum?
7. senātor multa verba dīxit. nōnne eī crēdis?
8. māter crūdēlis est; et fīliī et fīliae eius trīstēs sunt.

Further uses of cases: time phrases

So far, you have met the **accusative** case in time phrases that show **how long** an action lasted.

multōs annōs Rōmulus erat rēx.   **For many years** Romulus was king.

The **ablative** case is used in time phrases that show **when** an action took place.

prīmā hōrā servī cibum parāvērunt.   **At the first hour**, the slaves prepared food.

annō secundō mūrum aedificāvit.   **In the second year**, he built a wall.

Further uses of cases: place phrases

One of the odd quirks of Latin is that prepositions are not used with the **names of towns** if we need to express going **towards** a town, going **away from** a town, or being **at** or **in** a town.

Instead, the following three cases are used:

- **accusative** case: going **towards** a town.

    Rōmam festīnāvī.   I hurried **to** Rome.

- **ablative** case: going **away** from a town.

    Rōmā festīnāvī.   I hurried **from** Rome.

- **locative** case: being **at** or **in** a town.

    Rōmae manēbam.   I stayed **in** Rome.

> **Note that** the locative case only has this one use; as a result it is very rare and not listed in standard noun tables. Details of the **locative** case endings are on p226.

EXERCISE 7.4

1. tertiā hōrā domina etiam tum dormiēbat sed hōrā quartā ē vīllā exiit.

2. Rōmam adībō quod ibi sunt vīllae multae et magnae.

3. nōnne Rōmae mūrōs altōs et hortōs pulchrōs vīdistis?

4. ūnam hōram senātōrēs in forō ambulābant.

5. quod cīvēs īrātī erant, rēx crūdēlis Rōmā cucurrit.

6. decem annōs paucī lībertī auxilium amīcīs dabant.

7. diū Rōmae manēbās quod tabernae bonae erant.

8. Rōmā nūntius celeriter vēnit: ibi perīculum magnum est et cīvēs perterritī sunt.

9. sextō annō dominus omnēs servōs liberāvit.

10. pater meus Rōmae habitat: vīllam magnam habet et multōs servōs.

EXERCISE 7.5: PUBLIUS HORATIUS KILLS HIS SISTER

One of the more disturbing stories from the time of the Roman kings is the story of Publius Horatius and his sister. In the 7th century BC, the Romans went to war with the neighbouring city of Alba Longa. In order to avoid a long and unnecessary conflict, both sides decided that three Alban brothers would fight three Roman brothers. One of these Roman brothers was Horatius. Horatius won a remarkable victory but his glorious return to Rome was marred by the terrible murder of his own sister. She had been engaged to one of the Alban brothers and wept when she realized he was dead.

Horātius erat Rōmānus audāx et fortis. Horātius <u>frātrēs</u> duōs habēbat. frātrēs eius quoque fortēs erant et audācēs. eō <u>tempore</u> Rōmānī contrā <u>Albānōs</u> pugnābant. <u>inter</u> Albānōs quoque erant trēs frātrēs, <u>Cūriatiī</u> nōmine. 'pugnābimus,' clāmāvit Horātius, 'trēs frātrēs contrā trēs frātrēs: vincēmus et tum Rōmānī Albānōs regent!'   5

Cūriatiī fortiter pugnābant: Cūriatiī duōs frātrēs Horātiī interfēcērunt. tum ad Horātium ē Cūriatiīs frāter prīmus cucurrit: Horātius eum interfēcit! tum ad Horātium ē Cūriatiīs frāter secundus cucurrit: Horātius eum quoque interfēcit! tum Horātius cum ūnō pugnābat. tandem Horātius eum quoque interfēcit. Horātius laetus erat: 'eōs Cūriatiōs vīcī!' clāmāvit, 'et nunc Rōmānī Albānōs   10 regent!' Horātius arma Cūriatiōrum cēpit et Rōmam arma ferēns festīnāvit.

Horātius tamen <u>sorōrem</u> habēbat: soror eius ūnum ē Cūriatiīs amābat. soror, ubi Horātius Rōmam festīnābat, ad mūrōs Rōmae adiit et prope <u>Portam Capēnam</u> manēbat: ubi frātrem arma Cūriatiōrum ferentem vīdit, misera erat. 'arma <u>spōnsī</u> cōnspexī!' inquit lacrimāns. 'Horātius spōnsum meum interfēcit!'   15

Horātius, postquam sorōrem lacrimantem vīdit, īrātus erat: eam gladiō suō interfēcit. 'eam pūnīvī,' inquit Horatius, 'quod ubi cēterī Rōmānī laetī erant, soror mea lacrimābat.'

frāter, frātris, m	brother
tempus, temporis, n	time
Albānī, Albānōrum, m pl	the Albans
inter (+ acc)	among
Cūriatiī, Cūriatiōrum, m pl	the Curiatii
soror, sorōris, f	sister
Porta Capēna, Portae Capēnae, f	Capena Gate
spōnsus, spōnsī, m	fiancé

Pronouns: *hic, haec, hoc* and *ille, illa, illud*

Two other very common Latin **pronouns** are the words for **this, these** and **that, those**.

As with *is, ea, id,* both these pronouns have different forms depending on the **gender** and **number** of the noun they represent, but the **case** needed depends on their role in the sentence. Here are their different forms.

	masculine	feminine	neuter	masculine	feminine	neuter
nominative sg	hic – this	haec	hoc	ille – that	illa	illud
accusative sg	hunc	hanc	hoc	illum	illam	illud
genitive sg	huius	huius	huius	illīus	illīus	illīus
dative sg	huic	huic	huic	illī	illī	illī
ablative sg	hōc	hāc	hōc	illō	illā	illō
nominative pl	hī – these	hae	haec	illī – those	illae	illa
accusative pl	hōs	hās	haec	illōs	illās	illa
genitive pl	hōrum	hārum	hōrum	illōrum	illārum	illōrum
dative pl	hīs	hīs	hīs	illīs	illīs	illīs
ablative pl	hīs	hīs	hīs	illīs	illīs	illīs

Translating *hic, haec, hoc* and *ille, illa, illud*

> **Watch out!** It is important not to confuse the pronoun *hic, haec, hoc* with the adverb *hīc* meaning **here**.

- *hic* and *ille* can be used either with a noun or on their own; if they are used on their own, it is often necessary to translate them as **this man**, or **these women**, or **those things** etc., depending on their **gender** and **number**.

hic rēx est crūdēlis	**This king** is cruel.
hī Horātium laudābant sed **illae** īrātae erant.	**These men** were praising Horatius, but **those women** were angry.
cīvis **haec** audīvit.	The citizen heard **these things**.

- Sometimes – and especially to show a change of subject – *ille, illa, illud* is used to mean **he, she, it, they**.

Rōmānī cīvem malum pūnīvērunt: **ille** trīstis erat.	The Romans punished the bad citizen: **he** was sad.

EXERCISE 7.6

1. haec vīlla est magna, sed illa vīlla est parva.

2. paucī senātōrēs pecūniam illīs cīvibus dedērunt quod ex eīs auxilium volēbant.

3. cūr illīs ancillīs fessīs aquam nōn dedistī?

4. tum domina crūdēlis servōs pūnīēbat; nunc illī eam interficere volunt.

5. hic dominus multam pecūniam habet et vīllam pulchram: in hortō huius ambulāre volō.

6. hī cīvēs illum senātōrem per viās ambulantem salūtāvērunt.

7. dominus illum servum līberāvit quod saepe servus eī auxilium dabat.

8. cūr, senātōrēs, illīs cīvibus nōn persuāsistis?

9. festīnābitisne, ō amīcī, ad hanc urbem? hīc templa multa et pulchra vidēbitis!

10. fer cēnam et vīnum hīs nuntiīs! duās hōrās per viās cucurrērunt et nunc fessī sunt.

GRAMMAR HUNT

From Exercise 7.6, can you find each of the following?

1. hic, haec, hoc – genitive masculine sg

2. hic, haec, hoc – nominative masculine pl

3. hic, haec, hoc – accusative feminine sg

4. hic, haec, hoc – dative masculine pl

5. ille, illa, illud – nominative feminine sg

6. ille, illa, illud – dative masculine pl

7. is, ea, id – dative masculine sg

8. is, ea, id – ablative masculine pl

9. ille, illa, illud – used to mean *they*

10. the adverb which means *here*

EXERCISE 7.7: THE RAPE OF LUCRETIA

In 509 BC the rule of kings at Rome came to a sudden end. The final crime of the royal family was when Lucretia was raped by Sextus Tarquinius, son of the last king of Rome. Lucretia then committed suicide; she told her husband that she refused to live after her fidelity had been violated in this way. The Roman community was so enraged by Sextus Tarquinius' terrible behaviour that they rose up against the royal family and kings ruled at Rome no more.

rēx septimus Rōmānōrum habēbat fīlium, Sextum Tarquinium nōmine. hic fīlius audāx erat sed malus: uxōrem <u>Collātīnī</u> magnopere amābat. haec uxor, Lucrētia nōmine, erat fēmina pulchra et bona.

ōlim Sextus ad villam Collātīnī <u>clam</u> festīnāvit. Collātīnus aberat sed Lucrētia in vīllā dormiēbat. Sextus in <u>cubiculum</u> Lucrētiae cucurrit: 'Sextus Tarquinius   5
sum!' clāmāvit. 'gladium habeō: <u>aut</u> <u>mihī</u> <u>tē dēde</u> aut <u>tē</u> interficiam!' Lucrētia, ubi haec verba audīvit, perterrita erat quod Collātīnum amābat, nōn Sextum. 'abī!' clāmāvit Lucrētia. 'uxor Collātīnī sum.'

Sextus, tamen, erat crūdēlis: haec verba illī nōn persuāsērunt. quamquam Lucrētia hoc nōlēbat, illam fēminam <u>libīdine</u> crūdēlī vīcit.   10

Lucrētia, postquam Sextus haec fēcit, magnopere <u>dēspērābat</u>: Collātīnum vocāvit. ille ad vīllam celeriter festīnāvit: uxōrem in cubiculō lacrimantem cōnspexit. 'quamquam, Collātīne,' inquit Lucrētia, 'uxor tua sum, homō crūdēlis <u>mē</u> vīcit: corpus <u>violātum</u> est sed <u>anima</u> mea est <u>innocēns</u>.' tum Lucrētia gladium cēpit et hōc gladiō <u>sē</u> interfēcit.   15

Collātīnus magnopere īrātus erat: Sextum pūnīre volēbat. Rōmam festīnāvit et corpus uxōris mortuae cīvibus ostendit. per viās Rōmae corpus uxōris mortuae ferēns ambulābat. cēterī Rōmānī, ubi corpus illīus fēminae cōnspexērunt, īrātī erant. cēterī Rōmānī Sextum pūnīre volēbant. 'rēgēs nostrī malī sunt,' iterum et iterum in forō clāmābant. 'rēgēs nostrī crūdēlēs sunt et saevī; hī rēgēs   20 <u>terribilia</u> fēcērunt. rēgēs habēre nōlumus.' Sextus et pater timēbant: Rōmā abiērunt; numquam iterum Rōmae erant rēgēs. 'ā dominīs saevīs,' clāmāvērunt cīvēs, 'Rōmam līberāvimus.'

Collātīnus, Collātīnī, m	Collatinus (Lucretia's husband)
clam	secretly
cubiculum, cubiculī, n	bedroom
aut . . . aut. . .	either . . . or . . .
mihī (dative)	'to me'
tē dēde (imperative)	'surrender yourself'
tē (accusative)	'you'
libīdō, libīdinis, f	passion; lust
dēspērō, dēspērāre, dēspērāvī	despair
mē (accusative)	'me'
violātus, violāta, violātum	violated; abused
anima, animae, f	soul
innocēns, innocentis	innocent; blameless
sē (accusative)	'herself'
terribilis, terribile	terrible

> **Watch out!** It is important not to confuse the relative pronoun with the word *quod* meaning *because*.

Pronouns: *quī, quae, quod*

quī, quae, quod is known as the **relative pronoun**. It means *who* or *which*. It is used at the start of a **relative clause**.

A **relative clause** is a subordinate clause that gives information **relating** to a noun in the sentence.

He punished the citizens, **who** did not fight bravely.

main clause   relative clause

Here are the different forms of *quī, quae, quod*.

	masculine	feminine	neuter
nominative sg	quī – who	quae – who	quod – which
accusative sg	quem	quam	quod
genitive sg	cuius	cuius	cuius
dative sg	cui	cui	cui
ablative sg	quō	quā	quō
nominative pl	quī	quae	quae
accusative pl	quōs	quās	quae
genitive pl	quōrum	quārum	quōrum
dative pl	quibus	quibus	quibus
ablative pl	quibus	quibus	quibus

As with any other pronoun, the **gender** and **number** used for *quī, quae, quod* depend on the noun to which it relates.

As with any other pronoun, the **case** of *quī, quae, quod* depends upon its role in its own clause. Because the relative pronoun is used in a different clause from the noun to which it relates, it may have a different role in its own clause and so it may need a different case.

fēmina, **quam** senātor amābat, pulchra erat.

The woman, **whom** the senator loved, was beautiful.

EXERCISE 7.8

1. nūntius, quī haec verba dīxit, mox in forō iterum aderit.

2. omnēs lībertī tuī, quōs līberāvistī, ad forum īre volunt.

3. cīvis clārus, cuius hortus est magnus, multōs servōs et multās ancillās ēmit.

4. quandō ad templum, quod rēx aedificāvit, dōna ferentēs festīnāvistis?

5. domina, quae crūdēliter ancillās pūnīvit, nunc eās cēnam parāre iterum iūssit.

6. omnēs uxōrēs, quās cīvēs laudābant, laetī erant.

7. fīlius, cui pater pecūniam dedit, in tabernā multum vīnum ēmit.

8. deī et deae omnia dōna, quae cīvēs ad templum ferēbant, amābant.

9. cēterī cīvēs, quī in forō rīdēbant, verba nūntiī audīre nōn poterant.

10. māter, quod fīliī diū aberant, lacrimāvit.

GRAMMAR HUNT

From Exercise 7.8, see if you can find an example of each of the following forms of *quī, quae, quod*. For each of your answers, write out the noun to which the pronoun relates, and explain why each word is in its particular case.

1. nominative masculine pl

2. nominative feminine sg

3. dative masculine sg

4. accusative feminine pl

5. accusative masculine pl

6. accusative neuter pl

7. genitive masculine sg

8. Can you find the Latin words which mean *when* and *because*?

EXERCISE 7.9: CINCINNATUS IS CHOSEN AS DICTATOR

In times of crisis the Romans sometimes chose one man alone to govern them. This was contrary to the Republican principles of shared rule and discussion, but it was a practical response to the need in a crisis for decisions to be made quickly. Cincinnatus became dictator in 458 BC but solved Rome's crisis so quickly that he gave up the position after fifteen days. This story was used by the Romans as an example of the Republican principle that it was important that no man should wish to dominate for too long.

ōlim cōnsul, Minucius nōmine, et multī Rōmānī contrā Aequōs pugnābant. Aequī, tamen, fortiter pugnābant et Minucium terrēbant. Minucius et Rōmānī in castrīs diū manēbant quod perterritī erant. Minucius nūntiōs quīnque Rōmam festīnāre iūssit: 'auxilium petite, ō nūntiī!' clāmāvit Minucius. 'perīculum magnum adest!'

Rōmae cīvēs, postquam nūntiōs audīvērunt, magnopere perterritī erant: 'cōnsul   5
noster in perīculō est!' clāmāvērunt. 'volumus ūnum ducem quī fortis est et audāx! volumus ūnum ducem quī Aequōs vincet et cōnsulem nostrum ē perīculō līberābit. dictātōrem volumus!'

itaque senātōrēs nūntiōs ad Cincinnātum adīre iūssērunt: Cincinnātus erat Rōmānus clārus quī erat et fortis et audāx. Cincinnātus tamen ab urbe aberat   10
et in vīllā, quae procul erat, habitābat. nūntiī cōnspexērunt hominem quī in agrīs labōrābat: 'ille est Cincinnātus!' clāmāvērunt nūntiī. nūntiī, ad Cincinnātum festīnantēs, eum salūtāvērunt: 'ō Cincinnāte, Rōmam festīnā! volumus tē dictātōrem esse! Aequōs vince et cōnsulem nostrum ē perīculō līberā!'

celeriter Cincinnātus uxōrem vocāvit quae in vīlla labōrābat: 'fer togam meam!   15
Rōmam festīnābō!' Cincinnātus Rōmam adiit: prope mūrōs et in viīs multōs cīvēs, quī eum laudābant, cōnspexit: 'nunc, ō Cincinnāte,' inquiunt cīvēs, 'dictātor es; nunc es ille dictātor quī auxilium cōnsulī feret.' Cincinnātus et Rōmānī cum Aequīs quīndecim diēs fortiter pugnābant; Cincinnātus et Rōmānī Aequōs vīcērunt.   20

tum Cincinnātus dictātor esse nōlēbat: 'nōn iam dictātor sum; ad vīllam et ad agrōs ībō,' inquit. 'potestātem omnem habēre nōlō: volō multōs cīvēs potestātem habēre.'

cōnsul, cōnsulis, m	consul
Minucius, Minuciī, m	Minucius
Aequī, Aequōrum, m pl	Aequi (an Italian tribe east of Rome in the Apennines)
castra, castrōrum, n pl	military camp
dux, ducis, m	leader
dictātor, dictātōris, m	dictator
procul	far away
labōrō, labōrāre, labōrāvī	work
tē (accusative)	'you'
toga, togae, f	toga
quīndecim diēs (accusative)	'for fifteen days'
potestās, potestātis, f	power

Pronouns: *quis, quis, quid*

quis, quis, quid is a question word that means ***who. . .? what. . .? which. . .?***
It looks very similar indeed to the relative pronoun; in fact it only has different endings for its nominative singular (and neuter accusative singular) forms. These are listed in the table below.

	masculine	feminine	neuter
nominative sg	quis – who?	quis – who?	quid – what?
accusative sg	quem	quam	quid
for all other cases see p233			

As with any other pronoun, the **gender** and **number** depend upon the noun it represents.

As with any other pronoun, its **case** depends upon its role in the sentence.

quis, quis, quid can be used with a noun or on its own.

quis adest?	**Who** is here?
quem interfēcistī?	**Whom** did you kill?
quī cīvēs sunt audācēs?	**Which** citizens are bold?

EXERCISE 7.10

1. quis fīliam vestram amābit?

2. quōs amīcōs in forō salūtāvistī?

3. quam mātrem laudāvērunt?

4. quandō per viās urbis ambulāvērunt?

5. cui deae dōna dedistis?

6. quid nūntius dīxit? num senātor mortuus est?

7. quōs servōs līberāvit? nunc habet multōs lībertōs quī eum amant.

8. quid Rōmae cōnspexit? nōnne diū ibi manēbat?

9. quae verba cīvibus persuāsērunt? nunc fortiter pugnāre volunt quod nōn perterritī sunt.

10. quis est ille cīvis? eum in forō cōnspexī et nunc salūtāre volō.

EXERCISE 7.11: WHAT TO DO ABOUT HANNIBAL?

The political structure of the Roman Republic centred around discussion and debate, and later Roman historians often reimagined the great speeches that had taken place. One crucial debate happened in the 3rd century BC during the wars against Hannibal. Hannibal and the Carthaginians were Rome's greatest enemy; so great were Hannibal's successes that he managed to keep his army in Italy for 16 years.

In 205 BC Scipio, a famous military commander, became consul. He gave his first speech to a meeting of the senators held on the Capitoline hill. In this speech Scipio made the daring proposal to take the Roman army across to Africa and attack Carthage: his plan was to draw Hannibal out of Italy by forcing him to return to defend his own city. According to the historian Livy, there was a vigorous debate in the Roman senate: the ex-consul Quintus Fabius Maximus, one of the leading Romans of his day, was strongly opposed to the plan to strip Italy of Rome's army while Hannibal was still close at hand.

Hannibal erat <u>dux</u> Carthāginiensium. multōs annōs Hannibal et Carthāginiensēs cum Rōmānīs pugnābant. in <u>Ītaliam</u> et <u>ūsque</u> Rōmam adiērunt. Rōmānī perterritī erant.

multī senātōrēs dē Hannibale <u>disputābant</u>. <u>cōnsul</u>, Scīpiō nōmine, in <u>Āfricam</u>
5 cum multīs <u>mīlitibus</u> trānsīre volēbat. 'quod Hannibal abest,' inquit Scīpiō, 'quis Carthāginem <u>dēfendet</u>? quōs timēmus? quid <u>nōs</u> terret? quod Hannibal in Ītalia est, facile est Rōmānīs Carthāginem vincere.'

Scīpiō tamen omnibus senātōribus nōn persuāsit. senātor clārus, Quīntus Fabius Maximus nōmine, haec clāmāvit: 'quī mīlitēs Rōmam dēfendent? multī
10 mīlitēs in Āfricā erunt, nōn prope Rōmam! perīculum ingēns in Ītaliā est: <u>necesse</u> est in Ītaliā pugnāre, nōn in Āfricā. in Āfricā, quis auxilium Rōmānīs dabit? quī erunt amīcī nostrī? <u>melius</u> est in Ītaliā manēre.'

dux, ducis, m	leader
Carthāginiensis, Carthāginiense	Carthaginian
Ītalia, Ītaliae, f	Italy
ūsque (+ accusative)	right up to
cōnsul, cōnsulis, m	consul
disputō, disputāre, disputāvī	disagree
Āfrica, Āfricae, f	Africa
mīles, mīlitis, m	soldier
dēfendō, dēfendere, dēfendī	defend
nos (accusative)	'us'
necesse	'necessary'
melius (nominative neuter)	'better'

Fabius multīs senātōribus persuāsit quod <u>auctōritātem</u> magnam habēbat. Scīpiō, tamen, audāx erat: Hannibalem vincere volēbat. 'nōlī Hannibalem timēre!' clāmāvit. 'Rōmānī pugnāre, nōn timēre <u>solent</u>. nōn perterritus sum! Hannibalem 15 nōn timeō: fortiter pugnābō et Rōmam līberābō! in Āfricam ībō et Hannibal ex Ītaliā in Āfricam festīnābit. Hannibal urbem suam dēfendere volet. Rōmānī tamen Carthāginiensēs vincere poterunt quod Hannibal in Africam <u>sērō</u> festīnābit.'

diū Rōmānī disputābant. diū Rōmānī Scīpiōnem mīlitēs in Āfricam <u>dūcere</u> nōlēbant. tandem tamen Scīpiō Rōmānīs persuāsit quod mīles bonus erat. in 20 Āfricam mīlitēs dūxit et contrā Hannibalem audācter et fortiter pugnāvit. tandem Scīpiō Carthāginiensēs vīcit et Rōmam ā perīculō ingentī līberāvit. postquam Rōmam <u>rediit</u>, Rōmānī Scīpiōnem laudābant et nōmen novum Scīpiōnī dedērunt: 'nunc es Scīpiō <u>Āfricānus</u>,' inquiunt, 'quod in Āfricā audācter et fortiter pugnāvistī.' 25

auctōritās, auctōritātis, f	authority; influence
soleō, solēre	be accustomed
sērō	too late
dūcō, dūcere, dūxī	lead
redeō, redīre, rediī	return
Āfricānus (nominative)	'Africanus'

Chapter 7: Additional Language

SECTION A7: CHAPTER 7 VOCABULARY

Exercise A7.1: Vocabulary crossword

Complete the crossword below. Each clue is an English derivation of a Latin word found in the Chapter 7 vocabulary list. Write the Latin word in the crossword.

Next to each clue, you should also explain the link between the English word and the Latin verb. If you are unsure, you should look up the English word in a dictionary.

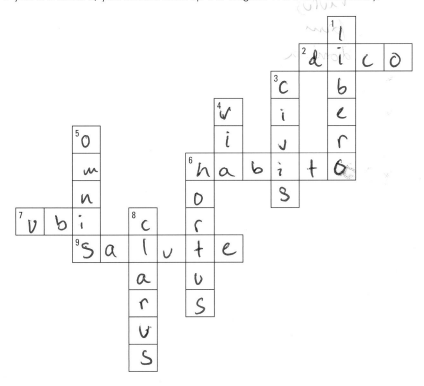

Across

2. dictate

6. habitat

7. ubiquitous

9. salute

Down

1. liberate

3. civilian

4. viaduct

5. omnipotent

6. horticulture

8. clarity

Exercise A7.2: Parts of speech

Sort the following words from Chapter 7 into the correct categories and write the meaning next to each word.

domina   antequam   ambulō   clārus   omnis
ubi   ille   habitō   hic   paucī
dicō   mūrus   forum   quī   postquam

verb	conjunction	noun	pronoun	adjective
ambulo dico	ubi	murus form domina	ille	Clarus

Exercise A7.3: Case endings (nouns and adjectives)

Circle the stem, and identify the declension of the following nouns and adjectives from Chapter 7. Then give the case requested.

	Latin	declension	
1	hortus, hortī, m		dative sg =
2	mūrus, mūrī, m		nominative pl =
3	nūntius, nūntiī, m		genitive pl =
4	forum, forī, n		ablative sg =
5	cīvis, cīvis, m		dative pl =
6	senātor, senātōris, m		accusative pl =
7	Rōma, Rōmae, f		accusative sg =
8	clārus, clāra, clārum		ablative masculine sg =
9	paucī, paucae, pauca		genitive feminine pl =
10	omnis, omne		accusative neuter sg =

Exercise A7.4: Verbs

Identify the tense of the Chapter 7 verbs in the table below and translate each one. Then change the form from singular to plural, or plural to singular, keeping the tense and person the same.

Remember that you need to look at the stem as well as the ending. Here are the principal parts for each verb so that you can see their different stems.

ambulō, ambulāre, ambulāvī
habitō, habitāre, habitāvī
līberō, līberāre, līberāvī
salūtō, salūtāre, salūtāvī
dīco, dīcere, dīxi

	Latin	tense	translation	new form
1	habitābant			
2	līberābimus			
3	salūtāvī			
4	dīcēbam			
5	ambulāvērunt			
6	habitāvistī			
7	līberātis			
8	salūtās			
9	dīxit			
10	dīcēmus			

SECTION B7: GRAMMAR

Exercise B7.1: *is, ea, id*

This exercise focuses on the forms of *is, ea, id* and the nouns you have met in the vocabulary list for Chapter 7.

Give the case, gender and number of the pronoun in **purple** and then translate the whole sentence.

1. lībertus **eam** salūtāvit.
2. dominus **eōs** līberāvit.
3. senātōrēs cum **eō** ambulābant.
4. nūntius **id** dīxit.
5. **eae** prope mūrum habitābant.
6. domina **ēius** in forum ambulāvit.
7. dominī **eōrum** clārī erant.
8. senātor **eīs** persuāsit.
9. quis **ea** dīxit?
10. **eō** annō **eum** amābāmus.

Exercise B7.2: *hic, haec, hoc*

This exercise focuses on the forms of *hic, haec, hoc* and the nouns you have met in the vocabulary list for Chapter 7.

Identify the case and gender of each pronoun and noun pair, and then give the plural form of the same case.

1. hic lībertus
2. hunc cīvem
3. hoc forum
4. huic dominō
5. haec domina
6. per hanc viam
7. huius dominī
8. huic senātōrī
9. in hāc viā
10. cum hōc senātōre

Exercise B7.3: *ille, illa, illud*

This exercise focuses on the forms of *ille, illa, illud* and the nouns you have met in the vocabulary list for Chapter 7.

Select the correct form of *ille* to translate the words in **purple** in the sentences below.

1. **That** forum is famous. (illud / ille)
2. **Those** messengers are walking in the forum. (illī / illōs)
3. Is the mistress walking away from **that** wall? (illā / illō)
4. The senator greeted **those** citizens. (illī / illōs)
5. The master of **those men** set that woman free. (illīus / illōrum)
6. What did you say to **that** freedman? (illī / illīs)
7. The master said **those things**. (illōs / illa)
8. On **that** road the citizen greeted the senator. (illō / illā)
9. The mistress loved **that** slave greatly. (illum / illud)
10. **That man** greeted those freedmen. (ille / illī)

Exercise B7.4: *quī, quae, quod*

This exercise focuses on the forms of *quī, quae, quod* and the nouns which you have met in the vocabulary list for Chapter 7.

Give the case, gender and number of the relative pronouns in **purple** in the sentences below, and then translate the sentence.

1. lībertus, **cui** domina multa dīxit, rīdēbat.
2. forum ingēns, **quod** dea amat, dēlēbimus.
3. senātōrī, **quem** cīvēs amant, crēde!
4. dominam, **cūius** pater īrātus erat, salūtāvī.
5. in forō, ex **quō** cīvēs cucurrērunt, manēbam.
6. via, in **quā** dominus ambulābat, pulchra erat.
7. dominōs, **quī** in forō multōs līberābant, spectābāmus.
8. nūntius dīxit omnia **quae** in forō audīvit.
9. ad mūrōs, prope **quōs** pugnābitis, currite!
10. dominae, **quārum** pātrēs sunt senātōrēs, clārae sunt.

Exercise B7.5: Mixed pronouns

This exercise focuses on all the pronouns you have met in Chapter 7.

Give the form requested for all four pronouns.

		is	hic	ille	quī
1	genitive neuter sg				
2	dative feminine pl				
3	ablative masculine sg				
4	accusative masculine sg				
5	accusative neuter pl				
6	genitive masculine pl				
7	nominative feminine sg				
8	accusative feminine sg				
9	nominative neuter sg				
10	dative masculine sg				

SECTION C7: ENGLISH TO LATIN SENTENCES

Exercise C7.1: Choosing pronouns: *is, hic, ille, quī, quis*

Translate each of the pronouns in **purple** into Latin.

1. The master greeted **him** in the garden.
2. **That woman** used to walk to the forum with a few slaves.
3. The river was deep. The citizens were afraid to go across **it**.
4. Because the master loved his slaves, he freed **them**.
5. **Those** masters, both cruel and savage, will never free these slaves.
6. Although they are sad, **these** slaves never cry.
7. **Their** fathers greeted the new senators.
8. **That** man is both bold and brave, although he killed few men in war.
9. **Which** citizens will greet the senator while he walks in the forum?
10. The slave **whom** the master praises is walking into the garden.
11. **To whom** will you give all these gifts, master?
12. **Whose** is this garden, which is both beautiful and large?

Exercise C7.2: Sentences to translate into Latin

1. Although the master had few slaves, he freed them all.
2. When the messenger came to the forum, he said words both many and good.
3. Who freed the slaves who lived on this street?
4. What did you say? Why were you angry? When did you shout?
5. Because the senators are famous, everyone wants to greet them.
6. Before the citizens walked into the forum, they greeted the senator who was near these walls.
7. Because the mistress gave the freedman a gift, the master did not praise her.
8. Although the angry citizens were shouting, we wanted to hear the senator.
9. While walking in the garden, the freedman said many words to that messenger.
10. This woman loved that man, who gave that gift to her.

SECTION D: CONSOLIDATION

Exercises for Additional Language Section D are available on the companion website. Exercises are structured by grammatical category, and cover all Core Vocabulary met so far within each category. For Chapter 7, these exercises are as follows:

- Exercise D7.1: 1st declension nouns
- Exercise D7.2: 2-1-2 adjectives
- Exercise D7.3: 1st conjugation verbs

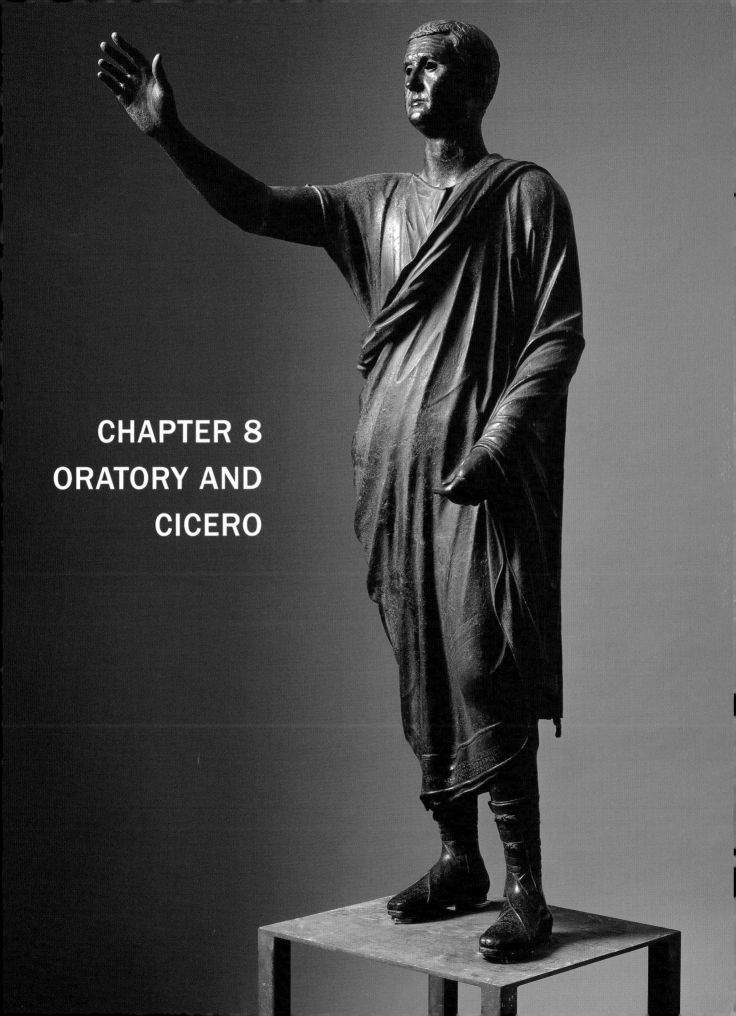

**CHAPTER 8
ORATORY AND
CICERO**

ⓒⓦ Chapter 8: Introduction

The cursus honorum

The principle of shared power in the Republic allowed many Romans to rise to the top. The career ladder by which they did this was known as the cursus honorum, and from the 2nd century BC it had increasingly strict rules. Romans had to be elected to the different magistracies in a particular order and there were wealth and age restrictions in place too. Before starting a political career, a Roman typically sought military experience by serving in the army from the age of 20. At 30 he could begin climbing the cursus honorum and, in theory, nobody could reach the top before the age of 40. The cursus honorum required a Roman to work his way through the following positions:

> The office of **aedile** was optional, and it was possible for Romans to progress directly from quaestor to praetor.

- quaestors – the magistrates responsible for supervising the state treasury and finances
- **aediles** – the magistrates responsible for maintaining public buildings and organizing public festivals
- praetors – the higher-ranked magistrates responsible for justice and the law courts
- consuls – the top magistrates in charge of leading debates in the senate and commanding the Republic's armies.

The cursus honorum was a steep pyramid and the fixed number of positions available decreased with each step. Although many young men would start at the bottom, they would not all reach the top. To do so, a Roman needed to prove his worth in a number of different areas, including civic planning, financial management and legal expertise. In addition, ambitious Romans needed the critical skills of military leadership and public speaking. In Chapter 9 we shall discuss the role of the army in the route to power; in this chapter we shall look at the role of oratory.

Oratory

Oratory, or the formal art of speaking persuasively, was an ancient skill and one that became very important in Rome from the 2nd century BC. Ambitious Romans needed to be able to speak well in order to win votes in an election, to persuade senators during debates, or to inspire their soldiers in the army. In addition, within the Roman legal system there were no professional lawyers, unlike today. Instead, Roman citizens had to argue their own cases or ask another citizen to speak on their behalf.

Oratory was considered so important that for hundreds of years it formed one of the main building-blocks of education, alongside logic and grammar. In Source 8.2 you can read an extract from one of the most famous textbooks for oratory, *de Oratore*, written by the famous statesman Cicero. Students of oratory would learn by studying the great speeches of the past, including those written by respected Greek orators such as Demosthenes. They also had to do many written exercises, such as composing a speech that praised a famous person, only to write another one straight afterwards which criticised them. In this way students learned how to develop both sides of an argument. A good memory was very important too, as orators were expected to speak, sometimes for hours, without any notes.

The Greek orator Demosthenes had said that the three most important things about public speaking were 'delivery, delivery, delivery': he rehearsed his speeches whilst walking up steep hills to manage his breathing and he made sure he strengthened the muscles in his mouth by practising speeches in his study with pebbles placed under his tongue. The Romans also believed that delivery and performance were an essential ingredient: the Roman orator Quintilian wrote at length about how to give a public speech well. To be truly persuasive, he wrote, a speaker needed to appeal to his audience's eyes as well as their ears. This meant he had to control his breathing, the pitch and tone of his voice, his hand gestures, body position and facial expressions. In Exercise 8.4 you will read a story about one of Rome's most famous speakers, Cato the Elder, and his excellent use of props to support his argument.

FIGURE 8.1 **An orator**

This bronze sculpture is nearly 2m tall and dates from the 2nd–1st centuries BC. It is now in the National Archaeological Museum in Florence, Italy. The type of boots the figure is wearing shows his high ranking as a senator. The extended right arm suggests that he is making a speech.

Cicero

Marcus Tullius Cicero was an exceptional Roman statesman and the most famous of Rome's orators. He was born in 106 BC and as a young man he worked hard to develop his oratorical skills. In 79 BC, he travelled to Rhodes to learn from the renowned Greek orator Apollonius Molon. When Cicero returned to Rome two years later, he began to climb the cursus honorum. Cicero won every election he entered, which was an extraordinary achievement, and he climbed each step of the cursus honorum as soon as he was old enough to run for the next office.

In 63 BC he was elected consul. This was a notable achievement, partly because it changed the future status of his family. The aristocratic label *nobilis* was used only for Romans who had an ancestor who had been a consul. Cicero's family did not: the label for him was not *nobilis*, but *novus homo*. As discussed in Chapter 7, a Roman's *auctoritas* depended partly on the status and achievements of their ancestors: it was particularly impressive therefore for any *novus homo* to make it to the top.

FIGURE 8.2 **Cicero**

This marble bust of Cicero was made in the 1st century AD. It is currently in the Hall of the Philosophers in the Capitoline Museums in Rome. Its location is a useful reminder that although Cicero is most famous for his oratory, he was also a prolific writer, whose works included private letters, poems and philosophical discussions.

Many of Cicero's personal letters and his political and legal speeches survive and they help us to reconstruct a vivid picture of his character and values, and the turbulent end of the Roman Republic. It is clear from his writing that Cicero was a committed and brave defender of the republican principle that power should be shared. He regularly spoke out against those nobles who he thought were trying to seize too much power for themselves, and – as we shall see in the sections which follow – he did so even when it brought significant personal danger for himself.

Consulship and the Catilinarian Conspiracy

The most famous episode in Cicero's life occurred when he was consul in 63 BC. Cicero claimed to have exposed a plot to kill both consuls. This plot was a brutal attempt to seize power and it is known as the Catilinarian Conspiracy. The leader of the conspiracy was a senator named Lucius Sergius Catilina, and in English he is referred to as Catiline. Catiline came from a distinguished patrician family that had fallen on hard times. He had lost to Cicero in the consular elections for 63 BC and he had begun to seek more violent ways of obtaining power.

When Cicero discovered this conspiracy, he took immediate action. He prevented a night-time attack on his life and summoned the senate the next day under an armed guard. In this meeting, Cicero eloquently denounced Catiline to his face with the first in a series of powerful and highly critical speeches. Catiline responded with contempt: he asked the senate if they really believed a *novus homo* such as Cicero over a *nobilis* from a distinguished family such as himself. Cicero, however, won the debate. Catiline fled from Rome and joined the small force he and his allies had been assembling outside the city. Cicero managed to persuade the senate to arrest the conspirators who were still in Rome. After a lengthy debate in the senate, the conspirators were put to death without trial. Catiline's army was soon destroyed in battle and Catiline was killed. Cicero was proclaimed a hero of the Republic and he was given the honorific title of *pater patriae*, the father of the fatherland.

In later years however, the mood changed. Cicero's decision to treat the conspirators as public enemies and to put them to death without trial became very controversial because it had violated the right to a legal trial that was held by every Roman citizen. In time, 63 BC proved to be both Cicero's most glorious year and one of the main causes of his downfall.

FIGURE 8.3   **Cicero denounces Catiline**

This painting was created in 1888 by Cesare Maccari. It is part of the collection in the Palazzo Madama in Rome. It captures the power of Cicero's speech against Catiline: Cicero holds the attention of the senate as he stands, arms outstretched, in command of his audience. In contrast, Catiline has been painted as an isolated figure, reduced to the shadows of the scene.

Decline and exile

In the years immediately after his consulship, Cicero was popular and influential. He soon received an invitation to join an informal alliance with three very powerful men: Julius Caesar, who had just been elected as one of the consuls for 59 BC, Pompey the Great, who was the Republic's most successful general at that time, and Crassus, who was the Republic's wealthiest man. Between them, these three men had more influence than anyone else.

These men wanted Cicero to join them and use his famous oratorical skills to ensure that the people and the senate supported the interests of the alliance, but Cicero was a great defender of Republican values and he refused their offer. Such an alliance between three powerful men did not fit with the Republican principle of shared and elected power and Cicero wanted nothing to do with it. This decision, however, marked the start of a steady decline in Cicero's career. Events in Rome moved on without him and despite Cicero's best efforts to defend the Republic by opposing the ruthless ambition of others he was ultimately unsuccessful.

As Cicero's power and status declined, he became an easier target for his political enemies who continued to attack the actions he had taken as consul during the Catilinarian Conspiracy. They said that Cicero's decision to put the conspirators, who were still Roman citizens, to death without trial was illegal. For this reason the people eventually turned against Cicero and in 58 BC he was exiled from Rome, his house was destroyed and he was forced to flee east to Thessalonica in Macedonia. Although Cicero was recalled from exile just one year later, he was a diminished public figure.

Cicero's death

Eventually civil war broke out between the power-hungry Julius Caesar and the senate in 49 BC. Cicero supported the senate, but this was the losing side. As we shall see in Chapter 9, Caesar won the civil war and became dictator in Rome until he was murdered in 44 BC. After Caesar's death, one of his closest associates, the powerful noble Mark Antony, continued to support the memory of Caesar. Cicero was an outspoken opponent of Antony and he wrote a series of speeches attacking him. These speeches were known as the *Philippics* and you can read an extract from them in Source 8.4. Antony did not forgive Cicero for these attacks, nor did he forget them.

In the aftermath of Caesar's death, Rome did not return to the normal rule of annually elected consuls. Instead, Rome once again was dominated by an alliance of three powerful men: this alliance was called the triumvirate. Unlike the informal alliance between Caesar, Crassus and Pompey, this was an official alliance formally declared in law and approved by the people. At the heart of the triumvirate was Cicero's enemy Mark Antony, who was joined by two others: Octavian and Lepidus. The triumvirs wielded more power than anyone else and, once again, Cicero opposed them on the grounds that the triumvirate was harmful to the Republic and the principle of shared power. Cicero's opposition to the triumvirate eventually cost him his life.

FIGURE 8.4 **Bust of Mark Antony**

Although Mark Antony was a famous and powerful Roman, very few images of him which were made during his lifetime have survived. This bust was created decades after Antony's death and it is now in the Vatican Chiaramonti Museum in Rome.

FIGURE 8.5 **The rostra in the Roman forum**

The rostra was a large platform built in the Roman forum on which orators would stand and address the Roman people. It gained its name in the 4th century BC from six captured warship prows (*rostra*) that were fixed to the platform as a symbol of the Republic's victory over its enemies. The tradition of showing the trophies of defeated enemies took a sinister turn when Antony ordered Cicero's hands and head to be displayed on the rostra in 43 BC.

Under the pretext of hunting down Caesar's murderers, the triumvirate drew up a list of their enemies, known as a proscription, and promised a reward in exchange for the death of anyone on the list or information about them. According to the historian Appian, 2,300 Romans were proscribed. Cicero's name was on this list, and, as we shall see in Exercise 8.10, he was hunted down and killed on Mark Antony's orders. As a symbolic gesture, Cicero's hands, which had written the *Philippics* against Antony, were cut off. These hands were sent to Rome, along with his head, and displayed in the forum. It is said that Antony's wife Fulvia pulled out Cicero's tongue and stabbed it with her hairpin, saying that his oratorical skills could not save him now. It was an ignoble end for such a distinguished individual.

Cicero's family

From Cicero's numerous surviving letters, we are able to understand much about his family life and the relationships he had with his friends. Extracts from these letters are printed in Source 8.3. Cicero's wife, Terentia, was a formidable woman: she came from a very wealthy family, and it is likely that she used her family's money to help fund Cicero's political career. Terentia and Cicero had two children: a daughter, Tullia, and a son, Marcus. When times grew hard for Cicero later in his career, their marriage became strained and eventually they divorced in 46 BC. Incredibly, Terentia is thought to have lived to the age of 103, outliving Cicero by almost half a century.

We know from Cicero's letters that he loved his children greatly, especially his daughter Tullia. Tullia lived a fairly difficult life: she was married three times, and her first marriage was in 62 BC when she was only 14 or 15. We hear in Cicero's letters that each marriage caused her sadness in different ways, and she died in 45 BC after giving birth to her second son. As we will see in Exercise 8.8, after Tullia's death Cicero was inconsolable. He wrote to his old friend Atticus saying that he had lost the one thing that made his life worth living.

CHAPTER 8: SOURCES TO STUDY

Source 8.1: Coin depicting Libertas and the rostra

This coin was made in 45 BC. On one side is the Roman deity Libertas. As we saw in Chapter 3, the Romans worshipped some deities who were the personification of qualities or values which were important to them. The Latin word libertas means freedom, but in the particular sense of the freedom to be involved in decision making. It refers to the freedom that was one of the factors which separated a citizen from a slave.

On the other side of the coin is the rostra, the name given to the speakers' platform in the forum. At the bottom of this side of the coin are images of the wooden prows (rostra) which were taken from captured enemy warships and fixed to the speakers' platform in the 4th century BC as a symbol of Rome's success. At the top of the coin appears the name Pallicanus. This probably refers to the Roman under whose authority the coin was made.

FIGURE 8.6 Roman denarius

Source 8.1: Questions

1 Why do you think Libertas and the rostra are shown on the same coin? What do you think the connection between them is supposed to be?
2 What statement do you think the Romans were making by displaying the prows from captured ships on their speakers' platform in the forum?
3 How would you have felt as a Roman citizen having this coin in your possession?
4 How would you have felt as a Roman slave handling this coin?
5 What else can you find out about the deity Libertas? Have other societies used images of a deity or figure like Libertas? What does this tell us about these societies?
6 Design a coin to represent the key aspects of our current political system: what images would you put on it and why?

Source 8.2: How to be a good speaker

In 55 BC Cicero finished writing a set of three books on oratory. This extract comes from the start of the first book. In it, he sums up the importance of oratory to the Romans, and the reasons why it was so difficult to master the art.

For after our rule over the whole world was established, and after the long-lasting nature of peace had given us more time for other things, nearly every young man was greedy for praise and thought that he should strive with every effort to be a speaker. Our community listened to Greek speeches, read Greek literature, employed Greek teachers and was fired with an incredible enthusiasm for speechifying. The importance, variety and quantity of lawsuits of every type spurred them on, and regular practice was added to the learning of theory. For this endeavour there used to be very sizeable rewards in relation to influence, to wealth or to status: indeed there still are today.

To be an excellent speaker, first one must have knowledge of the greatest number of things, without which the outpouring of words is trivial and laughable. The speech itself must be shaped, not just by the choice of words but also by their arrangement. All impulses of the human spirit must be understood in full, because all the power and craft of speech-making must be displayed in calming down or stirring up the feelings of the audience. As well as this, there must be a certain charm and wit, and the scholarship which befits a free-thinker, and a speed and punchiness both in rebutting and in attacking, and all this must work in conjunction with a subtle attractiveness and stylishness. What's more, all of history must be in one's grasp, and the capability to supply an example; knowledge of laws and civic rights must not be lacking. What more should I say about the delivery itself? This needs to be guided with the movement of the body, with gestures, with facial expressions, with the ability to maintain or to vary one's voice.

Cicero, *de Oratore* 1.IV.14–V.18 (with omissions)

Source 8.2: Questions

1 What does Cicero tell us about the relationship between Greek and Roman oratory?
2 What reasons does Cicero give us for the popularity of studying and then practising oratorical skills?
3 Write a list of the things Cicero says are necessary for a good speaker to have.
4 In this extract, Cicero refers to content, structure, style and delivery: which do you think would have been the most important of these aspects of oratory to a Roman, and why?
5 Television, radio and social media have had a transformatory impact on how politicians communicate with the public: what do you think have become the most important requirements for successful speech-making for modern-day politicians?

Source 8.3: Cicero attacks Mark Antony

The Philippics *are among Cicero's most famous speeches: in them Cicero delivered a stinging attack on Mark Antony. Cicero gave the first speech in the senate towards the end of 44 BC, after Julius Caesar's assassination. Antony was so enraged by this speech that Cicero withdrew to his country estate for the sake of his own safety. He circulated the second* Philippic *in written form. Throughout the second* Philippic, *Cicero attacks Antony's personal life as well as his political values, calling him a drunkard who has lived a life of vice. This sort of personal attack was not uncommon in Roman oratory.*

In the extract below, Cicero offers a scorching account of Antony's relationship with Caesar and his attempt to bring back the tyranny of one-man rule. After his victory in the civil war, Caesar had been made dictator, but Antony had suggested that he be declared king instead. As discussed in Chapter 7, this was a toxic label.

So, criminal, you alone were ready to propose that there should be a king at Rome; to transform your fellow-consul into your lord and master; and to inflict upon the Roman people this ultimate test of its capacity to suffer and endure. You even tried to move Caesar to pity when you hurled yourself at his feet as a suppliant. What were you begging for? To become his slave?

Nothing could have been more thoroughly deserving of the severest possible punishment. Are you a slave, cowering in expectation of a beating? If you have any feelings at all, you must be feeling the lash now: and my account of these events must surely be drawing blood. Seeing that the man who rejected the crown was killed, and was, by general consent, killed justly, it is appalling that the man who made him the offer should still be alive.

So I feel no surprise when you disturb the peace, when you shun Rome and the very daylight itself, when you drink with thieving riff-raff from early in one day until dawn of the next. For you, no refuge can be safe. Where could you possibly find a place in any community owning laws and law courts, since these are precisely what you have done your utmost to abolish and to replace with tyranny? Was this why Tarquin was expelled: to allow Antony, centuries after he was dead, to commit the forbidden evil of setting up a king at Rome?

Cicero, *Second Philippic* 85–87 (with omissions, trans. adapted)

Source 8.3: Questions

1 It was a common theme in Republican writing to compare the relationship between king and subject with the relationship between slave and master. In this extract, Cicero suggests that Antony acted like a slave because he wanted to have a king as his master. What details does Cicero give us which help us understand how horrendous it might have been to be a slave?

2 How does Cicero attack Antony's character? What are we told about how Antony spends his time?

3 Do you think the personal attack on Antony's character is relevant? Do you think this makes the speech more or less effective as a condemnation of Antony's actions in relation to Julius Caesar?

4 What do you think Cicero means when he writes that Antony was aiming to replace laws and law courts with tyranny?

Source 8.4: Cicero's letters to his family and friends

Cicero's letters show us much about his relationship with his family and friends. The extracts below are from three different letters. The first was written to his closest friend Atticus in 60 BC, the second was sent to Cicero by his brother Quintus in 53 BC, and the third was written by Cicero to his wife Terentia in 49 BC.

Extract 1: *in this extract Cicero tells Atticus how much he misses him. Atticus was a wealthy and highly educated Roman; he was Cicero's closest friend, but he had little interest in a political career and he spent much time away from Rome.*

> I must tell you that what I most badly need at the present time is a best friend, a friend with whom I could share all the things that give me any anxiety, a wise, affectionate friend to whom I could talk without pretence, or evasion or concealment. I am so utterly abandoned that my only moments of relaxation are those I spend with my wife, my little daughter and my darling **Marcus**. My self-serving, feigned friendships may make a fine show in public, but in private they bring no benefit. I go down to the forum surrounded by droves of friends, but in the midst of this great crowd I cannot find one with whom I can joke freely or whisper to with my guard down.

> Cicero, *Letters to Atticus,* A.18 (1.18) (with omissions, trans. adapted)

> **Marcus** was Cicero's son.

Extract 2: *this extract is from a letter sent to Cicero by his brother Quintus after he had heard the news that Cicero had decided to grant freedom to his former slave, Tiro. After Cicero's death, Tiro did much to secure the survival and publication of many of Cicero's letters.*

> I am most grateful because you decided that Tiro – who did not deserve the hand fate had dealt – should be our friend rather than our slave. Believe me, when I read your letter and Tiro's, I jumped for joy. Indeed, if **Statius**' trustworthiness and thriftiness are such a joy to me, then to how great an extent must these same qualities must be present in Tiro too, and – what's more – there is his literary skill, and his conversational skill, and his refinement, which are qualities worth more than those other attributes!

> Q. Cicero, *Letters to his Friends* F.44 (16.16) (with omissions)

> Cicero's brother had set free one of his own slaves, **Statius**, in 59 BC.

Extract 3: *in 49 BC the prospect of civil war hung over Rome. Cicero and his son Marcus decided to travel to Greece to join the Republican forces who were preparing to fight against Julius Caesar. The extract below is from a letter sent by Cicero to his wife, Terentia, as he set sail from Caieta, a port on the west coast of Italy.*

> I shall next write many letters to our friends, commending you and our **Tulliola** most earnestly to their care. I should give you words of encouragement to make you both braver if I had not found you braver than any man. First and foremost, I want you to take care of your health. Second, if you agree, please use the country houses which will be farthest away from the soldiers. The farm at Arpinum along with the household staff we have in Rome will be a good place for you if food prices go up. Darling Marcus sends you his best love. Once again, take care of yourself and goodbye.

> Cicero, *Letters to his Friends* F.155 (14.7) (with omissions, trans. adapted)

> **Tulliola** is an affectionate name for their daughter Tullia.

Source 8.4: Questions

1 Consider Extract 1.
   a. What does Cicero present as the ingredients of a true friendship?
   b. Cicero describes some of his friendships as 'self-serving' and 'feigned'. Cicero was extremely ambitious, and the Romans believed that the number and nature of one's friends served as a sign of success. Do you think that this is still true today?

2 Consider Extract 2.
   a. What talents and characteristics are we told that Tiro has?
   b. What does this extract show us about the relationship between some slaves and their masters?

3 Consider Extract 3: what does this letter show us of Cicero's relationship with his wife, daughter and son?

4 Overall, what impression do you get of Cicero's personality from these letters?

CHAPTER 8: QUESTIONS FOR DISCUSSION

1 Do you think that the cursus honorum was a good idea? What skills, experience or other qualities would a Roman need to reach the top?
You might like to consider
   - the time that it took to reach the top
   - the skills a Roman needed to succeed
   - the role of *auctoritas* and social class
   - whether elections were a reliable way of choosing the best candidates

2 From what you have read, do you think that Cicero's downfall was his own fault?
You might like to consider
   - his treatment of Catiline
   - his political principles and decisions
   - his personal enemies such as Mark Antony

3 Do you think that oratory should be an important part of political power?
You might like to consider
   - the connection between training and skill
   - the link between persuasiveness and truth
   - the different nature of public communication in the Roman world and our own

(CW) Chapter 8: Core Language Vocabulary List

appropinquō	appropinquāre, appropinquāvī + dative	approach; come near to
labōrō	labōrāre, labōrāvī	work; toil
legō	legere, lēgī	read; choose
scrībō	scrībere, scrīpsī	write
cupiō	cupere, cupīvī,	want; desire
conveniō	convenīre, convēnī	come together; gather; meet
exeō	exīre, exiī	go out from; go away
ineō	inīre, iniī	go into; enter
pereō	perīre, periī	die; perish
redeō	redīre, rediī	go back; come back; return
epistula	epistulae, f	letter
liber	librī, m	book
vir	virī, m	man; husband
magister	magistrī, m	teacher
clāmor	clāmōris, m	shout; shouting; noise
senex	senis, m	old man
longus	longa, longum	long
medius	media, medium	middle
nōtus	nōta, nōtum	well known; famous
stultus	stulta, stultum	stupid; foolish
ferōx	ferōcis	fierce; ferocious
nōbilis	nōbile	of noble birth; renowned
ego	meī	I, me
nōs	nostrum	we, us
tū	tuī	you (sg)
vōs	vestrum	you (pl)
sē	suī	himself, herself, itself, themselves
frūstrā		in vain
enim		for
quam		than; how; (+ superlative) as. . .as possible

People

Catō, Catōnis, m
234–149 BC

Cato the Elder was a respected orator and a senator who took pride in preserving the traditional customs of Rome.

Cicerō, Cicerōnis, m
106–43 BC

Cicero was Rome's greatest orator and a famous Roman statesman.

Catilīna, Catilīnae, m
108–62 BC

Catiline came from a distinguished but impoverished patrician family. He plotted an armed revolt and planned to murder Cicero as an attempt to seize power.

Marcus Antōnius, Marcī Antōniī, m
83–30 BC

Mark Antony was a powerful Roman noble. Cicero saw him as a threat to the Republican principles of shared power. The enmity between them led to Cicero's death in 43 BC.

Plīnius, Plīniī, m
AD 61–113

Pliny the Younger was a studious and intelligent man who was born a century after the end of the Republic. His personal letters reveal his belief in the importance of fine writing and speaking.

Pronouns: *ego, nōs, tū, vōs*

The words for *I, we, you* (sg) and *you* (pl) are known as **personal pronouns**. Here are their Latin forms:

nominative	ego – I	tū – you (sg)	nōs – we	vōs – you (pl)
accusative	mē	tē	nōs	vōs
genitive	meī	tuī	nostrum	vestrum
dative	mihī	tibī	nōbis	vōbis
ablative	mē	tē	nōbis	vōbis

Unlike other pronouns, they do not have different forms for different genders, but they do have different case endings. As with all other pronouns, their case depends upon their role in their clause.

ego tē amō et **tū mē** amās   I love **you** and **you** love **me**.

EXERCISE 8.1

Note that these pronouns are not used often in the nominative in Latin: if they are, it is usually to emphasize the subject of the verb.

1. nōs ad urbem nunc appropinquāmus sed tū abes.

2. 'dā mihī hunc cibum!' puella frūstrā clāmāvit.

3. cūr magister librum meum tibī nōn ostendit?

4. frūstrā nōs erāmus amīcī vōbis; nōbis enim nōn in bellō auxilium dedistis.

5. ō senēs! vōs in forō ambulantēs cōnspexī!

6. 'numquam tē laudābō, quod mala dīxistī!' clāmāvit senātor īrātus.

7. 'ō māter,' inquit puer miser, 'quandō mē vocāvistī? tē nōn audīvī.'

8. multās hōrās per viās longās festīnābāmus quod tē cōnspicere volēbāmus.

9. tandem servī fessī cēnam bonam nōbis parāvērunt.

10. nōs in agrīs labōrābāmus; vōs tamen in vīllā dormiēbātis.

Pronouns: *sē*

You have met the pronoun for *he, she, it, they* already (*is, ea, id*). This pronoun is known as the **3rd person pronoun**, because it is used to refer to the **3rd person** of the verb.

sē is also a 3rd person pronoun, but it can only be used **reflexively**: this means that it has to refer back to the noun that is subject of the verb.

The king killed **himself**.	rēx **sē** interfēcit.
I killed **him**.	**eum** interfēcī.

Because *sē* is reflexive, it cannot work on its own as the subject and so it has no nominative form. Surprisingly, its endings are the same in the singular and the plural, and it does not have different genders.

accusative sg / pl	sē – himself, herself, itself, themselves
genitive sg / pl	suī
dative sg / pl	sibi
ablative sg / pl	sē

EXERCISE 8.2

1. saepe Cicerō, quod senātor nōtus erat, sē laudābat.

2. servī et ancillae auxilium dominis, nōn sibi, dabant.

3. uxor ferōx et virum et sē interfēcit.

4. quamquam servus meus diū dormiēbat, ego nōlēbam eum pūnīre: cūr ille servōs suōs pūnīvit?

5. puellae ad templum appropinquābant: eās per viās ambulantēs cōnspexī.

6. in epistulīs suīs Plinius saepe dē sē scrībēbat.

7. deī templa sibi cupiēbant.

8. 'hunc librum lege!' puer fessus sibi inquit.

9. līberī librōs suōs ferre possunt: eīs auxilium nōn dabō.

10. ubi subitō clāmāvit, cīvis stultus sē terruit.

Further notes on Latin word order

There are several important principles for Latin word order. As mentioned in Chapters 1 and 2, the most important of these are:

- a basic sentence is typically written as subject, object, verb
- prepositions come before their nouns.

Here are some others:

- **adjectives** are usually next to the noun they describe
- **adverbs** are usually before the verb or words to which they relate
- **clauses** within a sentence often place events in temporal order. This means that the first event often comes first in the sentence, then the second, and so on.

These word-order patterns help to make the meaning of the sentence clear: words that work together are usually next to each other, and the most important words (the subject and the main verb) are positioned at the start and end of the sentence because words placed here often carry more weight than the others.

It is possible, however, to abandon these principles: in Latin, words are often put in unusual places in order to draw attention to these words. Sometimes a Latin sentence or clause starts or ends with a word which is not its subject or the main verb, and this technique puts **emphasis** on the relevant word.

Cicerō multōs librōs scrīpsit.	v.	Cicerō librōs scrīpsit **multōs**.
Cicero wrote many books.	v.	Cicero wrote books, **many of them.**

English can do this too, for example:

The giant came into the room.	v.	Into the room came the giant.

PRACTISE YOUR ENGLISH!

Have a go at recasting the following English sentences so that you use English word order and word patterns to emphasise each of the words in bold.

1. I am approaching the **well-known** senator.

2. The **children** were writing letters.

3. The boys **bravely** approached the angry old man.

4. **You** are the woman whom I love.

5. This **cruel** man lives here.

Further notes on *eō*

eō is one of Latin's most common irregular verbs.

It is often met in **compounds**: the table below lists the most common compounds of *eō*. You met some of these compounds in Chapter 3; the others are part of the Chapter 8 vocabulary list.

Look it up! The endings for *eō* are listed in full on p245.

abeō, abīre, abiī	go away from
trānseō, trānsīre, trānsiī	go over; cross
adeō, adīre, adiī	go to; approach
exeō, exīre, exiī	go out from; go away
ineō, inīre, iniī	go into; enter
pereō, perīre, periī	die; perish
redeō, redīre, rediī	go back; come back; return

The **perfect tense** of *eō* is usually *īvī,* but it is usual for these compounds to use *-iī* instead.

The **present participle** of *eō* is very unusual: the nominative form is ***iēns***, but the stem used for the other cases is ***eunt***-.

puer flūmen **trānsiēns** clāmōrēs audīvit.	The boy, **crossing** the river, heard the shouts.
puerum flūmen **trānseuntem** vīdī.	I saw the boy **crossing** the river.

EXERCISE 8.3

1. subitō senex ē vīllā exiēns amīcum cōnspexit.

2. quandō fīliōs montēs trānseuntēs spectāvistī?

3. magister lūdum iniit et puerōs laudāvit.

4. num virī ab urbe redībant antequam fīlius rēgis periit?

5. ad ancillās fēlīcēs ā templō redeuntēs appropinquāvimus.

6. frūstrā puer fortis magnum perīculum adiit; deinde periit.

7. cūr nōbīs flūmen trānseuntibus auxilium nōn dedistī?

8. subitō paucī agricolae equum agrōs ineuntem vīdērunt.

9. nunc fīlia vestra perit: nōnne eam vīdēre vultis?

10. quod saepe nōs terruistī, abībimus.

EXERCISE 8.4: CATO THE ELDER

Cato the Elder was a respected Roman statesman and a famous orator who lived in the 3rd to 2nd century BC. He had a reputation for speaking about the importance of agriculture and warfare, and the virtues of hard work, physical toughness and courage. Cato often spoke of the damage caused to these traditional Roman customs by the vices of greed and luxury, and the corrupting influence of aspects of Greek culture. You will get an idea of Cato's speeches from the story below.

At the end of the story is an example of the way that even the best speeches can be helped by a well-chosen prop. Cato repeatedly argued for a final military campaign against Carthage, and on one famous occasion he made dramatic use of some fresh figs to demonstrate how near to Rome the threat of Carthage was.

Catō erat vir clārus. multī Rōmānī eum laudābant quod in bellīs fortiter pugnābat, dē lēgibus multa intellēxit et ōrātiōnēs bonās scrībēbat. quamquam Rōmae auctōritātem magnam habēbat, saepe in agrīs suīs labōrāre mālēbat. saepe Catō sē laudābat: 'ego sum cīvis Rōmānus, sed quoque agricola: is quī agrōs suōs amat patriam suam quoque amat. ego sum cīvis bonus.' 5

eō tempore multī Rōmānī pecūniam multam habēre volēbant: 'illī quī pecūniam habent,' inquiunt multī cīvēs, 'potestātem magnam quoque sibi habent.' 'vōs pecūniam habēre vultis,' inquit Catō, 'quod potestātem et luxuriam amātis. ego pecūniam habeō sed et patriam et glōriam amō. luxuriam nōn amō. cīvis bonus sum. itaque in bellīs pugnābō et in agrīs labōrābō; tum magnam glōriam habēbō.' 10

eō tempore multī Rōmānī quoque librōs Graecōs legēbant: 'Graecī erant cultissimī,' inquiunt hī Rōmānī. 'nōs quoque cultissimī erimus.' 'ego Graecōs librōs legere nōlō,' inquit Catō. 'Graecī nōn fortiter pugnābant; in bellīs nōn vīcērunt. ego sum fortis et audāx et saepe in agrīs meīs labōrō: is quī cultissimus est et semper librōs Graecōs legit nōn fortiter pugnat.' 15

diū Catō contrā Carthāginiensēs pugnāre volēbat. 'Carthāginiensēs semper erunt hostēs nōbis,' saepe clāmābat. 'Carthāgō dēlenda est.' ōlim, quod senātōribus persuādēre volēbat, ficōs pulchrās eīs ostendit: 'vidēte hās ficōs!' magnō cum clāmōre inquit Catō. 'hae sunt fīcī Carthāginiensēs: etiam nunc pulchrae sunt, quod iter nōn erat longum; iter erat sōlum trīduī. ego 20 Carthāginiensēs timeō quod celeriter Carthāginiensēs Rōmae adesse possunt.'

Prep 18/5/2022

lēx, lēgis, f	law
intellegō, intellegere, intellēxī	understand
ōrātiō, ōrātiōnis, f	speech
auctōritās, auctōritātis, f	authority; influence
mālō, mālle, māluī	prefer
patria, patriae, f	fatherland; (one's own) country
tempus, temporis, n	time
potestās, potestātis, f	power
lūxuria, lūxuriae, f	extravagance
glōria, glōriae, f	glory
cultissimus, cultissima, cultissimum	most refined
hostis, hostis, m	enemy
dēlenda est	'must be destroyed'
fīcus, fīcī, f	fig
iter, itineris, n	journey
sōlum	only
trīduī	'three days (long)'

Superlative adjectives

You have met three different types of adjectives so far.

• īrātus, īrāta, īrātum	2-1-2 adjective
• fortis, forte	3rd declension adjective
• audāx, audācis	3rd declension adjective

Each of these also has a **superlative** form: this is a form which means **very. . .** or **the most. . .**

The most common **superlative** ending is **-issimus, -issima, -issimum**.

• īrātissimus, īrātissima, īrātissimum	very angry
• fortissimus, fortissima, fortissimum	very brave
• audācissimus, audācissima, audācissimum	very bold

For some adjectives the ending **-errimus** or **-illimus** is used instead.

• celerrimus, celerrima, celerrimum	very fast
• facillimus, facillima, facillimum	very easy
• difficillimus, difficillima, difficillimum	very difficult

As in English, some of Latin's most common adjectives, however, have **irregular** superlative forms as shown in the table below.

> **Note that** all superlative adjectives have 2-1-2 endings: to see these in full, see pp229 and 231.

bonus, bona, bonum – good	optimus, optima, optimum – best
malus, mala, malum – bad	pessimus, pessima, pessimum – worst
magnus, magna, magnum – big	maximus, maxima, maximum – greatest; largest; biggest
multus, multa, multum – much; many	plūrimus, plūrima, plūrimum – most; very many
parvus, parva, parvum – small	minimus, minima, minimum – smallest; least

EXERCISE 8.5

1. cīvēs nōbilēs plūrimam pecūniam et vīllās maximās habēbant.
2. ubi clāmōrēs audīvit, magister īrātissimus līberōs pessimōs pūnīvit.
3. plūrimī Rōmānī contrā rēgem saevum frūstrā pugnāvērunt.
4. 'stultissimī estis!' clāmāvit pater, 'equum enim optimum interfēcistis!'
5. facillimum est epistulam scrībere sed difficillimum est senibus persuādēre.
6. hic dominus crūdēlissimus est: minimum cibum servīs dedit.
7. miserrima sum et tu quoque trīstissimus es: quid faciēmus?
8. quod cīvēs perīculum timēbant, mūrī hūius urbis altissimī sunt.

EXERCISE 8.6: CICERO AND CATILINE

63 BC was the year of Catiline's notorious conspiracy to murder the Roman consuls and seize power. Catiline won support by the promise that he would secure the cancellation of all debts. This made him immediately popular among the citizens who were stuck in the grip of the high level of interest charged by some senators for money they had lent. Cicero was consul at the time: he stood firm against Catiline's plots and was praised as Rome's saviour.

In many ways, this was Cicero's finest hour, but as the years rolled on, his decision to inflict the death penalty upon some of the conspirators without fair trial became increasingly contentious and ultimately resulted in his own exile from Rome.

Catilīna erat vir nōbilis sed ferōcissimus. clam Catilīna et multī cīvēs convēnērunt. 'interficite cōnsulēs!' clāmāvit Catilīna. 'potestātem capite! contrā senātōrēs pugnāte et mē cōnsulem facite! tum nōn senātōrēs pecūniam plūrimam habēbunt sed nōs pecūniam habēbimus!' multī cīvēs habēbant pecūniam
5   minimam; hīs cīvibus Catilīna persuāsit.

Cicerō tamen erat cōnsul. 'Catilīna est homō stultissimus,' inquit Cicerō, 'et cīvis pessimus. ego tamen sum cōnsul optimus. Catilīna mē nōn interficiet. quod Catilīna cōnsulēs Rōmānōs interficere vult, eum pūniam.'

Cicerō et cēterī senātōrēs convēnērunt: 'nunc Catilīna nōn est cīvis nōbilissimus,'
10   inquit Cicerō īrātissimus. 'nunc Catilīna nōbīs est hostis audācissimus! nōs – quod Rōmānī et fortēs sumus – semper hostēs interficere cupimus; nunc tempus est Catilīnam interficere, quod est homō saevissimus.' multī Rōmānī contrā Catilīnam pugnāvērunt: mox Catilīna erat mortuus. 'tū, ō Cicerō,' inquiunt cīvēs, 'senātor es optimus! urbem nostram līberāvistī! tū, ō Cicerō, es pater patriae.' Cicerō
15   laetissimus erat et sē magnopere laudāvit: 'nunc clārissimus sum quod ego urbem nostram ē perīculō maximō līberāvī.'

postea tamen, cīvēs Cicerōnem nōn laudābant: 'Catilīna, quamquam pessimus erat, nōn hostis sed cīvis erat: erat nefās cīvem interficere. tū, ō Cicerō, cīvēs interficere volēbās. tū es cīvis pessimus; nunc tē pūniēmus.' Rōmānī Cicerōnem
20   Rōmā exīre iussērunt. Cicerō miserrimus erat. 'Rōmam servāvī,' inquit, 'sed frūstrā: Rōmānī enim mē pūnīvērunt.'

clam	in secret
cōnsul, cōnsulis, m	consul
potestās, potestātis, f	power
hostis, hostis, m	enemy
tempus, temporis, n	time
patria, patriae, f	fatherland; (one's own) country
postea	afterwards
nefās	'crime', 'wrong'
servō, servāre, servāvī	save

Comparative adjectives

A **comparative** adjective means *more.* . . or *rather* or *too.* . .

Here are the endings for **laetior**, which means **more happy, rather happy** or **happier**:

> **Note that** all comparative adjectives use these endings.

	masculine / feminine	neuter
nominative sg	laet-**ior**	laet-**ius**
accusative sg	laet-**iōrem**	laet-**ius**
genitive sg	laet-**iōris**	laet-**iōris**
dative sg	laet-**iōrī**	laet-**iōrī**
ablative sg	laet-**iōre**	laet-**iōre**
nominative pl	laet-**iōrēs**	laet-**iōra**
accusative pl	laet-**iōrēs**	laet-**iōra**
genitive pl	laet-**iōrum**	laet-**iōrum**
dative pl	laet-**iōribus**	laet-**iōribus**
ablative pl	laet-**iōribus**	laet-**iōribus**

As with superlative adjectives, some adjectives have **irregular** forms for their comparatives, as shown in the table below. Although these comparatives are irregular in their stems, they use the same case endings as *laetior*.

bonus, bona, bonum – good	melior, melius – better
malus, mala, malum – bad	peior, peius – worse
magnus, magna, magnum – big	maior, maius – bigger; larger; greater
parvus, parva, parvum – small	minor, minus – smaller
multus, multa, multum – much; many	plūs – more (see p138)

Comparing nouns

Latin has two ways of comparing nouns:

● the **ablative** case can be used to mean **than**

Catō fortior erat **Cicerōne**.   Cato was braver **than Cicero**.

● *quam* can be used to mean **than**; the two nouns compared will be in the **same case**

hic vīlla pulchriōr est
    quam ille hortus.

This house is more beautiful
    than that garden.

If the comparative adjective applies directly to the noun that is the focus of the comparison, this is known as **direct comparison.** If one noun is compared to another via something else, this is known as **indirect comparison.**

● The master is happier
    than his slave.   **direct comparison**
● This master has more slaves
    than that master does.   **indirect comparison**

The ablative of comparison can only be used for **direct** comparison. *quam* can be used for either **direct** or **indirect** comparison.

The ablative adjective ***multō*** can be used with a comparative to mean *much* or *by much.*

nunc **multō** laetior sum!   I am **much** happier now!

EXERCISE 8.7

1. pater laetior erat quam māter.

2. hī puerī multō ferōciōrēs sunt illīs.

3. maiōrem equum ēmī quam tū.

4. cūr ille senātor cīvibus peiōribus persuādēre cupiēbat?

5. 'domina mea est multō saevior quam domina tua,' lacrimāns inquit servus miser.

6. melius est aquam bibere quam vīnum.

7. 'numquam Graecī fortiōrēs erunt quam nōs!' clāmāvērunt Rōmānī.

8. cūr per viam longiōrem ambulāmus? fessus sum. ad vīllam redīre et dormīre cupiō.

9. 'hī iuvenēs sunt stultiōrēs,' clāmāvit magister. 'semper librōs frūstrā legunt.'

10. Cicerō, ubi Rōma exiit, saepe miserior erat quam amīcī.

EXERCISE 8.8: CICERO AND HIS DAUGHTER

In 45 BC Cicero's daughter died in childbirth. The letters Cicero wrote at the time record the grief he felt at her death. This grief was made worse because, in the midst of the decline of his political career, he said he had little else to give him cause for joy.

Cicerō fīliam <u>cārissimam</u> habēbat. Cicerō hanc fīliam magnopere amābat. fīlia, tamen, ubi fīlium <u>pariēbat</u>, subitō periit. Cicerō trīstissimus erat et magnopere lacrimābat. multās epistulās ad amīcum, <u>Atticum</u> nōmine, scrībēbat. in hīs epistulīs Cicerō sīc scrīpsit: 'nunc multō miserior sum quam eram. nunc ego et amīcī meī nōn convenīmus; nunc magnopere lacrimō et in silvīs ambulō; nunc   5
mihī <u>sōlitūdō</u> est amīcus.'

Cicerō ad vīllam Atticī adiit. Atticus plūrimōs librōs Graecōs habēbat. Cicerō hōs librōs Graecōs legēbat: 'librōs, quōs virī dē <u>dolōre</u> scrīpsērunt, legere volō,' inquit Cicerō. 'hī librī meliōrēs sunt mihī quam librī quōs virī dē <u>laetitiā</u> scrīpsērunt. mihī hī librī magistrī erunt.' Cicerō, postquam dē dolōre lēgit, librum suum   10
scrīpsit: 'nunc ego quoque sum vir quī dē dolōre scrīpsit: huic librō novō nōmen est 'cōnsōlātiō'.'

multī amīcī Cicerōnis ad eum epistulās scrīpsērunt: 'nōlī semper lacrimāre,' scrīpsērunt amīcī. 'omnēs hominēs <u>interdum</u> lacrimant; sed tum <u>necesse</u> est
<u>alia</u> facere.'   15

'ego sum trīstior quam illī hominēs,' respondit Cicerō. 'illī hominēs erant nōbilēs et clārī; ego nōn iam sum <u>cōnsul</u>, nōn iam cīvēs mē laudant; nunc senex sum. mihī fīlia cārior erat quam omnia. nunc fīlia mea est mortua. nunc <u>nihil</u> habeō.'   20

cārus, cāra, cārum	dear
pariō, parere, peperī	give birth to
Atticus, Atticī, m	Atticus
sōlitūdō, sōlitūdinis, f	solitude
dolor, dolōris, m	pain; grief
laetitia, laetitiae, f	happiness
cōnsōlātiō, cōnsōlātiōnis, f	consolation; comfort
interdum	sometimes
necesse	'necessary'
alia (accusative neuter pl)	'other things'
cōnsul, cōnsulis, m	consul
nihil	'nothing'

Comparative and superlative adverbs

Adverbs also have **comparative** and **superlative** forms; as with normal adverbs, the endings for each of these do not change.

Here are some examples:

	comparative adverb	superlative adverb
fortiter – bravely	fortius – more bravely	fortissimē – most bravely
celeriter – quickly	celerius – more quickly	celerrimē – most quickly
ferōciter – fiercely	ferōcius – more fiercely	ferōcissimē – most fiercely
saepe – often	saepius – more often	saepissimē – most often
diū – for a long time	diūtius – for rather a long time	diūtissimē – for a very long time
magnopere – greatly	magis – more	maximē – very greatly

If **quam** is used with a **superlative** adverb, it means **as. . . as possible**.

quam celerrimē festīnāvī.   I hurried **as quickly as possible**.

EXERCISE 8.9

1. hae puellae celerius labōrant quam illae.

2. 'fortissimē perībō!' clāmāvit cīvis audāx.

3. Rōmam quam celerrimē festīnāre cupiō.

4. Cicerō, quod verba plūrima et optima dīxit, saepius senātōribus persuāsit.

5. cōnspexistīne virum meum? ā vīllā diūtius abest.

6. hic senātor illa verba stultissimē dīxit: mihī nōn persuāsit.

7. Rōmānī, quod Rōmam amābant, in multīs bellīs ferōcissimē pugnābant.

8. fīlius meus Rōmam saepius adiit quam ego.

9. 'in forō conveniēmus,' clāmāvērunt cīvēs, 'et quam fortissimē contrā rēgem crūdēlem pugnābimus!'

10. diūtissimē agricola in agrīs labōrābat magis quam fīliī.

EXERCISE 8.10: CICERO'S DEATH

Despite the decline in his political career, Cicero continued to stand up for Republican values and oppose those who were trying to seize too much power for themselves. One of these men, Mark Antony, he attacked vociferously in a series of speeches known as the Philippics.

Antony, however, soon formed a powerful alliance with two of Rome's most ambitious nobles. This alliance was known as the triumvirate. Antony and his allies ruthlessly hunted down their political enemies, among whom was Cicero. Cicero was brutally murdered by Antony's soldiers in 43 BC.

Rōmae erant multī nōbilēs quī <u>potestātem</u> habēre cupiēbant. Cicerō hōs nōbilēs nōn laudābat et saepe haec scrīpsit: 'nōn bonum est paucīs cīvibus potestātem habēre; bonum est plūribus cīvibus potestātem habēre.' <u>inter</u> hōs nōbilēs erat Marcus Antōnius. Cicerō Antōnium nōn laudāvit et multās <u>ōrātiōnēs</u> contrā Antōnium ferōcissimē scrīpsit: 'Antōnius est cīvis saevissimus et pessimus,' 5
inquit Cicerō, 'Antōnius potestātem omnem sibi cupit; Antōnius sē, nōn Rōmam, amat. volō Antōnium esse mortuum.'

Antōnius, tamen, amīcōs nōbilēs et nōtōs habēbat: duo ex hīs amīcīs, <u>Octāviānus</u> et <u>Lepidus</u> nōmine, auxilium Antōniō dedērunt. 'nunc nōs sumus amīcī trēs,' laetī inquiunt, 'et plūs potestātis habēmus quam cēterī cīves. nunc est <u>tempus</u> 10
interficere omnēs quī nōbis nōn <u>favent</u>.' Antōnius et Octāviānus et Lepidus <u>trecentōs</u> senātōrēs interficere cupiēbant; Antōnius <u>praesertim</u> Cicerōnem interficere cupiēbat.

Cicerō perterritus erat. 'nunc Antōnius <u>nimium potestātis</u> habet,' trīstis inquit. 'nunc Rōmā exībō; numquam iterum redībō.' Cicerō Rōmā celerrimē exiit sed 15
Antōnius <u>mīlitēs</u> eum <u>invenīre</u> iussit. hī mīlitēs Cicerōnem ad <u>nāvem</u> festīnantem invēnērunt. Cicerō <u>cervīcem</u> mīlitibus ostendit: 'hīc!' clāmāvit Cicerō, 'hīc mē interficite! perībō, sed quam nōbilissimē perībō.'

mīlitēs <u>caput et manūs</u> Cicerōnis Rōmam tulērunt. in mediō forō Antōnius caput et manūs omnibus cīvibus saevissimē ostendit. 'hoc caput,' inquit, 'et hae 20
manūs contrā mē multās ōrātiōnēs fēcērunt: quamquam nunc iterum adsunt, numquam iterum ōrātiōnem facient.' cīvēs erant perterritī: 'Antōnius Cicerōnem saevius interfēcit; nunc Antōnium maximē timēmus.'

potestās, potestātis, f	power
inter (+ accusative)	among
ōrātiō, ōrātiōnis, f	speech
Octāviānus, Octāviānī, m	Octavian
Lepidus, Lepidī, m	Lepidus
tempus, temporis, n	time
faveō, favēre, fāvī (+ dative)	support
trecentī, trecentae, trecenta	300
praesertim	especially
nimium potestātis	'too much power'
mīles, mīlitis, m	soldier
inveniō, invenīre, invēnī	find
nāvis, nāvis, f	ship
cervīx, cervīcis, f	throat
caput et manūs	'head and hands'

> You have not met these endings yet, but the forms ***caput et manūs*** can be either **nominative** or **accusative**.

The pluperfect tense

You have met two **past tenses** so far: the **perfect** and the **imperfect** tense.

Latin has one more past tense: the **pluperfect tense**. This tense is translated as follows:

rēxeram   I **had** ruled

All verbs (including the irregular verbs) form their **pluperfect** in the same way: they use their **perfect stem** and the following endings.

I had ruled	rēx**eram**
you (sg) had ruled	rēx**erās**
he / she / it had ruled	rēx**erat**
we had ruled	rēx**erāmus**
you (pl) had ruled	rēx**erātis**
they had ruled	rēx**erant**

The pluperfect tense is used for actions which are **more** in the past than another past action.

Rōmulus Rōmānōs rēxerat; postquam periit, Rōmānī trīstēs erant.
Romulus **had ruled** the Romans; after he died, the Romans were sad.

N.B. English often uses the pluperfect tense in subordinate clauses, but in Latin the perfect is much more common. This means that sometimes a Latin perfect tense will be translated into the pluperfect tense in English.

ubi librum **lēgistī,** mihī dedistī.   **Latin perfect**
When **you had read** the book, you gave it to me.   **English pluperfect**

EXERCISE 8.11

1. hic servus cēnam optimam parāverat sed dominus diūtius in forō manēbat.

2. magister librum nōn lēgerat: verba stultissima līberīs dīxit.

3. agricola, quod amīcus equum iam ēmerat, pecūniam plūrimam habēbat.

4. cīvēs mūrōs altōs nōn aedificāverant; itaque perīculum maximum erat.

5. vīnum optimum bibere cupiēbāmus sed amīcī nostrī omne vīnum – et optimum et pessimum – iam biberant.

6. Rōmānī, ubi arma mortuōrum cēpērunt, laetissimī erant.

7. 'cūr celerius nōn labōrās?' māter īrāta clāmāverat, sed tum fīliam lacrimantem cōnspexit et misera erat.

8. ubi in mediō forō convēnimus, laetissimī erāmus.

EXERCISE 8.12: PLINY PREFERS TO STUDY

Even after the end of the Roman Republic, oratory remained an important way for Romans to prove their worth and it continued to be a central part of Roman education. The story below is an example of one Roman's commitment to learning the best way to use words effectively.

One of the most famous writers of Latin prose in the 1st century AD was Pliny the Younger. As a young man, Pliny spent time with his uncle, Pliny the Elder, who was a respected Roman writer and also the commander of the Roman fleet. When Mount Vesuvius erupted in AD 79, Pliny the Elder made a heroic effort to sail across the Bay of Naples in an attempt to rescue the people who were living near to the volcano. In his letters, Pliny explained his choice to prioritize his education instead of joining in with the rescue mission.

Plīnius erat vir nōtus et clārus: multōs librōs et plūrimās epistulās scrīpsit. <u>avunculus</u> Plīniī erat quoque vir nōtus et clārus. ōlim Plīnius, ubi iuvenis erat, quod avunculus multōs librōs scrīpserat et erat magister bonus, <u>apud</u> avunculum manēbat. 'librōs plūrimōs legam!' inquit Plinius. 'tum nōn stultus erō!'

5 prope vīllam avunculī erat mōns ingēns, <u>Vesuvius</u> nōmine. subitō ex hōc monte <u>flammae</u> altissimae <u>ērūpērunt</u>. Plīnius et avunculus clāmōrēs audīvērunt. '<u>fortasse</u> multī pereunt,' inquit avunculus. 'fortasse perīculum maximum est. ego tamen nōn perterritus sum. hīs hominibus auxilium dabō.' Plīnius tamen, ubi clāmōrēs audīvit, librum legēbat. 'vīsne ad montem īre?' rogāvit avunculus.

10 'nōlō,' respondit Plīnius.

Plīnius ad montem īre nōlēbat quod avunculus librum optimum eī dederat. 'hic liber,' inquit Plīnius, 'est optimus. <u>Līvius</u> hunc librum scrīpsit. Līvius hunc librum <u>ēlegantissimē</u> scrīpsit. Līvius multōs librōs ēlegantissimē scrīpsit quod Līvius <u>ipse</u> librōs multōs lēgerat. Līviō illī librī erant magistrī, sed nunc mihī Līvius est

15 magister meus. Līvius est magister optimus. ego quoque multōs librōs et <u>ōrātiōnēs</u> ēlegantissimē scrībere volō. nōn ad montem ībō sed hīc – hunc librum optimum legēns – manēbō.'

avunculus, avunculī, m	uncle
apud (+ accusative)	at the house of
Vesuvius, Vesuviī, m	Mt Vesuvius
flamma, flammae, f	flame
ērumpō, ērumpere, ērūpī	burst forth
fortasse	perhaps
Līvius, Līviī, m	Livy (a famous Roman historian)
ēlegantissimus, ēlegantissima, ēlegantissimum	most elegant
ipse (nominative masculine sg)	'himself'
ōrātiō, ōrātiōnis, f	speech

Chapter 8: Additional Language

SECTION A8: CHAPTER 8 VOCABULARY

Exercise A8.1: Derivations

Complete the table using the Chapter 8 vocabulary list.

	derivation	explanation	Latin word	meaning
1	frustration			
2	notable			
3	library			
4	virile			
5	senile			
6	egotist			
7	legible			
8	labour			
9	convention			
10	script			

Exercise A8.2: Parts of speech

Sort the following words from Chapter 8 into the correct categories and write the meaning next to each word.

nōtus	senex	epistula	nōbilis
frūstrā	ego	vir	nōs
ferōx	sē	stultus	magister

nouns	pronouns	adjectives	adverbs

Exercise A8.3: Case endings (nouns and adjectives)

Circle the stem and identify the declension of the following nouns and adjectives from Chapter 8. Then give the new form requested.

	Latin	declension	
1	liber, librī, m		accusative sg =
2	senex, senis, m		nominative pl =
3	epistula, epistulae, f		ablative pl =
4	vir, virī, m		accusative pl =
5	clāmor, clāmōris, m		ablative sg =
6	magister, magistrī, m		genitive pl =
7	ferōx, ferōcis		dative feminine pl =
8	nōbilis, nōbile		nominative neuter sg =
9	stultus, stulta, stultum		accusative masculine pl =
10	longus, longa, longum		dative masculine sg =
11	medius, media, medium		genitive feminine sg =
12	nōtus, nōta, nōtum		nominative masculine pl =

Exercise A8.4: Verbs

Identify the tense of the Chapter 8 verbs in the table below and translate each one. Then change the form from singular to plural, or plural to singular, keeping the tense and person the same.

Remember that you need to look at the stem as well as the ending. Here are the principal parts for each verb so that you can see their different stems.

appropinquō, appropinquāre, appropinquāvī
labōrō, labōrāre, labōrāvī
legō, legere, lēgī
scrībō, scrībere, scrīpsī
cupiō, cupere, cupīvī
conveniō, convenīre, convēnī
exeō, exīre, exiī
ineō, inīre, iniī
pereō, perīre, periī
redeō, redīre, rediī

> The irregular endings for **eō** and its compounds are listed on p245.

	Latin	tense	translation	new form
1	labōrābant	imperfect	they were working	laborabaut
2	lēgī	present perfect	I read	legimus
3	scrīpserāmus	present	we had written today are working	scripseram
4	cupiam	present future	they I shall want	cupiemus
5	conveniunt	present	they gather	convenit
6	exībās	imperfect	you were going out	etibatis
7	init	perfect	he (she) it goes in	inium
8	perībant	imperfect	they were digging	peribaut
9	rediīmus	perfect	we returned	redii
10	appropinquābit	future	he shall approach	appropinquabaut

SECTION B8: GRAMMAR

Exercise B8.1: Pronoun endings

This exercise focuses on the pronouns you have met in Chapter 8.

Complete the table with the correct form of each pronoun.

		accusative	genitive	dative	ablative
1	ego				
2	tū				
3	sē				
4	nōs				
5	vōs				

Exercise B8.2: Pronouns in sentences

This exercise focuses on the pronouns and verbs you have met in the vocabulary list for Chapter 8.

Give the correct form of the pronoun for the words in **purple** in the sentences below. You will need to think about the case that follows each verb and whether or not a preposition is needed.

1. My father **approached us**.
2. O freedmen, they read a letter **to you**.
3. **We** approached the fierce teacher but **you (pl)** went away.
4. Books are excellent **for us**, O Romans.
5. Because **you (sg)** were working, I read a book.
6. Don't go away from **us**!
7. He chose a book **for himself**.
8. They returned to **me**.
9. It is stupid **for us** to write this letter.
10. You (sg) have worked for a long time **for yourself**.

> Remember that **appropinquō** is followed by a dative noun or **ad** + accusative.

Exercise B8.3: Superlative adjectives

This exercise focuses on the superlative forms of adjectives you have met in Chapter 7 and Chapter 8, and the irregular superlatives you met in Chapter 8.

Complete the sentence with the correct form of the superlative adjective and translate the whole sentence.

1. per viam (longissima / longissimam / longissimae) ambulāvimus.
2. 'sum senātor (clārissimum / clārissimī / clārissimus),' inquit Cicerō.
3. ille servus verba (stultissimōs / stultissima / stultissimus) dīxit.
4. haec dea est (ferōcissima / ferōcissimō / ferōcissimae).
5. senātōrēs cīvibus (nōbilissimōs / nōbilissimīs / nōbilissimae) crēdēbant.
6. 'ō domina,' inquit puer, 'tū es ūna ē fēminīs (optimīs / optimus / optimōs)!'
7. illa est uxor magistrī (pessimī / pessimae / pessima).
8. convēnimus quod clāmōrem (maximus / maximum / maximōrum) audīvimus.
9. līberī librōs (plūrimōs / plūrimī / plūrimus) in vīllā legēbant.
10. nūntius (nōtissimōs / nōtissimus / nōtissimās) ē forō exiit.

Exercise B8.4: Comparative adjectives

This exercise practises the comparative forms of adjectives you have met in Chapter 7 and Chapter 8, and the irregular comparatives you met in Chapter 8.

Complete the table below.

	comparative adjective	meaning	
1	longior, longius		dative masculine sg =
2	clārior, clārius		accusative feminine pl =
3	stultior, stultius		nominative neuter pl =
4	ferōcior, ferōcius		genitive masculine pl =
5	nōbilior, nōbilius		genitive feminine sg =
6	nōtior, nōtius		ablative neuter sg =
7	melior, melius		dative feminine sg =
8	maior, maius		ablative feminine pl =
9	peior, peius		dative masculine pl =
10	minor, minus		accusative neuter sg =

Exercise B8.5: The pluperfect tense

This exercise practises the pluperfect tense of verbs you have met in the vocabulary list for Chapter 8.

Give the pluperfect of the following verbs in the form requested.

	principal parts	pluperfect
1	labōrō, labōrāre, labōrāvī	you (sg) had worked =
2	legō, legere, lēgī	I had read =
3	scrībō, scrībere, scrīpsī	we had written =
4	cupiō, cupere, cupīvī	you (pl) had desired =
5	conveniō, convenīre, convēni	they had gathered =
6	appropinquō, appropinquāre, appropinquāvī	they had approached =
7	redeō, redīre, rediī	you (pl) had returned =
8	pereō, perīre, periī	he had perished =
9	exeō, exīre, exiī	she had gone out from =
10	ineō, inīre, iniī	we had gone into =

Exercise B8.6: Irregular verbs in the pluperfect tense

This exercise practises the pluperfect of the irregular verbs you first met in Chapter 3 and Chapter 4.

Give the pluperfect of the following verbs in the form requested.

	principal parts	pluperfect
1	sum, esse, fuī	she had been =
2	possum, posse, potuī	we had been able =
3	volō, velle, voluī	you (sg) had wanted =
4	ferō, ferre, tulī	they had brought =
5	nōlō, nōlle, nōluī	you (pl) had not wanted =
6	eō, īre, īvī / iī	I had gone =

SECTION C8: ENGLISH TO LATIN SENTENCES

Exercise C8.1: Sentences to translate into Latin

1. The citizen, who had written long letters to the senator, greatly desired to praise him.
2. Although they fought as fiercely as possible for a long time, our men died in vain.
3. The letters were more famous than that man who had written them.
4. This old man is more stupid than that old man!
5. O children, I want you to approach the rather fierce teacher bravely.
6. In vain the very stupid children read the rather long books.
7. The old man had desired to greet the other old men in the **middle** of the forum.
8. I shall read letters to you often, but you will read these books more often.
9. The boy and the girl, working in the house, wept because they had the worst father.
10. Were the Greeks fiercer than the Romans? The Romans conquered more kings.

> **medius** is an adjective, so it agrees with the noun it describes e.g. *in mediā silvā* – in the middle of the wood.

SECTION D: CONSOLIDATION

Exercises for Additional Language Section D are available on the companion website. Exercises are structured by grammatical category, and cover all Core Vocabulary met so far within each category. For Chapter 8, these exercises are as follows:

- Exercise D8.1: 2nd declension nouns
- Exercise D8.2: 2nd conjugation verbs

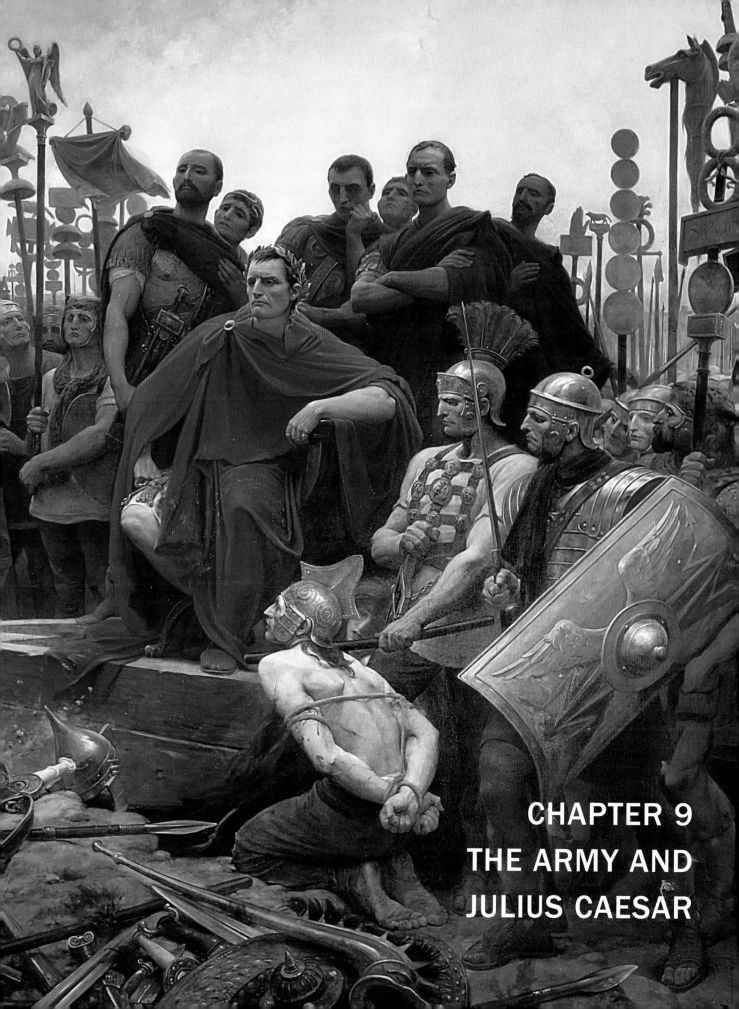

CHAPTER 9
THE ARMY AND
JULIUS CAESAR

Ⓒ Chapter 9: Introduction

The Roman army

The Romans were famous for being excellent soldiers. They combined tough training and discipline with even better planning and organization. The Romans understood that having a big army meant nothing if the soldiers were hungry, tired or suffering from illness. As you can see from Source 9.2, they built excellent camps to ensure that when the time came to fight, their soldiers were in good health and had eaten and slept well. They were brilliant military planners and often defeated much bigger enemy armies.

FIGURE 9.1   **A replica of a scene from Trajan's Column**

One of the most famous manoeuvres of the Roman army was the testudo, or tortoise formation: the Romans were trained to work as a group and use their shields like the shell of a tortoise in order to protect themselves from airborne weapons such as javelins, or to hold their ground defensively. This image of a testudo is from a column built in celebration of the emperor Trajan's military success in the 2nd century AD. A copy of the column is in the Victoria and Albert Museum in London.

Marius' reforms

At the end of the 2nd century BC, Rome's best general was Gaius Marius: he was consul seven times and you read a story about him in Chapter 6. He was so successful in battle that he was praised as being an additional founder of Rome. Marius introduced significant reforms to the Roman army. He realized that the army was marching too slowly because they had to wait for the mules that were used to transport equipment and supplies. As you will read in Exercise 9.2, to fix this he trained his soldiers to march carrying all their own weapons, armour, food and equipment, about 25kg in total. Marius could now move his army much faster: their increased speed meant they could gain the advantage of a surprise attack.

Marius' reforms went beyond training and equipment: they also tackled recruitment. As shown in Source 9.1, Roman soldiers had traditionally supplied their own equipment and their role in the army was determined by their wealth. By the end of the 2nd century BC, the Romans found that under these rules there were no longer enough citizens who owned enough property to serve as soldiers. As you will see in Exercise 9.2, Marius was worried that unless the rules changed Rome would not have enough soldiers to call upon if the Republic was attacked by multiple enemies at once. To address this, Marius removed the property and wealth restrictions of military service, a reform which greatly increased the number of soldiers available to the Republic.

The consequences of success

The success of the Roman army meant that Roman territory expanded greatly over time. During the early Republic, Rome's wars were fought in Italy, against local rivals. As you have read in some of the stories in previous chapters, in the 3rd century BC the Romans came into conflict with Carthage, a significant Mediterranean power. By the middle of the 2nd century BC Rome had conquered Carthage, and had also acquired territory in Sicily, Sardinia, Spain, Africa and Greece.

By the 1st century BC the Romans were fighting battles as far away as modern-day Armenia and Azerbaijan, more than 1,700 miles from Rome. The distances involved brought with them another major change for the army: the rules that had traditionally limited the power of the generals had to be relaxed. Rome was too far away to make it practical to wait for approval before major military decisions were taken, and some generals were given the power even to sign treaties before a decision had been discussed in the senate. In addition, although the yearly election of magistrates in Rome continued, a general could remain in power far longer. The limits to individual power in Rome no longer applied to the same degree for the generals in the army.

FIGURE 9.2 **Marius**

Marius had a brilliant military career and he was one of Rome's most famous generals. This bust of him was made in the late 1st century BC. It is currently held in the Glyptothek in Munich, Germany.

The generals: status, wealth and power

As discussed in Chapter 8, military experience was usually an essential part of any ambitious Roman's career and senior magistrates such as praetors and consuls were often expected to command armies. The growing power of Roman generals, however, had drastic implications for the health of the Republic. As the army became more successful, the prizes from victory grew greater and greater. Ambitious men were ever more hungry for individual success, and this pulled against the Republican principles of shared and limited power.

Success on the battlefield brought with it glory and *auctoritas*. Throughout Roman history, if a general's victory was impressive enough, the senate could grant him a public celebration known as a triumph. The victorious general would enter Rome before vast crowds riding a four-horse chariot at the head of his army, followed by a procession displaying the treasures he had plundered and the prisoners he had captured. The general would wear a crown of laurel and a special purple and gold triumphal toga, and he might even paint his face red to look like Mars, the god of war. As the wars grew bigger, so did the triumphs: as you will read in Exercise 9.5, triumphal processions could be on an enormous scale. The games and festivities which followed could last for days.

In addition, military success brought wealth not just to Rome but to the generals too. When the Romans conquered a city, they could plunder its wealth and the greatest share of this went to the general. Generals also had the right to take prisoners of war, who could then be sold for profit as slaves. In Exercise 9.5 you will read about the enormous wealth gained by a general named Lucullus, and how he paraded this wealth to gain status at Rome.

This increase in wealth meant that generals had the raw power to go beyond the laws and structures of the Republic. Crassus, the richest man in the 1st century BC, once boasted that a man could not consider himself truly wealthy until he could pay for an army. This boast had a dangerous reality behind it. Marius' reforms had allowed poor citizens, whose only income came from soldiering, to join the army. It was all too easy for a wealthy general to buy loyalty to himself, rather than the state. In 88 BC, the general Lucius Cornelius Sulla became the first Roman to march an army into Rome, killing and burning as he went, and all for the sake of his own agenda. Sulla had set an example for the next generation of generals. He showed that violence and military strength could be used to override any of Rome's laws or political structures in the name of personal ambition.

FIGURE 9.3 **The modern-day site of the gardens of Lucullus**

Pictured here is a temple in the middle of the lake in the Villa Borghese gardens in Rome. These gardens, built in 1605, are thought to have been constructed on top of the lavish and ostentatious gardens of the wealthy general Lucullus.

Julius Caesar

Julius Caesar is arguably the most famous Roman to have ever lived. He came from one of the most noble families in Rome and he claimed descent from the Roman hero Aeneas and also, therefore, from the goddess Venus herself. He was an excellent orator and, like Cicero, he had been taught by Apollonius Molon in Rhodes. Caesar was ruthless in pursuit of success. In 63 BC he stood as a candidate for the politically prestigious role of chief priest in Rome. His rivals were much older and more established than he was. To secure victory, he borrowed huge sums of money to bribe voters. Caesar won comfortably, but illegally. The historian Plutarch recorded two other stories which show the extent of Caesar's ambition. In 69 BC, Caesar had visited Spain, where he saw a statue of the 4th century BC Macedonian king, Alexander the Great. When Caesar realized that he was already the same age as Alexander had been when he conquered the known world, he wept in grief that he had not matched or surpassed Alexander's achievements. On another occasion, Caesar and his companions passed through a small village in the Alps. When his friends mocked the local people and jokingly wondered whether there were high-level political struggles even in this village in the middle of nowhere, Caesar told them, 'I would rather be first here than second at Rome.'

Caesar is most famous for his military success. As you will read in Source 9.4, many viewed him as the greatest of Rome's generals. In 47 BC, King Pharnaces II of Pontus attacked and defeated a Roman army near the Black Sea. At that time Caesar had just won a war in Egypt. He marched immediately to avenge the defeat, covering an enormous distance very quickly. By then, Caesar's reputation was so fearsome that Pharnaces immediately sent messengers to ask for peace. Caesar refused. When he arrived, Caesar annihilated Pharnaces' much larger army in only five days. Caesar's victory was so swift and total that the report he wrote back to a friend in Rome consisted of just three words: *veni, vidi, vici* – I came, I saw, I conquered.

FIGURE 9.4   Julius Caesar

This marble bust shows Caesar as a mature man. The date of the bust is unknown; it is part of the collection in the Vatican Museums in Rome.

Consulship, Gallic Wars and the expedition to Britain

Caesar's actions and achievements also show us the darker side of power. When he was elected as one of the consuls for 59 BC, his behaviour in office was highly unusual and he often used armed men to get his way and even intimidate the other consul into supporting the laws he wanted. The Roman historian Suetonius recorded that because Caesar passed laws without his consular colleague's agreement, many Romans joked that anything that happened in 59 BC was done during 'the consulship of Julius and Caesar'.

At the end of his consulship, Caesar was made governor of territory in Northern Italy, Southern France, Slovenia and Croatia, where he was put in charge of four Roman legions to defend Rome's borders and keep the peace. Caesar decided to invade Gaul (modern-day France and Belgium), where he spent almost ten years waging war against the tribes there and beyond. As you will read in Exercise 9.7, he was the first Roman to try to invade Britain:

FIGURE 9.5 **Vercingetorix surrenders**

This painting was created by Lionel Royer in 1899. It shows the aftermath of the Battle of Alesia, the battle that completed Caesar's conquest of Gaul. The Gauls' chieftain, Vercingetorix, rode out to meet Caesar, stripped the armour and weapons from his body and threw them down at Caesar's feet. This painting movingly captures Vercingetorix's brave acceptance of his defeat and Caesar's unyielding demeanour. Vercingetorix was later strangled in his prison cell after he had been paraded humiliatingly in Rome during Caesar's triumph. The painting is now in the Crozatier Museum in France.

he made two attempts by crossing the channel in 55 BC and 54 BC. It would be another hundred years before a Roman army tried to invade Britain again, as we will see in Chapter 12. In his decade-long conquest of Gaul, Caesar killed hundreds of thousands with bloodthirsty indifference. Source 9.4 puts the death toll at one million. This involved the destruction of entire tribes and the slaughter of men, women and children. In Exercise 9.9 you will read about Caesar's merciless brutality at the siege of Alesia.

Civil war

During his time in Gaul and Britain, Caesar's relationship with the senate at Rome deteriorated. They believed he had become too powerful as a general, whereas he thought they did not show him the respect he deserved. The senate asked him to disband his army and return to Rome. He refused. In 49 BC, Caesar gathered his army and crossed the Rubicon, the river that marked the boundary between Gaul and Italy. This counted as a declaration of civil war on Rome itself. As Caesar crossed the river, he is supposed to have said *alea iacta est* – the die has been cast – once again showing the risk-taking attitude he had demonstrated throughout his life.

Caesar and his soldiers were battle-hardened and experienced. The newer, less experienced armies who opposed him stood no chance. In light of his success, Caesar was appointed dictator. The senate repeated the appointment several times, and at the fourth appointment, they declared him dictator for life. The Roman Republic, with its annual elections of two consuls, seemed well and truly dead. Many of the senators thought that Caesar was starting to behave like a king, something they believed that no Roman should ever do. A large group, who called themselves the Liberators, began to plot against him.

Assassination and aftermath

The 15th March 44 BC is one of the best-known dates in Roman history: in accordance with the conventions of the Roman calendar, it is known as the Ides of March. On this day, 60 senators surrounded Caesar in the Theatre of Pompey and stabbed him 23 times. Nobody is sure what Caesar's final words were. Some say that when he saw his friend Brutus amongst the assassins he said, 'You too?' Others say Caesar simply groaned and accepted his fate by covering his head with his robe.

Many Romans were upset that Caesar had been killed. When he gave Caesar's funeral oration, Mark Antony was able to whip the masses into a frenzy against Caesar's assassins. During the games given in Caesar's honour, a comet was seen in the sky for seven days. It was believed to represent Caesar's immortal soul and he was deified and worshipped as a god. With such strong views about Caesar on either side, it is no wonder that the aftermath of his death was a chaotic period in Roman history. Caesar had won one civil war but now another one, the Liberators' civil war, took its place. Caesar's supporters wanted to hunt down the Liberators and punish them. On the other side, men like Cicero thought the Liberators should be praised for freeing the Republic from Caesar's tyranny.

In Chapters 10 and 11 we will explore what happened next, how Antony formed a powerful alliance with Caesar's heir Octavian and how Octavian eventually became the sole ruler of the Roman world, the man known as the first emperor, Augustus.

FIGURE 9.6 The death of Caesar

This painting by Jean-Léon Gérôme was completed in 1867, and is now part of the collection in the Walters Art Museum in Baltimore, USA. The painting focuses on the moments after Caesar's public and violent assassination. The senators who stabbed him leave the scene victoriously, while the dead body of Caesar lies bleeding and alone.

CHAPTER 9: SOURCES TO STUDY

Source 9.1: Polybius describes the Roman army before the Marian reforms

Polybius was a 2nd century BC historian who found himself in a unique position. He was born in Greece but when he was a young man he was given to the Romans as a hostage and spent 17 years living among them. This first-hand experience makes Polybius' account of the Roman army in the late 2nd century BC a valuable one.

The passage below shows the connection between a soldier's wealth and his role in the army, and it also demonstrates the importance of equipment.

They choose the youngest and poorest to form the *velites*; the next to them are made *hastati*; those in the prime of life *principes*; and the oldest of all *triarii*.

The youngest soldiers or *velites* are ordered to carry a sword, javelins and a shield. The shield is strongly made and sufficiently large to afford protection, being circular and measuring three feet in diameter. They also wear a plain helmet, and sometimes cover it with a wolf's skin or something similar both to protect and to act as a distinguishing mark by which their officers can recognise them and judge if they fight pluckily or not. The wooden shaft of the javelin measures about two **cubits** in length and is about a finger's breadth in thickness; its head is a span long hammered out to such a fine edge that it is necessarily bent by the first impact, and the enemy is unable to return it. If this were not so, the missile would be available for both sides.

> A **cubit** was a unit of length, roughly equivalent to the length of a forearm.

The next in seniority called *hastati* are ordered to wear a shield, the convex surface of which measures two and a half feet in width and four feet in length, the thickness at the rim being a palm's breadth. It is made of two planks glued together, the outer surface being then covered first with canvas and then with calf-skin. Its upper and lower rims are strengthened by an iron edging which protects it from descending blows and from injury when rested on the ground. It also has an iron boss fixed to it which turns aside the most formidable blows of stones and heavy missiles in general. Besides the shield they also carry a sword, hanging on the right thigh. This is excellent for thrusting, as the blade is very strong and firm. In addition they have two javelins, a brass helmet and protection for their shins. Finally they wear as an ornament a circle of feathers with three upright purple or black feathers about a cubit in height, the addition of which is to make every man look twice his real height, and to give him a fine appearance, such as will strike terror into the enemy.

The *principes* and *triarii* are armed in the same manner except that instead of the javelins the *triarii* carry long spears.

Polybius, *The Histories*, 6.21–23 (with omissions, trans. adapted)

Source 9.1: Questions

1 Write a list of the four different classes of soldiers and the equipment that each soldier carried.

2 How was the javelin carried by the *velites* made particularly effective for the Romans?

3 What are the differences between the shields carried by the *velites* and the *hastati*?

4 What does the description of the *hastati*'s equipment tell us about the importance of appearance when it came to armour?

5 In the standard Roman battle formation at this time, the Romans arranged their army in a threefold battle line: the *hastati* were positioned at the front, the *principes* formed the middle battle line and the battle-hardened *triarii* were positioned at the back. The *velites* moved around in front of the main battle line: their role was to soften the enemy with missiles before the main engagement. Do you think it was right or fair that wealth and age affected a soldier's role in the army in this way?

Source 9.2: A plan of a Roman army camp

When a Roman army made a camp, whether as a temporary shelter for the night or as a long-term base, they typically built it to the same design. Camps almost always had four gates divided by two main streets. The via praetoria *ran from the main gate to the headquarters* (principia)*, and the* via principalis *ran from the two side gates through the centre of the camp. The commanding officer's accommodation (*praetorium*) was next to the headquarters. Around the inside of the whole camp ran the* via sagularis. *Barracks for the soldiers were placed at the front of the camp, nearer the main gate. To the rear of the camp, the Romans housed their cavalry. The hospital and food store were placed in the middle, next to the headquarters.*

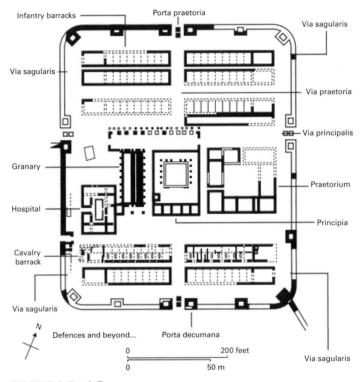

FIGURE 9.7 **A Roman army camp**

Source 9.2: Questions

1 What are the main features of the design of a Roman camp?
2 In what ways was the layout of a Roman camp sensible? Are there any parts of the design that you think are not sensible?
3 What do you think were the advantages and disadvantages of building a camp to a fixed design?
4 Consider the space allocated to different areas within the camp: what does this tell you about the needs and priorities of the Roman army?

Source 9.3: Julius Caesar attacks Britain

Julius Caesar wrote his own accounts of his campaigns. These have been of much interest to readers partly because his Latin is admired for its crisp and clear style. He writes in the third person and often refers to the Roman forces as 'our soldiers' or 'our ships'.

When Caesar planned his first invasion of Britain in 55 BC, he had originally intended to land at Dover, but as the Romans approached they found the Britons ready and waiting. Caesar sailed north, and it is thought that the invasion took place near Deal.

Caesar himself reached Britain with the first ships about nine o'clock in the morning, and saw the enemy's forces posted on all the hills. The lie of the land at this point was such that javelins could be hurled from the cliffs right on to the narrow beach enclosed between them and the sea. Caesar thought this a quite unsuitable place for landing, and therefore stayed at anchor until three o'clock, in order to give the rest of the ships time to come up. Meanwhile he assembled the officers and explained his plans. He warned them that skill in warfare, and particularly naval operations, in which things move rapidly and the situation is constantly changing, required the instant execution of every order. On dismissing the officers he found that both wind and tidal current were in his favour. He therefore gave the signal for weighing anchor, and after proceeding about seven miles ran his ships aground on an evenly sloping beach, free from obstacles.

The natives, on realising his intention, had sent forward their cavalry and a number of the chariots which they are accustomed to use in warfare; the rest of their troops followed close behind and were ready to oppose the landing. The Romans were faced with very grave difficulties. The size of the ships made it impossible to run them aground except in fairly deep water. The soldiers were unfamiliar with the ground, their hands were full, and they were weighed down by the heavy burden of their arms, and they had at the same time to jump down from the ships, get a footing in the waves, and fight the enemy, who, standing on dry land or advancing only a short way into the water, fought with all their limbs unencumbered and on perfectly familiar ground, boldly hurling javelins and galloping their horses, which were trained to this kind of work. These dangers frightened our soldiers, who were quite unaccustomed to battles of this kind, with the result that they did not show the same speed and enthusiasm as they usually did in battles on dry land.

Caesar, *Gallic Wars*, 4.23–24 (with omissions, trans. adapted)

Source 9.3: Questions

1 Why did Caesar have to abandon his plan to land at the first location?
2 Why did Caesar have to wait at anchor for six hours when he first reached Britain?
3 What advice did Caesar give to his officers?
4 Why was it so difficult for the Romans to disembark successfully at the second location?
5 This account was written by Caesar. What picture of himself do you think he intended to present?

Source 9.4: Caesar's achievements in Gaul

Caesar's campaigns in Gaul lasted from 58 to 51 BC. In this time he conquered vast areas of land and butchered the tribes who opposed him. The Greek writer Plutarch lived in the 1st–2nd century AD: he is known for his biographies of famous Romans. In this extract Plutarch compares Caesar's achievements with those of other Roman generals.

If we compare him with such men as Fabius and Scipio and Metellus, or with those who were either his contemporaries or lived a little before his time, such as Sulla, Marius, the two Luculli, or even with Pompey himself, whose fame for every kind of military excellence was, at this period, in full flower and reaching up to the skies, we shall find that Caesar's achievements surpass them all. He may be considered superior to one because of the difficulty of the country in which he fought; to another because of the extent of his conquests; to another because of the numbers and strength of the enemy forces which he defeated; to another because of the savage and treacherous character of the tribes whose goodwill he won; to another because of the reasonable and considerate way in which he treated prisoners; to another because of the gifts he gave to his soldiers and his acts of kindness to them; and he surpassed them all in the fact that he fought more battles than any of them and killed greater numbers of the enemy. For, though his campaigns in Gaul did not last for as much as ten complete years, in this time he took by storm more than 80 cities, subdued 300 nations, and fought battles at various times with three million men, of whom he destroyed one million in the actual fighting and took another million prisoner.

Plutarch, *Life of Caesar,* 15

Source 9.4: Questions

1 In your own words, explain why Plutarch thinks that Caesar's achievements were greater than those of any other Roman general.
2 Plutarch suggests that Caesar was a popular figure: detail the actions or qualities which contribute to this image.
3 Plutarch says that Caesar killed or captured millions of people in less than ten years. What does this tell us about Caesar and the Romans? How do you feel about this?
4 Shortly after Caesar was assassinated, Cicero described his character as 'an amalgamation of genius, method, memory, culture, thoroughness, intellect, and industry' and adds that 'his achievements in war, though disastrous for our country, were nonetheless mighty'. Does this change your reaction to the version of Caesar's character presented by Plutarch?

CHAPTER 9: QUESTIONS FOR DISCUSSION

1 What qualities do you think a Roman soldier needed to have, and to what extent do you think they changed over time?

You might like to consider
- personality / character
- physical strengths
- wealth
- family

2 What qualities do you think a Roman general needed to have?

You might like to consider
- previous military experience
- political experience and connections
- oratorical skills
- personal wealth
- character and values

3 Although Caesar was assassinated, there were many who strongly supported him, even after his death. Do you think we should be impressed or appalled by the actions and achievements of Caesar?

You might like to consider
- his political actions
- his military actions
- his training and education
- the outcomes of his campaigns and the territory he conquered

ⓒⓦ Chapter 9: Core Language Vocabulary List

Verbs are now listed with four principal parts. This is explained on p94.

invītō	invītāre, invītāvī, invītātum	invite
necō	necāre, necāvī, necātum	kill
occupō	occupāre, occupāvī, occupātum	take possession of; occupy
oppugnō	oppugnāre, oppugnāvī, oppugnātum	attack
superō	superāre, superāvī, superātum	overcome; overpower
vulnerō	vulnerāre, vulnerāvī, vulnerātum	wound; injure
dēleō	dēlēre, dēlēvī, dēlētum	destroy
moveō	movēre, mōvī, mōtum	move
dēfendō	dēfendere, dēfendī, dēfēnsum	defend
dūcō	dūcere, dūxī, ductum	lead; take
gerō	gerere, gessī, gestum	wear (clothes); wage (war)
incendō	incendere, incendī, incēnsum	burn; set on fire
mittō	mittere, mīsī, missum	send
occīdō	occīdere, occīdī, occīsum	kill
trādō	trādere, trādidī, trāditum	hand over; hand down
rapiō	rapere, rapuī, raptum	seize; grab
custōdiō	custōdīre, custōdīvī, custōdītum	guard
incola	incolae, m	inhabitant
patria	patriae, f	country; homeland
cōpiae	cōpiārum, f pl	forces; troops
oppidum	oppidī, n	town
proelium	proeliī, n	battle
scūtum	scūtī, n	shield
comes	comitis, m/f	comrade; companion
dux	ducis, m	leader
hostis	hostis, m	enemy
mīles	mīlitis, m	soldier
mors	mortis, f	death
bene		well
deinde		then

People and places

Marius, Mariī
157–86 BC

Marius was the Roman general who reformed the Roman army in the 2nd century BC. His reforms had long-lasting consequences.

Lūcullus, Lūcullī, m
118–56 BC

Lucullus was a Roman general who became extraordinarily wealthy as a result of war plunder.

Pompēius, Pompēiī, m
106–48 BC

Pompey was a dazzlingly brilliant general who bent or broke nearly all the rules of the cursus honorum and became one of the most powerful Romans of his day. In 49 BC he led the forces of the senate against Julius Caesar in a civil war.

Caesar, Caesaris, m
100–44 BC

Julius Caesar is arguably the most famous Roman: he gained wealth and power from military success. He drove the Republic to a civil war in 49 BC from which he emerged as the sole victor.

Gallia, Galliae, f
Gallī, Gallōrum, m pl

Gaul is the Roman name for a huge area which included modern-day France, Luxembourg, Belgium and parts of Switzerland, Italy, the Netherlands and Germany. The people who lived there were known as the **Gauls**. Caesar's victory against the Gallic chieftain **Vercingetorix** in 52 BC was seen as the final battle in Caesar's conquest of Gaul.

Vercingetorīx,
Vercingetorīgis, m
82–46 BC

Britannia, Britanniae, f
Britannī, Britannōrum, m pl

The **Britons** were the collection of Celtic tribes who lived in **Britain**. Caesar led an invasion of **Britain** in 55 BC.

Consolidation: the present participle

Remember, a **participle** is a form of a verb which behaves like an **adjective**.

In Latin, the **present participle** uses the **present stem** of the verb and so there are differences in vowels across the different conjugations.

1st conjugation	am**ā**ns, am**antis** – loving
2nd conjugation	terr**ē**ns, terr**entis** – terrifying
3rd conjugation	reg**ē**ns, reg**entis** – ruling
4th conjugation	aud**iē**ns, aud**ientis** – hearing
mixed conjugation	cap**iē**ns, cap**ientis** – taking

Participles have to **agree** with the nouns they describe.

mīlitēs **pugnantēs** erant fortēs. The **fighting** soldiers were brave.
mīlitem **pugnantem** vīdī. I saw the **fighting** soldier.

It is often better in English to translate a **participle** with a **clause**.

mīlitēs oppidum **oppugnantēs** dūxī.

→ I led the soldiers **who were attacking** the town.
I led the soldiers **while they were attacking** the town.

> **Note that** each participle changes its case endings like the 3rd declension adjective **ingēns**. These endings are listed in full on p243.

EXERCISE 9.1

1. vīdistīne mīlitēs hunc incolam vulnerantēs?

2. antequam dux oppidum dēlēvit, incolae – scūta et gladiōs ferentēs – ad mīlitēs Rōmānōs cucurrērunt.

3. clāmōrēs cīvium mūrōs dēfendentium audīvimus.

4. deinde dux – audācter clāmāns – mīlitibus persuāsit.

5. senex puerōs cibum rapientēs invēnit.

6. incolae auxilium hominibus mūrōs altōs dēlentibus nōn dedērunt.

7. domina ancillās lacrimantēs pūnīvit.

8. cūr cīvem patriam dēfendentem nōn laudāvit?

9. erant multae mortēs mīlitum nōn bene pugnantium.

10. cōnspexī hostēs ducem nostrum occīdentēs.

EXERCISE 9.2: MARIUS REFORMS THE ROMAN ARMY

Wealth traditionally determined a soldier's role in the Roman army: his position depended on his ability to buy weapons, armour and other equipment. By the end of the 2nd century BC, however, the Romans did not have enough soldiers to fight the growing number of battles in different places in their empire. Marius, Rome's most successful general at that time, introduced some radical reforms which enlarged and improved the Roman army.

ōlim mīlitēs Rōmānī erant illī quī pecūniam suam habēbant. 'nostrī mīlitēs,' inquiunt ducēs Rōmānī, 'et gladiōs et scūta et arma emere possunt. nostrī mīlitēs – sua arma optima habentēs – fortiter pugnāre possunt.'

Rōmānī tamen, quod timēbant multōs hostēs quī in multīs locīs erant, plūrēs
5   mīlitēs habēre volēbant. 'saepius hostēs nōs vulnerāvērunt,' inquit Marius, quī tum erat dux, 'et nunc multī mīlitēs mortuī sunt. plūrimī cīvēs, quod pecūniam suam nōn habent, mīlitēs esse nōn possunt; quī nunc mīlitēs erunt?'

Marius erat dux et audāx et <u>ingeniōsus</u>. 'pecūniam mīlitibus dabimus,' inquit, 'et tum etiam illī quī <u>pauperēs</u> sunt mīlitēs esse poterunt.' <u>cōnsilium</u> Mariī erat bonum: plūrimī cīvēs mīlitēs esse volēbant quod multam pecūniam habēre volēbant. mox Rōmānī plūrēs mīlitēs habēbant quam <u>anteā</u>. multōs annōs hī mīlitēs fortiter pugnābant quod ducēs <u>stīpendium</u> magnum eīs dabant.   10

Marius cōnsilia multa et bona habēbat: 'volō mīlitēs Rōmānōs celerrimē <u>contendere</u>! saepe mīlitēs, quī prīmī in terram novam veniunt, illam terram occupāre possunt. anteā nōn celerrimē contendimus quod <u>mūlī</u> <u>impedīmenta</u> ferēbant. mīlitēs tamen multō celerius festīnāre possunt quam mūlī impedīmenta ferentēs. nunc omnēs mīlitēs et cibum suum et arma sua ferentēs contendent. nunc quam celerrimē in loca nova mīlitēs movēbō.'   15

Marius etiam volēbat mīlitēs <u>valēre</u>. senātōribus sīc persuāsit: 'mīlitēs, quī nōn fessī sunt, diūtius et audācius pugnant quam hostēs. anteā mīlitēs, ubi cum hostibus nōn pugnābant, ad agrōs suōs redībant et, <u>ut</u> agricolae, labōrābant. nunc semper mīlitēs Rōmānī in <u>castrīs</u> nōn in agrīs suīs labōrābunt! nōn ad agrōs suōs redībunt sed hīc in castrīs manēbunt. prope castra labōrantēs mūrōs aedificābunt et viās facient. <u>cotīdiē</u> arma ferentēs et gladiōs habentēs current et tum valēbunt.'   25

ingeniōsus, ingeniōsa, ingeniōsum	talented; clever
pauper, pauperis	poor
cōnsilium, cōnsiliī, n	plan
anteā	before; previously
stīpendium, stīpendiī, n	military pay
contendō, contendere, contendī	march; hurry
mūlus, mūlī, m	mule
impedīmenta, impedīmentōrum, n	baggage; equipment
ut	as
valeō, valēre, valuī	be strong; hardy
castra, castrōrum, n pl	military camp
cotīdiē	every day

The passive

All the verbs you have met so far have been **active**: this label is given to verbs whose subject **does the action**.

For some forms of the verb, however, the subject **experiences** or **suffers** the action because someone / something else does it to them.

> **I was wounded** by a spear.

We call these forms of the verb **passive**.

From now on, it will be important to think of the **subject** as the **noun the sentence is about**. The subject will only be the noun which does the action if the verb is active.

- **active verbs** – subject (nominative) **does** the action
- **passive verbs** – subject (nominative) **suffers** the action

EXERCISE 9.3

For each of the following sentences identify the noun which is the nominative subject, and say whether the verb is active or passive.

1. The slave was killed by the slave girl.

2. The city is being defended by the citizens.

3. The farmer was moving the horse.

4. The soldiers will be led by the brave general.

5. The fields were destroyed by the enemy.

6. The money is handed over to me by the inhabitant.

7. We were defending our homeland bravely.

8. The house is being burned by the inhabitants.

9. The children were being guarded by the slaves.

10. The leader had been wounded in the battle.

The 4th principal part and perfect passive participles

From now on, you will see verbs listed with **four** principal parts.

> dūcō, dūcere, dūxī, ductum   lead; take

The 4th principal part is known as the **supine**, and from it we get a new **stem** for each verb.

> dūcō, dūcere, dūxī, **duct**um   the **supine stem** is *duct-*

This stem is used for the **perfect passive participle**.

> duct-us, duct-a, duct-um   having been led

> **Note that** English derivations are often from the **supine stem**.

This participle is often referred to as the **PPP**. It is a **2-1-2 adjective**, like *īrātus*, and describes a noun as having had an action done to it. The endings for 2-1-2 adjectives are printed in full on p229.

Like the present participle, the **perfect passive participle** behaves like an **adjective** and has to **agree** with the noun it describes.

The literal meaning of the PPP is very cumbersome in English. Like the present participle, it is often best to translate the PPP with a **clause** instead.

dux **vulnerātus** periit	The **having been wounded** commander died. → **After he had been wounded**, the commander died.
epistolam **scriptam** legō	I am reading the **having been written** letter → I am reading the letter, **which has been** written.

Intransitive verbs

Not every verb has passive forms. These verbs are known as **intransitive**.

Intransitive verbs often have a **supine** but they do not have a PPP in the same way as other verbs. For example:

> veniō, venīre, vēnī, ventum   come

veniō has a supine, but it does not have a PPP: it is clearly impossible to think of describing a person or thing as *having been come*.

The supine is still listed for intransitive verbs because its stem is used for other (active) forms of the verb which you will meet if you continue to study Latin.

EXERCISE 9.4

1. Caesar Gallōs captōs necāvit.

2. fīlius patrem necātum vīdit et lacrimāvit.

3. ex oppidō occupātō cīvēs quam celerrimē cucurrērunt.

4. paucī incolae mīlitēs prope mūrōs mōtōs cōnspexērunt.

5. senātor ad vīllam dēlētam nōn redībit.

6. mors ducis vulnerātī mīlitēs terruit.

7. senātor mīlitēs superātōs nōn laudāvit.

8. hoc scūtum – ex hostibus raptum – pulcherrimum est.

9. hostēs oppidum ā cīvibus bene dēfēnsum nōn occupāvērunt.

10. ō servī, aquam equō vulnerātō ferte!

PRACTISE YOUR ENGLISH!

Each of the following English sentences contains a perfect passive participle. As you can see, the perfect passive participle is very unwieldy in English. Rewrite each sentence into better English.

1. He killed the having been wounded man.

2. Having been moved away from the town, we ran into the wood.

3. Having been guarded by the soldiers, we did not want to eat the food.

4. Have you seen the having been killed horse?

5. I want the having been seized money!

6. The slaves having been handed over to their master were terrified.

7. Where are the having been overpowered inhabitants?.

8. The having been invited friends are here!

EXERCISE 9.5: LUCULLUS IS DENIED A TRIUMPH

Generals who won an impressive enough victory were granted a parade, known as a triumph, through the streets of Rome in celebration of their success. Leading this triumphal procession gave Roman generals significant prestige. Ambitious Romans were often jealous of their rivals' power and status and tried to make sure that their rivals did not outdo them in this regard.

Two such rivals were the generals Pompey and Lucullus. Lucullus was a successful general, but Pompey managed to persuade the other nobles to deny Lucullus a triumph. Lucullus decided, therefore, not to return to Rome, but to flaunt his wealth and power in other ways.

In 63 BC the senate changed their mind, and Lucullus was finally granted permission to celebrate his triumph. Not to be outdone, two years later Pompey celebrated a triumph on a scale more lavish than had ever been seen before.

Lūcullus erat dux clārissimus. plūrimōs hostēs superāvit et plūrimam pecūniam cēpit. ubi Rōmam rediit, <u>triumphum agere</u> volēbat. cēterī tamen senātōrēs <u>potestātem</u> Lūcullī timēbant: 'Lūcullus <u>dīvitior</u> est quam cēterī nōbilēs,' inquit Pompēius īrātus. '<u>nimis</u> potestātis habet. nōlō eum triumphum agere; nōlō cīvēs Lūcullum hostēs captōs dūcentem vidēre; nōlō cīvēs Lūcullum laudāre.'   5
saepissimē amīcī Pompēiī quoque senātōribus haec dīxērunt. tandem Pompēius et amīcī cēterīs nōbilibus persuāsērunt.

Lūcullus īrātus erat: '<u>extrā</u> Rōmam manēbō,' inquit, 'et, quod pecūniam plūrimam habeō, multa et optima emam.' Lūcullus vīllam <u>splendidam</u> aedificāvit, hortōs <u>māgnificentiōrēs</u> fēcit, librōs optimōs ā Graecīs scrīptōs ēmit. saepe   10
amīcōs plūrimōs ad vīllam invītāvit. Lūcullus et amīcī cēnās <u>sūmptuōsissimās</u> cōnsūmpsērunt. 'pecūniam plūrimam habeō,' inquit Lūcullus, 'itaque potestātem plūrimam habeō. omnēs amīcī mē laudant quod dīvitissimus sum.'

ōlim servī cēnam parātam ad Lūcullum tulērunt. Lūcullus īrātissimus erat: 'haec cēna nōn sūmptuōsissima est!' magnō cum clāmōre inquit. 'cūr cēnam   15
meliōrem nōn parāvistī?' '<u>hodiē</u>,' inquiunt servī, 'amīcī tuī absunt. cēnam tibī, nōn multīs, parāvimus.' 'ō stultissimī!' clāmāvit Lūcullus, 'ego clārissimus sum quod dīvitissimus sum; semper <u>apud</u> Lūcullum cēnae sūmptuōsissimae sunt. etiam hodiē apud Lūcullum cēnam cōnsūmō: fer mihī cēnam meliōrem. etiam hodiē cēnam sūmptuōsissimam cōnsūmam.'   20

trēs annōs Lūcullus extrā Rōmam habitābat. tandem Rōmam rediit et triumphum ēgit. Pompēius, tamen, quoque dux clārissimus et dīvitissimus erat. Pompēius, ubi hostēs plūrimōs multīs in locīs superāvit, triumphum multō maiōrem ēgit quam triumphum Lūcullī. Rōmae Pompēius per viās hostēs ferōcēs captōs dūxit et aurum plūrimum et arma optima rapta cīvibus ostendit: 'numquam,' inquiunt   25
cīvēs, 'triumphum <u>tam</u> māgnificum vīdimus; Pompēius est ē nōbilibus optimus.'

triumphum agō, agere, ēgī	celebrate a triumph
potestās, potestātis, f	power
dīves, dīvitis	rich
nimis (+ genitive)	too much
extrā (+ accusative)	outside
splendidus, splendida, splendidum	splendid
māgnificus, māgnifica, māgnificum	magnificent
sūmptuōsus, sūmptuōsa, sūmptuōsum	lavish
hodiē	today
apud (+ accusative)	at the house of
tam	so

Perfect passive

You have learned 5 tenses of the Latin verb.

future tense (active)	I shall love	amābō
present tense (active)	I love	amō
imperfect tense (active)	I was loving	amābam
perfect tense (active)	I loved	amāvī
pluperfect tense (active)	I had loved	amāveram

Each of these is **active**: the subject **does** the action.

Each of these tenses also has a **passive** form: in the **passive**, the subject **suffers** or **experiences** the action.

One of the most common **passive tenses** is the **perfect passive**. All verbs in Latin form the **perfect passive** in the same way. Two words are needed: the **PPP** and the relevant form of *sum, es, est, sumus, estis, sunt.*

I was ruled / I have been ruled	rēctus sum
you (sg) were ruled / you (sg) have been ruled	rēctus es
he was ruled / he has been ruled	rēctus est
we were ruled / we have been ruled	rēctī sumus
you (pl) were ruled / you (pl) have been ruled	rēctī estis
they were ruled / they have been ruled	rēctī sunt

The **PPP** always has to agree with the noun it describes, and so its endings change depending on its **subject**. For example:

| **he** was ruled | **she** was ruled | **it** was ruled | **we** (f) were ruled |
| rēct**us** est | rēct**a** est | rēct**um** est | rēct**ae** sumus |

Agent and instrument

The **subject** of a **passive** verb **suffers** or **experiences** the action. It is often necessary to say who or what did that action too.

- The **ablative** case is used for **instruments**, i.e. things.

  dux **gladiō** interfēctus est.   The commander was killed **by a sword**.

- **ā / ab + ablative** is used for **agents**, i.e. people.

  mīlitēs **ab incolīs** interfēctī sunt.   The soldiers were killed **by the inhabitants**.

EXERCISE 9.6

1. hoc oppidum ā iuvenibus et senibus fortiter dēfēnsum est.

2. quod in proeliō vulnerātī sumus, hostēs nōn superābimus.

3. ubi vīlla incēnsa est, līberī lacrimāvērunt.

4. ubi oppidum occupātum est, mīlitēs cibum et pecūniam ā cīvibus rapuērunt.

5. diū bene pugnāvistī sed nunc gladiō vulnerātus es.

6. 'pūnīta sum,' inquit fīlia magnopere lacrimāns, 'quamquam servus erat ille quī vīnum bibit.'

7. amīcī ad vīllam nostram invītātī sunt: nunc cēnam optimam parābimus et laetissimē eōs salūtābimus!

8. et fortiter et audācter pugnantēs, ō mīlitēs, ab hostibus occīsī estis!

9. ubi comes sagittā necātus est, scūtum eius mihī trāditum est.

10. quod vōs dē perīculō monēre volēbam, epistula Rōmam celeriter missa est.

EXERCISE 9.7: CAESAR LAUNCHES AN INVASION OF BRITAIN

Julius Caesar was one of Rome's greatest generals. He spent ten years fighting in Gaul, and he was the first Roman to attempt an invasion of Britain. To the Romans, Britain was a distant and mysterious place, but Caesar had heard reports that Britain was a country rich in valuable metals and that the Britons were providing help for the Gauls in their battles against him.

Caesar made two attempts to invade Britain. Neither was particularly successful. In the first, bad storms destroyed much of the Roman fleet and forced an early return to Gaul. Caesar's second attempt was slightly better, but the need to make progress in his conquest of Gaul caused him to redirect his attention back to there.

In Source 9.3 you can read an extract from Caesar's own account of the invasion.

Caesar erat dux clārissimus, cuius mīlitēs saepe hostēs necāvērunt et multa oppida occupāvērunt. decem annōs Caesar in Galliā bellum gerēbat. in Galliā erant multae <u>gentēs</u> quae ferōciter oppida sua dēfendēbant. 'difficile est Gallōs vincere,' inquit Caesar. 'multa oppida fortiter dēfēnsa sunt quod Gallī multōs comitēs et amīcōs habent. quamquam multī Gallī ā mīlitibus meīs vulnerātī 5 sunt, saepe hī amīcī auxilium Gallīs dant.'

<u>inter</u> hōs amīcōs erant Britannī. 'in Britanniam īre volō,' inquit Caesar, 'et incolās superāre. tum facilius erit Gallōs superāre. in Britanniā est <u>plumbum album</u>: incolās superābō et plumbum album rapiam. <u>nūllus</u> Rōmānus in Britanniam trānsiit. in Britanniam trānsībō et clārissimus erō.' difficile tamen erat in 10 Britanniam trānsīre. perīculum magnum erat <u>nāvibus</u> mare trānseuntibus. Caesar suōs ad <u>ōram</u> Britanniae dūxit: ibi Caesar multōs Britannōs in ōrā manentēs cōnspexit. hī Britannī mīlitēs Caesaris terruērunt.

quamquam Rōmānī cum Britannīs fortiter pugnāvērunt, Britannī nōn victī sunt. tum in <u>tempestāte</u> magnā multae nāvium Rōmānārum dēlētae sunt. 'hīc 15 manēre,' inquit Caesar, 'nōn bonum est. quamquam <u>neque</u> incolae superātī sunt <u>neque</u> plumbum album raptum est, in Galliam redībimus et nāvēs meliōrēs aedificābimus.' ubi nāvēs meliōrēs factae sunt, iterum Caesar suōs in Britanniam dūxit. quamquam mīlitēs Caesaris iterum fortiter pugnāvērunt, iterum Britannī nōn victī sunt. 'nunc meōs in Galliam dūcām,' inquit Caesar, 'et ibi in multīs 20 proeliīs Gallōs vincam: melius erit cum Gallīs pugnāre quam cum Britannīs.'

Caesar, ubi in Galliā manēbat, epistulās Rōmam mīsit: in hīs epistulīs multa dē Britannīs scrīpsit. 'Britannī sunt <u>barbarī</u> saevissimī,' scrīpsit Caesar; 'omnēs Britannī corpora sua <u>caerulea</u> <u>pingunt</u>; omnēs Britannī <u>pellēs</u> gerunt; saepe patrēs et fīliī uxōrēs <u>commūnēs</u> habent.' Rōmānī Caesarem laudābant: 'forte 25 erat in Britanniam īre quod ibi incolae sunt saevissimī.'

gēns, gentis, f	tribe
inter (+ accusative)	among
plumbum album, plumbī albī, n	tin
nūllus, nūlla, nūllum	no; not any
nāvis, nāvis, f	ship
ōra, ōrae, f	coast
tempestās, tempestātis, f	storm
neque . . . neque . . .	neither . . . nor . . .
barbarī, barbarōrum, m pl	barbarians
caeruleus, caerulea, caeruleum	dark blue
pingō, pingere, pinxī	paint
pellis, pellis f	animal skin
commūnis, commūne	shared; communal

Consolidation: the imperfect active

It is very important not to get the meaning of the **imperfect active** and the **perfect passive** confused.

imperfect active	I was leading	dūcēbam
perfect passive	I was led	ductus sum

Remember that the **imperfect active** can be translated in several different ways.

Caesar contrā Gallōs **pugnābat**.   Caesar **was fighting** against the Gauls.
Caesar **used to fight** against the Gauls.
Caesar **began to fight** against the Gauls.

For verbs where the action naturally lasts for some time, the **imperfect active** is very rarely translated as *was / were* because it is natural in English to use the perfect tense instead.

senātor in vīllā magnā **habitābat**.   The senator **lived** in a big house.
Rōmānī Britannōs **timēbant**.   The Romans **feared** the Britons.
pugnāre **volēbam**.   **I wanted** to fight.

EXERCISE 9.8

1. multī cīvēs patriam dēfendere volēbant.

2. per viās currēbam quod in tabernā diūtius mānseram.

3. agricola, ubi in agrīs labōrābat, subitō ab equō suō necātus est.

4. oppidum occupātum est quod cīvēs nōn bene custōdiēbant.

5. mīlitēs ā duce pūnītī sunt quod dormiēbant.

6. comitēs ad proelium vocātī sunt quod multī mīlitum iam mortuī erant.

7. cōpiae urbem vestram dēlēbant et uxōrēs et fīliās occīdēbant.

8. ducēs pecūniam mīlitibus suīs dabant.

9. postquam incolae in proeliō ferōcissimō superātī sunt, haec oppida incēnsa sunt.

10. multōs annōs rēgēs Rōmānōs regēbant.

EXERCISE 9.9: CAESAR CONQUERS VERCINGETORIX AND ALL OF GAUL

Gaul was inhabited by a large number of different tribes, and it took Julius Caesar ten years to conquer the territory. The most famous of the Gallic chieftains was Vercingetorix. He persuaded many of the other Gauls to join forces in a combined attempt to fight against Caesar. To begin with, Vercingetorix's strategy was sound: he aimed to reduce Caesar's fighting capacity by destroying his food supply.

Later, however, Vercingetorix established a military base in the town of Alesia. Caesar was skilled in siege warfare, and gradually he starved Vercingetorix and his men into defeat. The story below is taken from Caesar's own account of the campaign. It shows Caesar's tactical brilliance, but also his ruthlessness in the pursuit of victory.

in Galliā multōs annōs Caesar manēbat et in multīs proeliīs cum Gallīs pugnābat. Gallī ducēs multōs et ferōcēs habēbant; ex hīs ducibus ferōcissimus erat Vercingetorīx.

'vōs bene dūcam,' Vercingetorīx cēteris Gallīs inquit, 'et Rōmānōs vincēmus.
5 cibum et viās dēlēbimus et tum Caesar suōs contrā nōs dūcere nōn poterit.'
Vercingetorīx cēterīs Gallīs persuāsit. itaque in agrīs cibus incēnsus est et <u>pontēs</u> multōrum flūminum dēlētī sunt.

pōns, pontis, m   bridge

in oppidō, <u>Alesia</u> nōmine, Vercingetorīx et cōpiae manēbant. mīlitēs tamen Caesaris hoc oppidum ferōciter oppugnābant et diū prope mūrōs oppidī manēbant. Gallī miserī erant: 'quod oppidum <u>obsidētur</u>,' lacrimantēs inquiunt,   10 'exīre nōn possumus. cibus omnis ā nōbis cōnsūmptus est; quid nunc cōnsūmēmus?' Gallī, quod nōn <u>satis</u> cibī habēbant, fēminās et līberōs ē mūrīs mīsērunt. '<u>fortasse</u>,' inquiunt Gallī, 'Caesar fēminās et līberōs capiet et cibum eīs dabit. quamquam fēminae et līberī servī erunt, <u>saltem</u> non mortuī erunt.'

fēminae et līberī ā Caesare vīsī sunt. 'nōlīte, ō mīlitēs,' magnō cum clāmōre   15 inquit Caesar, '<u>veniam</u> dare!' Vercingetorīx, ubi verba Caesaris audīta sunt, magnopere <u>dēspērābat</u>: 'ē mūrīs, ō Gallī, omnēs exīte! nunc enim <u>tempus</u> est nōbis <u>suprēmum</u> pugnāre.' in hōc proeliō, cōpiae Vercingetorīgis victī sunt: 'iam, Gallī,' inquit Vercingetorīx miserrimus, 'victī sumus. mē Caesarī trādite <u>aut</u> mortuum <u>aut</u> <u>vīvum</u>.'   20

Vercingetorīx erat Gallōrum dux optimus. 'cōpiae nostrae superātae sunt,' inquiunt Gallī magnopere lacrimantēs, 'et dux noster captus. nunc patriam dēfendere nōn possumus. Vercingetorīx victus est et nunc victa est Gallia omnis.'

Alesia, Alesiae, f	Alesia
obsidētur	'he / she / it is being besieged'
satis (+ genitive)	enough
fortasse	perhaps
saltem	at least
venia, veniae, f	mercy
dēspērō, dēspērāre, dēspērāvī	despair
tempus, temporis, n	time
suprēmum	'for the last time'
aut . . . aut . . .	either . . . or . . .
vīvus, vīva, vīvum	alive

Pluperfect passive

The **pluperfect passive** is formed in a way that is very similar to the perfect passive: the **PPP** is used with the relevant form of ***eram, erās, erat, erāmus, erātis, erant***.

I had been ruled	rēctus eram
you (sg) had been ruled	rēctus erās
he had been ruled	rēctus erat
we had been ruled	rēctī erāmus
you (pl) had been ruled	rēctī erātis
they had been ruled	rēctī erant

As with the **perfect passive,** the **PPP** has to agree with its **subject**.

he had been ruled	**she** had been ruled	**it** had been ruled	**we** (f) had been ruled
rēct**us** erat	rēct**a** erat	rēct**um** erat	rēct**ae** erāmus

Like the **pluperfect active**, in Latin the **pluperfect passive** is not as widely used as in English. This is especially true in subordinate clauses: Latin often will use a **perfect** tense verb instead. This means that sometimes a Latin perfect tense will be translated into the pluperfect tense in English.

postquam dux **captus est**, mīlitēs lacrimāvērunt.	**Latin perfect passive**
After their commander **had been captured**, the soldiers wept.	**English pluperfect passive**

EXERCISE 9.10

1. quod mūrī altissimī aedificātī erant, cīvēs oppidum bene dēfendēbant.

2. in proeliō dux occīsus erat, sed mīlitēs etiam tum fortiter pugnābant.

3. hastae iactae erant; deinde cīvēs hostēs gladiīs vulnerābant.

4. quod agrī incēnsī erant, agricolae lacrimābant.

5. antequam oppidum oppugnātum est, incolae scūta et gladiōs cēpērunt et ad hostēs cucurrērunt.

6. mīlitēs, quod pecūnia eīs trādita erat, laetissimī erant.

7. līberī parvī ab equō vulnerātī erant: et pater et māter lacrimābant.

8. mīlitēs, postquam incolae necātī sunt, aurum et uxōrēs rapuērunt.

EXERCISE 9.11: CIVIL WAR IN ROME

At Rome many nobles feared the power and influence that Julius Caesar had won through his success in Gaul. Fearful of Caesar's power, in 49 BC the senate ordered that Caesar disband his army before returning to Rome. Pompey, another brilliant and highly successful general, seems to have been the driving force behind the opposition to Caesar. When Caesar refused to follow the senate's instructions, a brutal civil war began between Caesar and Pompey.

Caesar emerged as victor: his power was undeniable and he was appointed dictator, a post which granted him supreme power at Rome. No doubt the peace that this brought to Rome was welcome, but the Republican principles of shared power were severely shaken.

quod Gallia victa erat, Caesar erat dux clārissimus. 'multa oppida incēnsa sunt,' inquit Caesar, 'et plūrimī Gallī necātī sunt. aurum raptum est. mīlitēs meī mē amant quod pecūniam plūrimam eīs dedī. nunc Rōmam mīlitēs dūcam: ibi, quod cīvis et nōbilissimus et optimus sum, <u>potestātem</u> magnam habēbō.'

Rōmae, tamen, multī nōbilēs Caesarem timēbant: 'Caesar,' inquiunt, '<u>glōriam</u>   5 et potestātem amat; Caesar patriam nōn amat. Caesar vult esse dux nōn mīlitum suōrum sed omnium Rōmānōrum.' senātōrēs epistulam ad Caesarem mīsērunt: 'nōlī Rōmam cum mīlitibus redīre: Rōmae cīvis nōn <u>imperātor</u> eris.'

10   verba tamen senātōrum Caesarī nōn persuāsērunt. Caesar, quod ā senātōribus nōn laudātus erat, īrātus erat. 'erit bellum <u>cīvīle</u>,' magnō cum clāmōre inquit. 'nunc contrā cīvēs Rōmānōs nōn contrā hostēs pugnābō.' deinde mīlitēs trāns flūmen, <u>Rubicōnem</u> nōmine, et in <u>Ītaliam</u> dūxit. 'nunc,' inquit Caesar, '<u>alea</u> iacta est.' Rōmae Pompēius et cēterī senātōrēs īrātissimī erant: 'cum Caesare pugnābimus,' clāmāvit Pompēius. 'Caesar nōn erit dux omnium Rōmānōrum!'

15   in bellō cīvīlī erant multa proelia et multae mortēs. multī cīvēs vulnerātī et occīsī sunt; multae vīllae dēlētae sunt; multī agrī incēnsī sunt. Caesar, tamen, quod dux melior erat quam Pompēius, mīlitēs Pompēiī tandem superāvit. cīvēs miserī erant: 'cīvēs cum cīvibus pugnābant; multī patrēs et fīliī mortuī sunt. multa <u>terribilia</u> facta sunt. nunc ā Caesare victī sumus. nunc melius est

20   Caesarem laudāre quam cum cīvibus pugnāre.'

deinde Caesar <u>dictātor</u> factus est: Rōmae Caesar plūs potestātis habēbat quam omnēs cēterī. multī Rōmānī Caesarem laudābant, sed plūrimī <u>ānxiī</u> erant: 'nunc patria nōn est <u>rēs pūblica</u>,' inquiunt cīvēs, 'nunc iterum rēgem habēmus.'

potestās, potestātis, f	power
glōria, glōriae, f	glory
imperātor, imperātōris, m	commander
cīvīlis, cīvīle	civil; belonging to a citizen
Rubicō, Rubicōnis, m	the river Rubicon
Ītalia, Ītaliae, f	Italy
alea, aleae, f	a game of dice; die
terribilis, terribile	terrible
dictātor, dictātōris, m	dictator
ānxius, ānxia, ānxium	anxious
rēs pūblica (nominative sg)	'a republic'

Chapter 9: Additional Language

SECTION A9: CHAPTER 9 VOCABULARY

Exercise A9.1: Derivations crossword

English derivations often come from the stem of the 4th principal part of a verb.

Each of the clues below is a derivation from one of the verbs in the vocabulary list for Chapter 9 and shares the same stem as the Latin verb's 4th principal part.

The answer to each clue is the 4th principal part that the clue derives from. Next to each clue, you should also explain the link between the English word and the Latin verb. If you are unsure, you should look up the English word in a dictionary.

Across

4. rapt
6. invitation
7. motion
9. incensed
10. aqueduct

Down

1. occupation
2. delete
3. tradition
5. defensive
8. mission

Exercise A9.2: Verb stems and conjugations

Highlight the 3 stems (present, perfect and supine) shown by these principal parts from the verbs for Chapter 9. Then give the meaning of each verb and its conjugation.

	principal parts	meaning	conjugation
1	superō, superāre, superāvī, superātum		
2	rapiō, rapere, rapuī, raptum		
3	custōdiō, custōdīre, custōdīvī, custōdītum		
4	invītō, invītāre, invītāvī, invītātum		
5	dēleō, dēlēre, dēlēvī, dēlētum		
6	occupō, occupāre, occupāvī, occupātum		
7	mittō, mittere, mīsī, missum		
8	occīdō, occīdere, occīdī, occīsum		
9	trādō, trādere, trādidī, trāditum		
10	moveō, movēre, mōvī, mōtum		

Exercise A9.3: Case endings (nouns)

Circle the stem, give the meaning and identify the declension of the following nouns from Chapter 9. Then give the case requested.

	Latin	meaning	declension	
1	patria, patriae, f			accusative sg =
2	oppidum, oppidī, n			nominative pl =
3	cōpiae, cōpiārum, f pl			genitive pl =
4	proelium, proeliī, n			accusative pl =
5	mors, mortis, f			ablative pl =
6	incola, incolae, m			ablative sg =
7	mīles, mīlitis, m			genitive pl =
8	scūtum, scūtī, n			accusative pl =
9	comes, comitis, m/f			dative sg =
10	dux, ducis, m			dative pl =

Exercise A9.4: Case endings (participles)

The participles in the table below are all from the verbs from Chapter 9.

Circle the stem and give the meaning and declension of each participle. Then give the case requested.

	Latin	meaning	declension	
1	custōdiēns, custōdientis			accusative masculine pl =
2	superāns, superantis			accusative feminine sg =
3	incendēns, incendentis			nominative masculine pl =
4	oppugnāns, oppugnantis			dative feminine pl =
5	trāditus, trādita, trāditum			nominative feminine pl =
6	gestus, gesta, gestum			accusative neuter pl =
7	ductus, ducta, ductum			ablative masculine pl =
8	necātus, necāta, necātum			genitive feminine pl =

Exercise A9.5: Verbs

Identify the tense of the Chapter 9 verbs in the table below and translate each one. Then change the form from singular to plural, or plural to singular, keeping the tense and person the same.

Remember that you need to look at the stem as well as the ending. Here are the principal parts for each verb so that you can see their different stems.

mittō, mittere, mīsī, missum
necō, necāre, necāvī, necātum
dēleō, dēlēre, dēlēvī, dēlētum
rapiō, rapere, rapuī, raptum
occīdō, occīdere, occīdī, occīsum

	Latin	tense	translation	new form
1	mīsit			
2	necant			
3	necābunt			
4	dēlet			
5	dēlēvit			
6	rapuimus			
7	rapimus			
8	occīdis			
9	occīdēs			
10	occīdistī			

SECTION B9: GRAMMAR

Exercise B9.1: The passive voice

This exercise focuses on the nouns and verbs you have met in the vocabulary list for Chapter 9.

These sentences contain active and passive verbs. For each of the sentences:

- underline all the words that make up the verb and then identify the verb as active or passive
- identify the case of the nouns in **purple**

1. The **shield** was seized by the leader of the enemy.
2. The **enemy** were wounded by the soldiers.
3. After we attacked the town, the **inhabitants** were killed by our companions.
4. With shield and sword they were defending the **town** bravely.
5. The **town** was defended by many brave troops.
6. The enemy waged **war** often, but soon they were destroyed by our forces.
7. They were wounded and killed. They did not overpower **our soldiers**.
8. Our **troops** were sent into the town of the enemy.
9. The **inhabitants** of the town were guarding the **enemy** who had been overpowered in battle.
10. Although they had been invited into the town, the **soldiers** attacked it.

Exercise B9.2: The 4th principal part and the PPP

Give the meaning of each of the following verbs from Chapters 6–8. Then use the vocabulary reference list to look up the 4th principal part for each. Use this to work out each verb's perfect passive participle. Then translate the participle.

	verb	meaning	PPP	meaning of the PPP
1	rogō			
2	moneō			
3	videō			
4	emō			
5	līberō			
6	salūtō			
7	dīcō			
8	legō			
9	scrībō			
10	cupiō			

Exercise B9.3: Translating the PPP

All these PPPs are from the verbs you have met in the vocabulary list for Chapter 9. Find the verb which these PPPs come from and then translate them.

	PPP	which verb?	meaning of the PPP
1	necātus, necāta, necātum		
2	oppugnātus, oppugnāta, oppugnātum		
3	superātus, superāta, superātum		
4	vulnerātus, vulnerāta, vulnerātum		
5	dēlētus, dēlēta, dēlētum		
6	mōtus, mōta, mōtum		
7	dēfēnsus, dēfēnsa, dēfēnsum		
8	ductus, ducta, ductum		
9	raptus, rapta, raptum		
10	custōdītus, custōdīta, custōdītum		

Exercise B9.4: Noun and participle pairs

This exercise focuses on nouns and PPPs from the vocabulary lists for Chapters 7–9.

Work out the case needed for each noun and PPP pair in **purple** and then pick the correct Latin translation.

1. The **letter read** by the slave was excellent.
     (epistula lēcta / epistulam lēctam)
2. I read the **books written** by my father.
     (librī scrīptī / librōs scrīptōs)
3. The **wounded leader** was very brave.
     (ducem vulnerātum / dux vulnerātus)
4. Where is the **freedman sent** by the farmer?
     (libertum missum / libertus missus)
5. The father of the **seized soldier** was very sad.
     (mīlitis raptī / mīlitem raptum)
6. We ran very quickly from the **overpowered inhabitants**.
     (incolās superātōs / incolīs superātīs)
7. **Greeted** savagely by her husband, the **mistress** cried for three hours.
     (domina salūtāta / dominam salūtātam)
8. The **enemy killed** by our men had been very daring.
     (hostēs necātōs / hostēs necātī)
9. In **attacked towns** the inhabitants are often both miserable and angry.
     (oppidī oppugnāti / oppidīs oppugnātīs)
10. We persuaded the **wounded messenger** with many words.
     (nūntium vulnerātum / nūntiō vulnerātō)

Exercise B9.5: Imperfect active and perfect passive

This exercise focuses on verbs from the vocabulary list for Chapter 9.

Choose the correct Latin for each of the verbs in **purple** in the sentences below.

1. **He was inviting** them to his homeland. (invītābat / invītātus est)
2. **They were invited** to a new place. (invītātī sunt / invītābant)
3. **They were guarded** by a cruel enemy. (custōdiēbant / custōdītī sunt)
4. **They were defending** the town in vain. Then they were defeated.
     (defēnsī sunt / dēfendēbant)
5. **They were led** into battle by an excellent leader. (ductī sunt / ducēbant)
6. A very brave soldier **was leading** his comrades into battle.
     (ductus est / ducēbat)
7. A sad and cruel war **was waged** in the homeland. (gerēbat / gestum est)
8. Often the Romans **waged** war against their enemies. (gerēbant / gesta sunt)
9. The letters of the captured men **were burned**. (incendēbant / incēnsae sunt)
10. The books written by the enemy **were seized**. (rapiēbant / raptī sunt)

Exercise B9.6: The perfect passive and pluperfect passive

This exercise practises verbs from the vocabulary list for Chapter 9.

Identify the tense and person of each of these passive verbs, and then translate each verb.

	verb	tense	person	translation
1	invītātus sum			
2	dēfēnsus erat			
3	ductī estis			
4	raptus erās			
5	necāta est			

SECTION C9: ENGLISH TO LATIN SENTENCES

Exercise C9.1: Sentences to translate into Latin

1. The soldier defended by his huge shield was not killed by the spears.
2. The town was set on fire. The houses and shops were destroyed quickly.
3. The inhabitants invited the wounded soldiers into their town.
4. Although our comrades were defending themselves bravely, they were easily conquered.
5. Weapons seized in the battle were handed over to the troops.
6. Overpowered and wounded, my comrades at last perished.
7. The leader was wounded by the sword seized by the bad soldier.
8. Very often our fathers waged wars and defended the homeland most bravely.
9. The inhabitants feared death because their town was destroyed.
10. Surely the soldiers who had fought most fiercely in many battles were not overpowered by spears and arrows?

SECTION D: CONSOLIDATION

Exercises for Additional Language Section D are available on the companion website. Exercises are structured by grammatical category, and cover all Core Vocabulary met so far within each category. For Chapter 9, these exercises are as follows:

- Exercise D9.1: 3rd declension nouns
- Exercise D9.2: 3rd declension adjectives
- Exercise D9.3: 3rd conjugation verbs

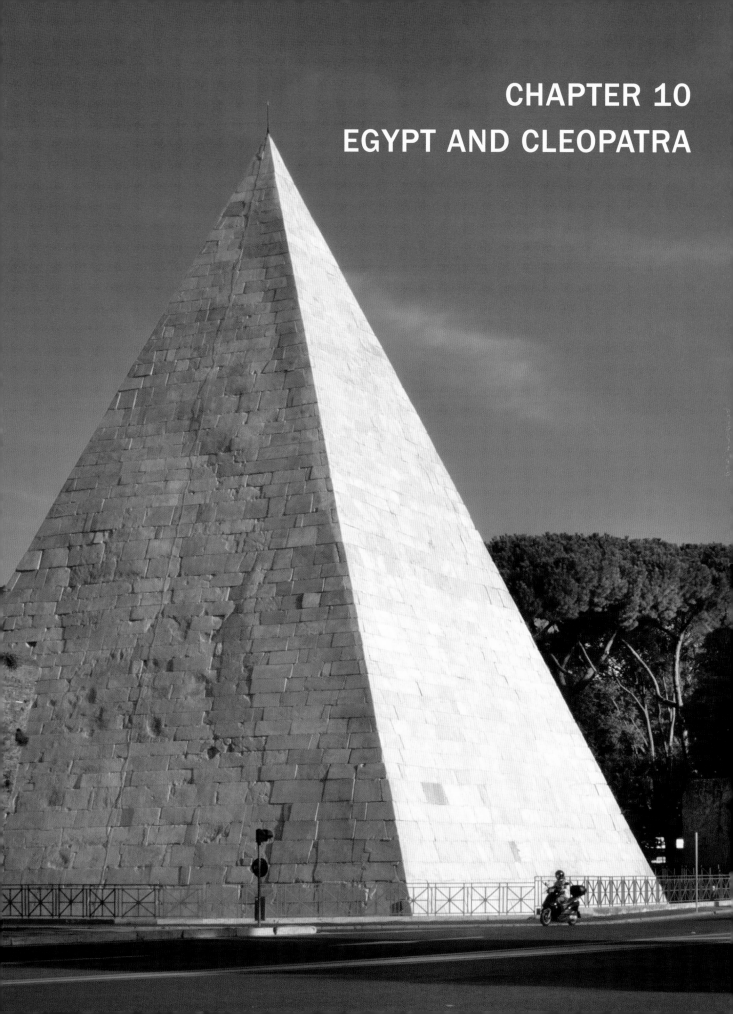

ⓒⓦ Chapter 10: Introduction

FIGURE 10.1 Cestius' pyramid

Perhaps surprisingly, this pyramid is in Rome at the Porta San Paolo. The pyramid was built at the end of the 1st century BC and it acted as a tomb for a wealthy Roman named Gaius Cestius. Cestius may have been involved in the Roman invasion of Nubian territory in 23 BC, where he would have seen similar pyramids. Displays of Egyptian culture such as this became fashionable in Rome after Egypt became a Roman province in 30 BC.

Egypt and Rome

The ancient community of Egypt is a fascinating one by any measure, but it had a particular importance to the Romans for two reasons. First, after Egypt became a Roman province in 30 BC, it supplied a large proportion of Rome's food. Second, the wealth and power of Egypt had played a central role in the civil wars which scarred the end of the Roman Republic. Two of Rome's most powerful generals, Julius Caesar and then later Mark Antony, had love affairs with Cleopatra, Egypt's most famous ruler. Cleopatra is described by ancient authors, such as Plutarch, as a woman of remarkable intelligence and beauty, but the phenomenal wealth and resources she had access to in Egypt must have offered a further attraction for these ruthlessly ambitious Romans.

Ancient Egypt

The history and culture of Egypt began over 7,000 years ago. The fertile plains alongside the river Nile are ideal for agriculture and helped to make Egypt a powerful and wealthy kingdom in the ancient world. The Egyptians were able to grow a surplus of food, and use this food to trade with other communities. The river Nile allowed goods to be moved easily and Egypt's location on the north coast of Africa made it a natural centre of trade in the Mediterranean.

Ancient Egypt was truly ancient. Before it became a Roman province in 30 BC, there had been more than thirty ruling dynasties in Egypt, covering almost 3,000 years between them. The growth of Egyptian civilization is divided into three periods of history known as

FIGURE 10.2 Section of a mosaic showing the river Nile

This floor mosaic was discovered in the Italian town of Palestrina, to the east of Rome. It measures roughly 5m by 4m and it is thought to date from around 100 BC. The Romans were fascinated by the exotic animals and culture of Egypt. The mosaic is now in the National Museum of Palestrina in Italy.

kingdoms. The Old Kingdom saw the construction of the great pyramids, in which the Old Kingdom Pharaohs were buried. The Middle Kingdom is seen as the golden age of Egypt's ancient language and literature. Finally, the 1500s BC marked the start of the New Kingdom. This was a period where military success increased the territory under Egyptian control. The wealth this brought contributed to the building of the great temples at Karnak and Luxor. All of this happened in Egypt before the civilizations of Rome and Greece had even begun. Part of Egypt's long history was documented by the Greek historian Herodotus, as you will see in Exercise 10.4.

Alexander, Alexandria and the Ptolemaic dynasty

In the 4th century BC, Alexander the Great, a Macedonian king, set out to conquer vast expanses of territory. He was undefeated in battle and built an empire that stretched from Greece to the Indian subcontinent in just 13 years. When Alexander died suddenly in 323 BC, his Macedonian generals began to fight amongst themselves to divide his vast empire between them. One of these generals, a man named Ptolemy, emerged as the ruler of Egypt and in 305 BC he officially adopted the Egyptian title of Pharaoh. His family, known as the Ptolemaic Dynasty, ruled Egypt until Cleopatra's death in 30 BC.

We shall see in Exercise 10.5 how Alexander the Great founded the city of Alexandria at the northwest edge of the Nile Delta in 331 BC. Alexandria quickly became one of the

FIGURE 10.3 **The burning of the library of Alexandria**

This image dates from 1876, but the artist is unknown. It shows the lighthouse and behind it the city and the library in flames. It is thought that these fires were lit by Julius Caesar in 48 BC during the Egyptian civil war. The flames grew out of control, destroying at least part of the library and its collection. In the foreground of the image is the imposing presence of the lighthouse. Waves crash dramatically at its base, while its beacon fire burns brightly at the top. The blue sky behind creates a contrast with the destructive flames belching smoke into the sky while the city burns.

FIGURE 10.4

Cleopatra VII

This Roman marble bust was made in the 40s BC, and it is now in the Altes Museum in Berlin, Germany. Cleopatra was described as remarkably attractive by ancient authors such as Plutarch and Cassius Dio. You can read more about this in Source 10.1.

most important cities in the ancient world, known in particular for its wealth and its status as a centre of trade and learning. It contained a number of famous buildings including the Great Lighthouse and the Great Library. The lighthouse at Alexandria was also known as the Pharos and it was considered to be one of the seven wonders of the ancient world. It was roughly 100m tall and guided ships safely into Alexandria's harbours. Alexandria's library was the base for some of the greatest scholars of the ancient world and it is believed to have housed a collection of nearly 500,000 texts, stored on papyrus scrolls.

Cleopatra

Cleopatra VII was born in 69 BC. She is known as the last Pharaoh of Egypt, but, as discussed above, the Ptolemaic dynasty was Greek in origin, and although she was born in Egypt, her native language was Greek. Cleopatra was extremely well educated. She spoke at least nine different languages and, according to Plutarch, was the first Ptolemaic ruler to learn Egyptian. During the final years of her father's reign, she had assisted him as co-ruler. When he died in 51 BC, he left his kingdom to the eighteen-year-old Cleopatra and her ten-year-old brother Ptolemy XIII.

Ptolemy was not old enough to co-rule with Cleopatra himself and so a regent was appointed to rule in his place until Ptolemy was old enough. This regent, Pothinus, despised Cleopatra, who was a popular queen. Pothinus soon turned Cleopatra's brother against her. In 48 BC she was forced to flee to Syria, where she raised an army, starting a civil war in Egypt.

Cleopatra and Julius Caesar

Egypt was not the only state in the middle of a civil war at the time. As we saw in Chapter 9, by crossing the Rubicon with an army in 49 BC, Julius Caesar had disobeyed the Roman senate and started a civil war. Roman fought against Roman on a scale never seen before. Eventually, at the Battle of Pharsalus in 48 BC, Caesar defeated the forces of the senate led by his rival Pompey. Caesar was then the most powerful man in Rome.

Following the battle, Pompey fled to Egypt where he hoped Ptolemy XIII would help him. Instead of finding help, however, Pompey was murdered. His head was kept by Ptolemy and Pothinus as a gift for Caesar, whose support they wanted in the civil war against Cleopatra. When Caesar arrived in Alexandria and gazed upon the head of his former rival, he was not pleased but furious with the boy king and his regent for treating such a brilliant Roman general in this terrible way. Ptolemy and Pothinus' plan to gain Caesar's support had failed.

By 48 BC, Cleopatra also wanted Caesar's help to reclaim her throne, on account of his military skill and powerful army. Hearing that Caesar was in Alexandria, Cleopatra needed a way to meet him without her brother's men stopping her. Exercise 10.7 describes one of the more fanciful stories about Cleopatra as told by the Greek biographer, Plutarch. In this story, Cleopatra made an ingenious plan: she had herself wrapped in a linen sack, smuggled into the royal palace and carried all the way to Caesar's room. As she suspected, nobody stopped the man carrying her and, when the young queen emerged before Caesar, he was amazed.

Despite the thirty-year age gap between them, Caesar and Cleopatra soon became lovers and she even visited Rome. In 47 BC Cleopatra gave birth to a son whom she named Caesarion, claiming that the father was Caesar. Not everyone was impressed with Cleopatra, however, and we know from Cicero's letters that he hated her because he thought she was haughty and arrogant.

Cleopatra and Mark Antony

Cleopatra was in Rome when Caesar was killed in 44 BC. His death put her in a vulnerable position. Although she hoped that Caesar's will would name Caesarion as his heir, Caesar chose his great-nephew Octavian instead. Realizing it was no longer safe for her to remain in Rome, Cleopatra fled back to Egypt with her son.

As discussed in Chapter 8, Caesar's newly appointed heir, Octavian, joined forces with two of Caesar's close friends, Mark Antony and Lepidus. This formal alliance was known as the triumvirate. Between them, they divided the Roman world into three parts and governed one each. Octavian governed the west, Lepidus governed Africa and Antony was given the eastern part, closest to Egypt. Antony soon summoned Cleopatra to visit him.

As you will read in Source 10.2 and Exercise 10.11, Cleopatra made quite an impression on Antony. She arrived dressed like the goddess Venus on her royal barge, which was covered in gold with fine purple sails and oars of silver. Aware of her own power, she refused to disembark and she made Antony come to her instead. Cleopatra entertained Antony and his men with two days of extravagant feasting aboard her richly adorned boat. He was so

FIGURE 10.5 Cleopatra's Needle

Cleopatra's Needle is an obelisk made from red granite. It is just over 20m tall and it dates from around 1450 BC. In 12 BC it was moved to Alexandria and put into the Caesareum, a temple built by Cleopatra to honour Caesar. In 1819 it was given by Egypt as a gift to Britain to commemorate British naval victories over the French. It now stands on the Victoria Embankment in London.

attracted to her that, when she invited him back to Egypt, he agreed to visit immediately. Like Caesar before him, Antony became Cleopatra's ally and lover and in 40 BC she gave birth to their twins. As you can read in Source 10.3, many Romans were appalled by this relationship.

The Battle of Actium

The alliance between Octavian, Antony and Lepidus soon became strained. Their individual ambition and desire for power meant the relationships they shared were tense. To try to improve the situation, Octavian and Antony had agreed that Antony would marry Octavian's sister, Octavia, in 40 BC. Understandably then, Octavian did not take kindly to Antony abandoning his sister in favour of Cleopatra. In 36 BC, Lepidus was involved in a dispute with Octavian over the province of Sicily. Octavian took the opportunity to overthrow Lepidus and strip him of his land and almost all of his official power. Finally, Antony officially divorced Octavia in 32 BC.

By 31 BC, the Roman empire was ruled by just two men whose personal relationship had deteriorated beyond repair. In the senate, Octavian portrayed himself and the west as being Roman and Antony and his foreign wife in the east as the enemy. When Octavian and the senate declared war on Cleopatra, they declared war on Antony by extension. The final confrontation came that year at the Battle of Actium. This sea-battle took place off the coast of western Greece. Although Cleopatra and Antony had the combined strength and wealth of Egypt and the Roman East at their disposal, it was not enough to defeat Octavian and Agrippa, his naval commander. Cleopatra and Antony both fled the battle and returned to Egypt.

FIGURE 10.6 **The death of Cleopatra**

Jean-André Rixens painted this scene in 1874. It is now part of the collection in the Musée des Augustins in Toulouse, France. Cleopatra lies dead on her bed, with a basket of figs on the floor beside her. Sprawled across her feet lies one of her attendants, while the other caresses her head. Cleopatra's pale and erotic beauty is the focal point of the scene.

Cleopatra's death

Octavian and Agrippa invaded Egypt in 30 BC. Antony realized he was beaten and committed suicide with his sword, thinking that Cleopatra had already killed herself. As he was dying, he found out that she was still alive. He was brought to her and died in her arms. Cleopatra was captured and taken to Octavian. Octavian promised, surprisingly, that he would spare her life. According to some ancient authors, this was no act of generosity on Octavian's part: Cleopatra feared that he wanted the glory of parading her through Rome as his prisoner. Cleopatra refused to be humiliated in this way and took her own life. Plutarch tells us that some people believed that Cleopatra used a basket of figs to smuggle a venomous asp into her room. Octavian, although he cannot have been pleased by what she had done, granted Cleopatra's final wish and allowed her to be buried with Antony.

CHAPTER 10: SOURCES TO STUDY

Source 10.1: Cleopatra and Julius Caesar

In 48 BC there was civil war in Egypt: Cleopatra was in the midst of a power struggle with her brother, Ptolemy XIII, and she was keen to enlist the help and resources of Julius Caesar. The passage below is an account of Cleopatra's first meeting with Caesar. Its author, Cassius Dio, was a Roman historian who wrote roughly 250 years later.

Caesar was a total womanizer, and he had fallen for ever so many other women – indeed doubtless for all who had come his way. As soon as Cleopatra learned that his nature was such, she sent a message to him that she was being betrayed by her friends and she asked that she be allowed to make her case to him in person. She did this not least because she was a woman of exceptional beauty, and at that time, when she was in the prime of her youth, she was most striking; she also possessed a most charming voice and a knowledge of how to make herself agreeable to everyone. She asked, therefore, to go to meet him, and when this was granted, she adorned and beautified herself so as to appear before him in the most majestic and pity-inspiring manner. When she had finished these preparations, she entered the city and, by night, without Ptolemy's knowledge, she went into the palace. When Caesar saw her and heard her first words, he was so immediately enslaved to her that at once, before dawn, he sent for Ptolemy and tried to reconcile them.

Cassius Dio, *Roman History*, Vol. IV, 42.34–35 (with omissions, trans. adapted)

Source 10.1: Questions

1 Explain why, according to this source, Cleopatra was so keen to meet with Julius Caesar in person.
2 List the attributes that Cassius Dio tells us Cleopatra possessed.
3 What preparations did Cleopatra make for her meeting with Caesar?
4 How did Caesar respond to Cleopatra?
5 How does this source affect your view of Cleopatra's character?
6 How does this source affect your view of Caesar?
7 This is a source written approximately 250 years after the meeting it describes. It was written by a man for a predominantly male audience. What effect does this context have on the way we might view it as evidence?

Source 10.2: Cleopatra sails to meet Mark Antony

In the 40s BC, Mark Antony was chosen to govern the eastern part of Rome's empire. He invited Cleopatra to meet him in Tarsus, a city in the south of modern-day Turkey and the capital city of the Roman province of Cilicia. Cleopatra sailed to meet Antony in her royal barge with her wealth and power on full display. Plutarch's account of their meeting was written more than a hundred years later, but he describes their meeting in lavish detail.

She received a whole succession of letters from Antony and his friends summoning her to visit him, but she treated him with such disdain that when she appeared it was as if in mockery of his orders. She came sailing up the river Cydnus in a barge with a stern of gold, its purple sails billowing in the wind, while her rowers caressed the water with oars of silver which dipped in time to the music of the flute, accompanied by pipes and lutes. Cleopatra herself reclined beneath a canopy of cloth of gold, dressed in the character of Venus, as we see her in paintings, while on either side to complete the picture stood boys costumed as Cupids, who cooled her with their fans. Instead of a crew the barge was lined with the most beautiful of her waiting-women attired as **Nereids** and **Graces**, some at the rudders, others at the tackle of the sails, and all the while an indescribably rich perfume, exhaled from innumerable incense-burners, was wafted from the vessel to the river-banks.

> **Nereids** were believed to be beautiful sea nymphs; **Graces** were female deities who personified characteristics such as grace, beauty and charm.

Great multitudes accompanied the boat along the river, some of them following the queen on both sides of the river from its very mouth, while others hurried down from the city of Tarsus to gaze at the sight. Gradually the crowds drifted away from the market-place, where Antony, sitting high on the speaker's platform, awaited the queen, until at last he was left sitting quite alone and the word spread on every side that Venus had come to revel with Bacchus for the happiness of Asia.

Antony then sent a message inviting Cleopatra to dine with him, but she thought it more appropriate that he should come to her, and so, as he wished to show his courtesy and goodwill, he accepted and went. He found the preparations made to receive him magnificent beyond words, but what astonished him most of all was the extraordinary number of lights. So many of these, it is said, were let down from the roof and displayed on all sides at once, and they were arranged and grouped in such ingenious patterns in relation to each other, some in squares and some in circles, that they created as brilliant a spectacle as can ever have been devised to delight the eye.

Plutarch, *Life of Antony*, 26 (trans. slightly adapted)

Source 10.2: Questions

1 What was Cleopatra's initial attitude towards Mark Antony?
2 List the details of Cleopatra's appearance and her boat which must have seemed exotic and extraordinary to Antony.
3 How did Cleopatra make sure that she controlled her meeting with Antony?
4 Plutarch writes that the rumour spread that 'Venus had come to dine with Bacchus for the happiness of Asia'. What does this suggest the locals thought about Cleopatra and Antony?
5 Imagine you were in the crowd when Cleopatra appeared on her barge. What would you think when you saw, heard and smelled the barge as it passed? Would you think it attractive to flaunt wealth like this?

Source 10.3: Roman outrage at the power of Cleopatra

According to many Roman writers, Mark Antony's relationship with Cleopatra caused outrage at Rome, and his love-affair with her was presented as a rejection of Roman values and customs. The extract below is from Cassius Dio's history of Rome and it was written roughly 250 years later. The extract starts just after the Roman people have found out that Antony intended to leave vast sums of money to the children he had had with Cleopatra and that he wished to be buried in Alexandria with her when he died.

The Romans were so outraged that they were willing to believe that the other rumours were equally true, namely that if Antony were victorious, he would hand over the city of Rome to Cleopatra and transfer the seat of government to Egypt. Public hostility became so intense that not only Antony's enemies but even his closest friends utterly condemned his actions. Cleopatra had, it was believed, enslaved Antony so completely that she was saluted by him as 'queen' and 'mistress', and she had Roman soldiers in her bodyguard, all of whom had her name inscribed upon their shields. She visited the market-place with Antony, presided with him over festivals and at the hearing of law suits, rode with him on horseback even in the cities, or else was carried in a litter, while Antony followed on foot together with the **eunuchs**. Antony sometimes carried an oriental dagger in his belt, wore clothes which were completely alien to Roman custom, and appeared in public seated on a gilded couch or chair. Indeed she so enchanted and enthralled not only Antony but all the others who counted for anything with him that she came to entertain the hope that she would rule the Romans as well, and whenever she took an oath, the most potent phrase she used were the words, 'So surely as I shall one day give judgement on the Capitol.'

> A **eunuch** is a man whose testicles have been removed before puberty.

Cassius Dio, *The Roman History*, Book 50.4–5 (with omissions)

Source 10.3: Questions

1 What does Cassius Dio suggest that the Romans were most angry about when they heard about Antony's commitment to his new Egyptian family?

2 Cassius Dio tells us that the Romans were appalled that Antony was the inferior half of an unequal relationship: which details from this source convey this?

3 Cassius Dio also tells us that Antony no longer dressed like a Roman: why do you think this mattered to the Romans?

4 The Capitol was an important hill in Rome, and often regarded as its political centre: what does Cleopatra's oath at the end of this source mean?

5 Do you think that a modern-day audience in a similar situation would react the same way as the Romans did to the rumours about Antony and Cleopatra?

Source 10.4: Cleopatra, the enemy of Rome

Horace was one of Rome's greatest poets. He lived at the end of the 1st century BC, and so he was a direct contemporary of Cleopatra. This poem celebrates Octavian's victory over Cleopatra in the Battle of Actium. The poem is famous for its picture of the eastern queen as a deranged drunkard, but noble still in her courageous suicide.

Salian feasts were known to be particularly sumptuous.

Caecuban wine was a very fine variety.

The **Capitol** was an important hill in Rome, and often regarded as its political centre.

Mareotic wine came from Egypt.

'Caesar' refers to Octavian; as heir to Julius Caesar he had taken his name.

Thrace was an area to the northwest of modern-day Turkey and to the northeast of Greece.

A **Liburnian** galley was a warship propelled by rowing.

Now we must drink, now we must
beat the earth with unfettered feet, now,
　　my friends, is the time to load the couches
　　　　of the gods with **Salian** feasts.

Before this it was a sin to take the **Caecuban**
down from its ancient racks, while the mad queen
　　with her contaminated flock of men
　　　　diseased by vice, was preparing

the ruin of the **Capitol** and the destruction
of our power, crazed with hope
　　unlimited and drunk
　　　　with sweet fortune. But her madness

decreased when scarce a ship escaped the flames
and her mind, which had been deranged by **Mareotic** wine,
　　was made to face real fears
　　　　as she flew from Italy, and **Caesar**

pressed on the oars (like a hawk
after gentle doves or a swift hunter
　　after a hare on the snowy plains
　　　　of **Thrace**) to put to chains

this monster sent by fate. But she looked
for a nobler death and did not have a woman's fear
　　of the sword, nor did she make
　　　　for secret shores with her swift fleet.

Daring to gaze with face serene upon her ruined palace,
and brave enough to take deadly serpents
　　in her hand, and let her body
　　　　drink their black poison,

fiercer she was in the death she chose, as though
she did not wish to cease to be a queen, taken to Rome
　　on the galleys of savage **Liburnians**
　　　　to be a humble woman in a proud triumph.

Horace, *Odes,* 1.37

Source 10.4: Questions

1 Horace writes that it is time to celebrate now that Cleopatra's threat to Rome has gone. In your own words, explain what he says this 'mad queen' had been preparing to do.

2 Which details from the poem do you think are most effective in characterizing Cleopatra negatively?

3 Horace writes that at the Battle of Actium Cleopatra was 'made to face real fears'. What do you think these were?

4 Horace uses two similes to describe Octavian during his pursuit of Cleopatra. To what does he compare Octavian and what does this suggest about Octavian's character?

5 Horace writes that Cleopatra chose death instead of being taken in chains to be paraded in a triumphal procession in Rome. What details does Horace use in the second half of the poem to present Cleopatra in a more admirable light?

6 This is a flamboyant and imaginative poem and its author, Horace, was Octavian's friend. It was written close to the time of the events it describes. Do you think this context makes it more or less useful as a source?

CHAPTER 10: QUESTIONS FOR DISCUSSION

1 Why was Egypt so important and so fascinating to Rome and its leading figures in the 1st century BC?
You might like to consider
- Egypt's wealth, agriculture and geographical position
- the history of Egypt
- the needs of the generals of the Roman civil war
- Cleopatra

2 Cleopatra lived an exciting but dangerous life. Would you have liked to have been Cleopatra?
You might like to consider
- Cleopatra's education and personal qualities
- Cleopatra's family and the civil war in Egypt
- Cleopatra's relationships with Julius Caesar and Mark Antony
- Cleopatra's death
- Cleopatra's reputation

3 What do you think the Roman attitude to Egypt and Cleopatra shows us about the Romans' sense of identity and their cultural values?
You might like to consider
- Julius Caesar and Mark Antony's love affairs with Cleopatra
- the reaction to these love affairs
- Egypt's role and image in the civil war between Octavian and Mark Antony
- the Egyptian influence on Roman art and architecture

Ⓒ Chapter 10: Core Language Vocabulary List

exspectō	exspectāre, exspectāvī, exspectātum	wait for; expect
nāvigō	nāvigāre, nāvigāvī, nāvigātum	sail
doceō	docēre, docuī, doctum	teach
teneō	tenēre, tenuī, tentum	hold
quaerō	quaerere, quaesīvī, quaesītum	search for; look for; ask
fugiō	fugere, fūgī, fugitum	run away; flee
inveniō	invenīre, invēnī, inventum	find
nauta	nautae, m	sailor
turba	turbae, f	crowd
marītus	marītī, m	husband
amor	amōris, m	love
coniūnx	coniugis, m/f	husband / wife
lūx	lūcis, f	light; daylight
mulier	mulieris, f	woman; wife
nāvis	nāvis, f	ship
parēns	parentis, m/f	parent
pars	partis, f	part
iter	itineris, n	journey
tūtus	tūta, tūtum	safe
alius	alia, aliud	other; another
aliī . . . aliī . . .		some . . . . others
mīrābilis	mīrābile	wonderful; extraordinary
circum	+ accusative	around
inter	+ accusative	among; between
post	+ accusative	after; behind
forte		by chance
statim		at once; immediately
-que		and
nihil		nothing
necesse		necessary
satis		enough

> *alius* has slightly unusual endings and it is used in slightly unusual ways; see Reference Grammar p250.

People and places

Aegyptiī, Aegyptiōrum, m pl
Aegyptus, Aegyptī, f

The **Egyptians** were one of the wealthiest and oldest communities in the ancient world. **Egypt** became a Roman province in 30 BC.

Hērodotus, Hērodotī, m
5th century BC

Herodotus was a Greek writer. He is often referred to as the father of history. His long account of the wars Greece fought against Persia includes a lengthy section about Ancient Egypt and its influence upon Greek culture and religion.

Alexander, Alexandrī, m
356–323 BC
Alexandrīa, Alexandrīae, f

Alexander the Great was a Macedonian king who was undefeated in battle until his sudden death, aged 32. He founded the great city of **Alexandria** in Egypt.

Cleopātra, Cleopātrae, f
69–30 BC

Cleopatra was the last Ptolemaic ruler of Egypt. She was famous for her wealth, beauty, intelligence and power. She had significant love affairs with two powerful Roman men: Julius Caesar and Mark Antony.

Caesar, Caesaris, m
100–44 BC

In this chapter you will read about **Julius Caesar**'s love affair with Cleopatra. Cleopatra came to live with Caesar in Rome until his death in 44 BC.

Marcus Antōnius,
 Marcī Antōniī, m
83 BC–30 BC

Mark Antony was appointed governor of Rome's eastern provinces in 42 BC. He became the second Roman noble to have a long-lasting love affair with Cleopatra.

Unusual words: *alius* and *-que*

In the vocabulary list for this chapter there are two words that behave slightly differently from other words you have met.

- *-que* means *and*, but unlike *et* it is written at the end of a word. It needs to translated **before** the word it is added to.

  Rōmānī pugnāvērunt vīcērunt**que**.   The Romans fought **and** won.

- *alius, alia, aliud* has slightly unusual endings. These are listed in the Grammar Reference section on p250. It means *other* or *another*, but it can also be used as follows.

  aliī oppidum fortiter dēfendēbant,   **Some** men were defending the town
      aliī fugiēbant.   bravely, but **others** were fleeing.

  aliī alia dīcunt.   **Different** men say **different** things.

> **Look it up!** The endings for **alius, alia, aliud** are listed in the Reference Grammar on p250.

EXERCISE 10.1

1. nautae nāvēsque prope mare manēbant.
2. aliī parentum līberōs laudāvērunt, aliī pūnīvērunt.
3. invēnī marītum inter nautās quī in tabernā bibēbant rīdēbantque.
4. post proelium aliī alia quaerēbant.
5. 'nunc aliam mulierem amābō,' inquit marītus īrātus.

Consolidation: adjectives and idiom

Idiom is the name we give to aspects of a language that are particular to that language. In the Latin sentences and stories so far, you have met quite a lot of **idiom**, especially **idiom** which relates to adjectives.

- **Word order**: it is typical for adjectives to follow their nouns, but adjectives that express **size** or **quantity** are often written **before** their nouns.

  mīlitēs **fortēs** adsunt.   Brave soldiers are here.
  maximum perīculum adest.   Very great danger is here.

- Adjectives can be used without a noun to refer to **men**, **women** or **things**.

  dux **suōs** in bellum dūxit.   The general led **his men** into war.

- **Neuter adjectives** can be used with an infinitive:

  forte est pugnāre.   It is brave to fight.

- **Two adjectives** in Latin are joined by *et* or *-que* but are often translated without the word *and*.

  equum **magnum fortemque** habeō.   I have a big, brave horse.

Emphatic word order patterns: the chiasmus

It is possible to break with the conventions for Latin word order and put adjectives in surprising places. This **emphasizes** the adjective.

fortēs erant prope flūmen nautae.   Brave were the sailors near the river.

One of Latin's favourite emphatic word order patterns is the **chiasmus**: this is the name given to a word order pattern which mirrors itself.

audāx   dux laudāvit mīlitēs fortēs.
adjective noun verb   noun   adjective

EXERCISE 10.2

1. laetī parentēs erant sed līberī miserī.
2. malum erat ducī suōs interficere.
3. marītus coniugem saevam et īrātam habēbat.
4. dux suōs prope nāvēs manentēs invēnit.
5. in vīllā mulier laeta parvōs līberōs tenēbat.

Adjectives: *necesse* and *prīmus*

necesse is an adjective, but it is met only in this form; it does not change its endings. **necesse** is often used with a **dative** and an **infinitive**.

necesse est **mihī**   It is necessary **for**
coniugem **invenīre**.   **me to find** my wife.

prīmus is an adjective like any other, but notice the following idiom.

līberī **prīmī** fūgērunt.   The children **were the first to** flee.

prīmō nauta lacrimāvit;   **At first** the sailor cried;
deinde rīsit.   then he laughed.

EXERCISE 10.3

1. mulier prīma virum quaesīvit.
2. necesse est tibī parentēs amāre.
3. prīmō nautae nāvem pulcherrimam aedificāvērunt.
4. necesse est turbae rēgem exspectāre.
5. necesse est magistrīs līberōs docēre, quamquam stultissimī sunt.

EXERCISE 10.4: HERODOTUS TRAVELS TO EGYPT

Herodotus was a Greek historian who lived in the 5th century BC. *He is often described as the father of history. He travelled widely and gathered a tremendous collection of stories about the communities he met. In his introduction to his famous work, the* Histories, *Herodotus wrote that he recorded the results of his enquiries so that human achievements might not be forgotten.*

Book 2 of the Histories *focuses on Egypt, and Herodotus describes the influence of the Egyptians upon Greek culture, and some of the remarkable differences between the Egyptians and the rest of the known world.*

inter Graecōs Hērodotus erat vir clārissimus: itinera longa multaque fēcit quod dē <u>gentibus</u> aliīs plūrima quaerere volēbat. postquam dē hīs gentibus multa mīrābiliaque invēnit, magnum librum scrīpsit.

ōlim Hērodotus in Aegyptum iter fēcit: ibi flūmen maximum, <u>Nīlum</u> nōmine, cōnspexit. 'hoc flūmen est mīrābile,' in librō scrīpsit Hērodotus, 'quod maximum   5
est! in agrōs, quī prope flūmen sunt, plūrimam aquam <u>fundit</u>. in hīs agrīs facile est cibum <u>colere</u>. nōn necesse est agricolīs in agrīs magnopere labōrāre quod flūmen eīs auxilium fert.'

Hērodotus Aegyptiōs magnopere laudāvit quod <u>antīquī</u> erant: 'hī Aegyptiī,' scrīpsit Hērodotus, 'prīmī nōmina deīs suīs dedērunt. nōs Graecī quoque hōs   10
deōs habēmus sed Aegyptiī prīmī nōmina hīs deīs dedērunt. postquam Aegyptiī nōmina deīs dedērunt, nōs Graecī nostrōs deōs invēnimus. Aegyptiī prīmī annum in <u>duodecim</u> <u>mēnsēs</u> <u>dīvīsērunt</u>. prīmī templa aedificāvērunt. haec templa mīrābilia sunt quod antīquissima altissimaque sunt. multae partēs hōrum templōrum aurō aedificātae sunt. in Aegyptō sunt templa quae <u>abhinc</u>   15
duo mīlia annōrum aedificāta sunt.'

dē Aegyptiīs virīs fēminīsque Hērodotus quoque multa quaesīvit: 'Aegyptiae in forum adeunt et <u>mercātūram</u> faciunt; Aegyptiī tamen in vīllīs manent et <u>textile</u> faciunt. <u>stantēs</u> Aegyptiae <u>ūrīnam</u> <u>mingunt</u>, sed Aegyptiī <u>sedentēs</u>. omnēs Aegyptiī in viīs sedentēs cibum cōnsūmunt. Aegyptiī <u>animālia</u> in vīllīs suīs   20
habitantia habent. in Aegyptō sunt multa mīrābilia.'

gēns, gentis, f	race; people
Nīlus, Nīlī, m	the river Nile
fundō, fundere, fūdī, fūsum	pour
colō, colere, coluī, cultum	grow; cultivate
antīquus, antīqua, antīquum	ancient
duodecim	twelve
mēnsis, mēnsis, m	month
dīvidō, dīvidere, dīvīsī, dīvīsum	divide
abhinc (+ accusative)	ago
mercātūra, mercātūrae, f	trade
textile, textilis, n	cloth
stō, stāre, stetī, statum	stand
ūrīna, ūrīnae, f	urine
mingō, mingere, minxī, mictum	pass (urine)
sedeō, sedēre, sēdī, sessum	sit down
animal, animālis, n	animal

EXERCISE 10.5: ALEXANDRIA

Alexandria was one of the most splendid cities of the ancient world. It was founded by Alexander the Great in 331 BC. He created a city of impressive proportions, with wide streets laid out in a grid system. The huge lighthouse built at Alexandria was one of the seven wonders of the ancient world. It was more than 100m tall, and the light which always shone from the fires burning inside could be seen more than 30 miles away.

Alexandria was an important place for trade, but it also became an intellectual epicentre and many famous scientific discoveries were made there. The Great Library at Alexandria became a base for scholarship and it is believed to have housed nearly 500,000 texts.

prope <u>Graeciam</u> erat <u>Macedonia</u>, ubi rēx optimus, Alexander nōmine, regēbat. multī hunc rēgem Alexandrum Magnum vocābant. hoc nōmen eī datum est quod Alexander plūrimās terrās vīcerat. in Aegyptum Alexander quoque suōs dūxit et mox Aegyptiōs vīcit. 'haec terra optima est!' inquit Alexander. 'in hāc terrā est aurum! hīc sunt agrī optimī! <u>hūc</u> multae nāvēs itinera faciunt. in hōc   5
locō urbem optimam aedificābō! huic urbī nōmen erit Alexandrīa. ego sum Alexander et nōtissimus sum: urbs mea quoque et nōtissima et clārissima erit. in hāc urbe multī <u>mercātūram</u> facient. in hāc urbe erit plūrima pecūnia.'

urbs pulcherrima ab Alexandrō aedificāta est. erant viae magnae <u>marmoreae</u>que; hae viae maiōrēs erant quam viae quae Rōmae erant. post mortem Alexandrī   10
<u>pharus</u> altissima quoque aedificāta est. 'haec pharus bona est,' inquiunt nautae laetī. 'lūx huius pharī semper clārissima est! nunc facile est multīs nāvibus itinera facere. nunc tūtum est nautīs prope terram nāvigāre.' pharus ā multīs sīc laudāta est: 'ex omnibus aedificātīs, haec pharus est optima!'

multae nāvēs multa mīrābilia Alexandrīam ferēbant: vīnum ferēbant et <u>aes</u> et   15
cibum <u>externum</u>. librōs quoque ferēbant quod Alexandrīae <u>bibliothēca</u> maxima aedificāta erat. virī, quī dē multīs doctī erant, ad hanc bibliothēcam conveniēbant. illī, librōs et legentēs et scrībentēs, <u>scientiam</u> novam quaerēbant. ūnus ex virīs doctissimīs erat <u>Aristarchus</u>. 'terra,' scrīpsit Aristarchus, 'circum <u>sōlem</u> circumit, nōn sōl circum terram!' aliī ex virīs doctissimīs in <u>tabulīs</u> locōs terrārum prīmī   20
<u>pinxērunt</u>.

Graecia, Graeciae, f	Greece
Macedonia, Macedoniae, f	Macedonia, a kingdom to the north of Greece
hūc	hither; to here
mercātūra, mercātūra, f	trade
marmoreus, marmorea, marmoreum	marble
pharus, pharī, f	lighthouse
aes, aeris, n	bronze
externus, externa, externum	foreign; exotic
bibliothēca, bibliothēcae, f	library
scientia, scientiae, f	knowledge; understanding
Aristarchus, Aristarchī, m	Aristarchus
sōl, sōlis, m	sun
tabula, tabulae, f	chart; map
pingō, pingere, pinxī, pictum	paint; draw

Imperfect passive

The **imperfect passive** is formed in a way which is very similar to the imperfect active: the only difference is the **person ending**.

imperfect active		imperfect passive	
I was ruling	regēba**m**	I was being ruled	regēba**r**
you (sg) were ruling	regēbā**s**	you (sg) were being ruled	regēbā**ris**
he / she / it was ruling	regēba**t**	he / she / it was being ruled	regēbā**tur**
we were ruling	regēbā**mus**	we were being ruled	regēbā**mur**
you (pl) were ruling	regēbā**tis**	you (pl) were being ruled	regēbā**minī**
they were ruling	regēba**nt**	they were being ruled	regēba**ntur**

The **imperfect passive** uses the **present stem**, and so the vowels used vary across the different conjugations.

1st conjugation	am**ā**bar	I was being ruled
2nd conjugation	terr**ē**bar	I was being terrified
3rd conjugation	reg**ē**bar	I was being loved
4th conjugation	audi**ē**bar	I was being heard
mixed conjugation	capi**ē**bar	I was being captured

Look it up! You can see the imperfect passive listed in full for all conjugations on p239.

Translating the imperfect active and passive

As with the **imperfect active**, the **imperfect passive** can be translated in a range of ways.

imperfect active	regēbam	I **was** ruling
		I **began to** rule
		I **used to** rule
imperfect passive	regēbar	I **was being** ruled
		I **began to be** ruled
		I **used to be** ruled

If the action naturally lasts for a long time, sometimes it is best to translate a Latin imperfect passive into an English perfect passive instead.

multōs annōs ā rege saevō **regēbantur**.   **Latin imperfect passive**
For many years **they were ruled** by a savage king.   **English perfect passive**

EXERCISE 10.6

1. marītus ā coniuge laetā amābātur.

2. līberī ā parentibus trīstibus quaerēbantur.

3. cūr ā magistrīs crūdēlibus docēbāmur?

4. haec terra ā rēgibus regēbātur; deinde rēgēs fūgērunt.

5. semper in bellō multī et fortēs occīdēbantur.

6. perterritus eram quod ab agricolā saevō tenēbar.

7. cūr, ō fīliī, ā parentibus pūniēbāminī?

8. in agrīs et silvīs equī fugientēs quaerēbantur.

9. exspectābārisne, ō nauta, ab aliīs nautīs?

10. templum aurō aedificātum ā multīs laudābātur.

EXERCISE 10.7: CLEOPATRA, QUEEN OF EGYPT

The Greek Ptolemaic dynasty ruled Egypt for nearly 300 years. Cleopatra, the most famous of the Ptolemies, was an impressive and notorious figure within the ancient world. Highly educated and extremely ambitious, she managed to win the civil war against her brother by enlisting help from the most powerful Roman at the time, Julius Caesar.

Plutarch, a Greek historian writing in the 2nd century AD, wrote an account of their first meeting. The anecdote retold below is a good example of Cleopatra's ruthless willingness to pursue her own agenda.

postquam Alexander Aegyptiōs vīcit, ā rēgibus <u>Macedoniīs</u> Aegyptus regēbātur. post mortem Alexandrī in Aegyptō <u>Ptolemaeus</u> erat rēx; Aegyptus ā <u>nepōtibus</u> eius <u>circiter</u> <u>trecentōs</u> annōs regēbātur. clārissima ex hīs rēgibus rēgīnīsque erat Cleopātra. Cleopātra et <u>frāter</u> Aegyptiōs regēbant. Cleopātra, quae dē multīs <u>linguīs</u> et dē multīs <u>gentibus</u> docta erat, ā multīs laudābātur et amābātur   5
quod fēmina <u>sagāx</u> et pulcherrima erat.

Cleopātra tamen ā frātre nōn amābātur: 'nōlō Aegyptiōs regere cum Cleopātrā,' inquit frāter. '<u>sine</u> Cleopātrā regere omnēs Aegyptiōs volō.' mox inter Cleopātram frātremque erat bellum <u>cīvīle</u>. 'nōn tūtum est,' inquit Cleopātra lacrimāns, 'in Aegyptō manēre; necesse est mihī in <u>Syriam</u> fugere.'   10

Cleopātra fēmina audācissima erat: frātrem vincere et omnem Aegyptum regere volēbat. 'Rōmānōrum,' inquit amīcō, <u>Apollodōrō</u> nōmine, 'fortissimus est Iūlius Caesar. Caesar multōs mīlitēs habet. forte Alexandrīae Caesar adest. necesse est mihī Alexandrīam redīre et Caesarem statim invenīre. Caesar, <u>sīcut</u> hominēs aliī, mē amābit; nōbīs auxilium dabit et tum frātre <u>potentior</u> erō.' 'ō   15
Cleopātra,' Apollodōrus respondit, 'est perīculum maximum. Alexandrīae circum nōs erunt hostēs quī tē interficere volent. num tūtī ad Caesarem ībimus?' '<u>textile</u> circum mē pōne,' inquit Cleopātra, 'et mē ad Caesarem fer. hostēs nostrī tē textile ferentem vidēbunt; tē mē ferentem nōn vidēbunt.'

itaque Cleopātra in Aegyptum nāvigāvit et ad Caesarem tūta lāta est. postquam   20
ā Caesare cōnspecta est, statim Caesar amōre magnō tenēbātur. 'Cleopātra fēmina pulcherrima et sagācissima est,' inquit Caesar, 'et Cleopātra est rēgīna terrae potentissimae. ego eī auxilium dabō et illa mihī quoque auxilium dabit. tum nōs potentiōrēs omnibus cēterīs erimus.'

Macedonius, Macedonia, Macedonium	Macedonian; from Macedonia
Ptolemaeus, Ptolemaeī, m	Ptolemy
nepōs, nepōtis, m	descendant
circiter (+ accusative)	around; about
trecentī, trecentae, trecenta	300
frāter, frātris, m	brother
lingua, linguae, f	language
gēns, gentis, f	nation; people
sagāx, sagācis	shrewd; clever
sine (+ ablative)	without
cīvīlis, cīvīle	civil; between citizens
Syria, Syriam, f	Syria
Apollodōrus, Apollodōrī, m	Apollodorus
sīcut	just as
potēns, potentis	powerful
textile, textilis, n	cloth

Further notes on the genitive and dative cases

- The **genitive** case connects two nouns: most often it shows that one noun **belongs** to another.

  nāvis **nautae** optima est.   The **sailor's** ship is excellent.

- Notice that *plūs* is followed by a **genitive**. This also happens with *satis.*

  plūs pecūniae quam tū habeō.   I have **more money** than you.
  satis cibī cōnsūmpsī   I ate **enough food**.

- The **dative** case is usually best translated using *to* or *for*. Sometimes, however, it is used to show **possession**.

  mihī nāvēs multae sunt.   literal translation: **There are to me** many ships.
                                 better translation: **I have** many ships.

EXERCISE 10.8

1. saepe plūs lūcis est in agrīs quam in silvīs.

2. fīliī mulierīs ē vīllā fugiēbant.

3. satis vīnī bibī et nunc dormīre volō.

4. nihil plūs aurī habet quam hoc templum nōtissimum.

5. Rōmānīs senātōrēs clārissimī et nōbilissimī erant.

6. nautae nāvis diūtius quaerēbantur.

7. marītus plūs pecūniae fīliō nōn dedit.

8. nōnne satis nāvium et nautārum habēs?

9. marītō mulierīque līberī et bonī et laetī erant.

10. nōlīte, ō ancillae, plūs cibī mihī ferre! satis cōnsūmpsī!

CASES QUIZ

Identify and explain the cases of each of the following nouns from Exercise 10.8.

1. lūcis (from Q1)

2. vīnī (from Q3)

3. Rōmānīs (from Q5)

4. nāvis (from Q6)

5. nāvium (from Q8)

Consolidation: the imperfect active, imperfect passive and perfect passive

It is very easy to get the translation of these three tenses confused.

imperfect active	regēbam	I was ruling
perfect passive	regēbar	I was being ruled
imperfect passive	rēctus sum	I was ruled

Watch out! It is also important to remember that the imperfect active and the imperfect passive can be translated in more than one way (see p135).

EXERCISE 10.9

1. hic puer ā patre doctus est.
2. illī servī per silvam fugiēbant.
3. ancilla ā dominō crūdēlī pūniēbātur.
4. in mediō forō omnēs senātōrem novum exspectābāmus.
5. nōnne iuvenēs ā senibus docēbantur?
6. multās hōrās per altum mare nāvigābāmus.
7. in bellō plūrimī cīvēs necātī sunt.
8. mīlitēs hastās longās ad hostēs iaciēbant.
9. dux gladiō suō necātus est.
10. ubi aurum inventum est? diūtissimē per viās agrōsque quaerēbam!

VERB QUIZ

Name the tenses of each of the following verb forms from Exercise 10.9.

1. doctus est
2. fugiēbant
3. pūniēbātur
4. docēbantur
5. necātī sunt

EXERCISE 10.10: CLEOPATRA AND JULIUS CAESAR

Cleopatra and Julius Caesar had a long love affair; Cleopatra bore Caesar a son and moved to Rome to live with him there. Many historians think that Cleopatra hoped that her son would inherit Caesar's wealth and power; Caesar, however, never officially acknowledged Caesarion as his son: after Caesar's death, his great-nephew Octavian was the chosen heir. Cleopatra, realizing that her future in Rome was no longer safe, returned to Egypt.

inter Cleopātram Caesaremque erat amor maximus. Cleopātra, postquam
mīlitēs <u>frātris</u> auxiliō Caesaris victī sunt, Caesarem magnopere amābat. 'ad
<u>Ītaliam</u> cum Caesare nāvigāre volō,' inquit Cleopatra. 'Caesarem marītum
meum esse volō. Rōmae cum Caesare habitāre cupiō. rēgīna nōtissima sum.
Rōmae multī mē laudābunt quod plūs pecūniae quam omnēs Rōmānī habeō. in   5
vīllā <u>māgnificā</u> habitābimus.'

Cleopātra ā Caesare magnopere amābātur: 'Cleopātra rēgīna et pulcherrima et
docta est; nihil mīrābilius Cleopātrā est. Cleopātra quoque <u>potentissima</u> est.
mihī nōn iam satis <u>potestātis</u> est. Rōmae ego et Cleopātra habitābimus,
maximam potestātem habēbimus et omnēs nōs laudābunt.'   10

Cleopātra et Caesar ad Ītaliam nāvigāvērunt. nōn omnēs, tamen, Cleopātram
laudāvērunt: 'Cleopātra,' inquit Cicerō, 'est rēgīna <u>externa</u>. Cleopātra est mulier
pessima quae aurum et <u>lūxuriam</u> amat. saepius Cleopātram sē laudantem
audīvī; saepissimē Cleopātra haec dīxīt: "ego clārior omnibus Rōmānīs sum."
Cleopātra nōn melior omnibus Rōmānīs est: multī Rōmānī clārissimī sunt, multī   15
Rōmānī nōbilissimī sunt: etiam ego Rōmānus clārissimus sum. nōn <u>sōlum</u>
Cleopātra mīrābilis est.'

mox Cleopātrae et Caesarī fīlius, <u>Caesariō</u> nōmine, erat. 'fīlius noster,' inquit
Cleopātra, 'Rōmae et Alexandrīae potentissimus erit.' Caesar, tamen, ab <u>inimīcīs</u>
necātus est. post mortem Caesaris omnis pecūnia <u>Octāviānō</u>, nōn fīliō   20
Cleopātrae, data est. 'Caesar Octāviānum potestātem habēre volēbat,' inquit
Cleopātra lacrimāns. 'fīlium nostrum potestātem habēre nōlēbat. nunc multī
inimīcī circum nōs adsunt. quamquam in Aegyptō rēgīna potentissima sum,
Rōmae nōbis nōn tūtum est manēre. multō melius est in Aegyptum redīre.'

frāter, frātris, m	brother
Ītalia, Ītaliae, f	Italy
māgnificus, māgnifica, māgnificum	magnificent
potēns, potentis	powerful
potestās, potestātis, f	power
Cicerō, Cicerōnis, m	Cicero
externus, externa, externum	foreign
lūxuria, lūxuriae, f	luxury
sōlum	only
Caesariō, Caesariōnis, m	Caesarion
inimīcus, inimīcī, m	(personal) enemy
Octāviānus, Octāviānī, m	Octavian

After Julius Caesar's death, the territories of the Roman Republic were divided between the three most powerful Romans at the time: Octavian, Lepidus and Mark Antony. Once Lepidus was removed from power in 36 BC, Octavian held sway in the west, and Antony in the east. Antony was keen to extend his eastern power and he needed money to fund his army. Cleopatra, together with the wealth of Egypt, was a natural choice of ally.

According to the historian Plutarch, at their first meeting Cleopatra flaunted her wealth, beauty and power. Antony was enthralled and the second famous love affair between the eastern queen and a Roman potentate began. You can read Plutarch's account of this meeting in Source 10.2.

post mortem Caesaris Cleopātra in Aegyptum rediit. paucōs post annōs, alius Rōmānus, Marcus Antōnius nōmine, auxilium Cleopātrae petīvit.

'mihī,' inquit Antōnius, 'Cleopātra erit amīca optima et comes <u>potentissima</u>: Cleopātrae plūrima pecūnia est. pecūniā Cleopātrae mīlitēs emam et multās terrās superābō.' itaque epistula ab Antōniō ad Cleopātram missa est. 'ab 5
Antōniō invītāta sum,' inquit Cleopātra, 'sed rēgīna potentissima sum: iubeō aliōs, nōn ab aliīs <u>iubeor</u>.' itaque in Aegyptō Cleopātra manēbat. iterum tamen Antōnius Cleopātram invītāvit. 'Antōnius mē vidēre magnopere vult,' inquit Cleopātra. 'itaque ad Antōnium nāvigābō et Antōniō ostendam <u>potestātem</u> meam maximam.' 10

Cleopātra nāvēs et multās et pulcherrimās habēbat. 'nāvem pulchriōrem omnibus nāvibus cēterīs habeō,' inquit Cleopātra, 'et in hāc nāve ad Antōnium nāvigābō.' postquam nāvis aurō et <u>argentō</u> parāta est, Cleopātra ad Antōnium nāvigāvit. ubi nāvis per flūmen nāvigāns cōnspecta est, magna turba per viās currēbat quod omnēs cīvēs nāvem pulcherrimam vidēre volēbant. Antōnius 15
tamen Cleopātram exspectāns in forō manēbat: diūtius Antōnius Cleopātram exspectābat. 'ego sum rēgīna potentissima,' inquit Cleopātra, 'et aliōs ad mē vocō, nōn <u>vocor</u> ab aliīs.' tandem Antōnius ad nāvem Cleopātrae adiit. ubi fēminam <u>tam</u> pulcherrimam, nāvem tam <u>splendidam</u>, <u>dīvitiās</u> tam maximās vīdit, tenēbātur maximō amōre. 'nihil melius Cleopātrā est,' inquit Antōnius 20
magnō cum amōre. 'Cleopātra coniūnx erit!'

potēns, potentis	powerful
iubeor	'I am ordered'
potestas, potestātis, f	power
argentum, argentī, n	silver
vocor	'I am called'
tam	so
splendidus, splendida, splendidum	splendid
divitiae, divitiārum, f pl	riches; wealth

Chapter 10: Additional Language

SECTION A10: CHAPTER 10 VOCABULARY

Exercise A10.1: Derivations

Translate these Latin words from Chapter 10, give an English derivation and explain the connection.

	Latin	meaning	derivation	explanation
1	turba			
2	marītus			
3	nāvis			
4	iter			
5	satis			
6	nāvigō			
7	doceō			
8	fugiō			
9	inveniō			
10	circum			

Exercise A10.2: Case endings (nouns and participles)

Circle the stem, and give the meaning and declension of the following nouns and participles from Chapter 10. Then give the case requested.

	Latin	meaning	declension	
1	nauta, nautae, m			accusative pl =
2	iter, itineris, n			nominative pl =
3	pars, partis, f			accusative sg =
4	parēns, parentis, m			dative sg =
5	turba, turbae, f			genitive pl =
6	marītus, marītī, m			dative sg =
7	nāvis, nāvis, f			ablative pl =
8	lūx, lūcis, f			ablative sg =
9	mulier, mulieris, f			dative pl =

	Latin	meaning	declension	
10	coniūnx, coniugis, m/f			genitive sg =
11	quaerēns, quaerentis			dative masculine sg =
12	fugiēns, fugientis			accusative neuter sg =
13	inveniēns, invenientis			nominative feminine pl =
14	tentus, tenta, tentum			ablative masculine sg =
15	doctus, docta, doctum			genitive feminine sg =

Exercise A10.3: Verbs

Identify the tense of the Chapter 10 verbs in the table below and translate each one. Then change the form from singular to plural, or plural to singular, keeping the tense and person the same.

Remember that you need to look at the stem as well as the ending. Here are the principal parts for each verb so that you can see their different stems.

> exspectō, exspectāre, exspectāvī, exspectātum
> navigō, navigāre, navigavī, navigatum
> doceō, docēre, docuī, doctum
> teneō, tenēre, tenuī, tentum
> quaerō, quaerere, quaesivī, quaesitum
> fugiō, fugere, fugī, fugitum
> inveniō, invenīre, invēnī, inventum

	Latin	tense	translation	new form
1	exspectābit			
2	nāvigāverāmus			
3	docuit			
4	docet			
5	tenuistī			
6	quaerit			
7	quaeret			
8	fugiam			
9	invēnērunt			
10	invenīmus			

SECTION B10: GRAMMAR

Exercise B10.1: Identifying voice and case

This exercise focuses on nouns and verbs from the vocabulary lists for Chapter 9 and Chapter 10.

These sentences contain active and passive verbs. For each of the sentences:

–   underline all the words that make up the verb
–   identify the verb as active or passive, and name the tense
–   identify the case of the nouns in **purple**

> *exspectō* – *I wait for* – is followed by an accusative noun. It is important not to confuse this with the *for* which signals the dative case.

1. The **woman** was **waiting for** her husband.
2. For a long time he waited for **light**.
3. We were sailing in a **boat** with the brave sailors.
4. They used to be taught by their excellent **parents**.
5. **Soldiers**, although you were wounded, you were running away.
6. Your **parent** has been found!
7. You were looking for **ships** for the **sailors**.
8. The **crowd** was overcome by love.
9. The **enemy** were burning the ships.
10. **War** was being waged by our comrades.

Exercise B10.2: Imperfect passive

This exercise focuses on verbs from the vocabulary lists for Chapter 9 and Chapter 10.

Translate these imperfect passive verbs into English.

	imperfect passive	translation
1	tenēbātur	
2	dēfendēbāmur	
3	necābantur	
4	vulnerābāris	
5	dūcēbāminī	
6	dēlēbātur	
7	inveniēbantur	
8	quaerēbar	
9	exspectābāris	
10	custōdiēbāmur	

Exercise B10.3: Conjugations and the imperfect passive

This exercise focuses on verbs from the vocabulary lists for Chapter 9 and Chapter 10.

Here is a reminder of the imperfect passive in all conjugations.

1st conjugation	amābar	I was being loved
2nd conjugation	terrēbar	I was being terrified
3rd conjugation	regēbar	I was being ruled
4th conjugation	audiēbar	I was being heard
mixed conjugation	capiēbar	I was being captured

Give the conjugation and the imperfect passive form requested for each verb.

	verb	conjugation	
1	teneō, tenēre		it was being held =
2	quaerō, quaerere		you (sg) were being searched for =
3	expectō, exspectāre		I was being waited for =
4	dēleō, dēlēre		you (pl) were being destroyed =
5	moveō, movēre		they were being moved =
6	necō, necāre		she was being killed =
7	rapiō, rapere		you (pl) were being seized =
8	custōdiō, custōdīre		we were being guarded =
9	dēfendō, dēfendere		it was being defended =
10	dūcō, dūcere		they were being led =

Exercise B10.4: Imperfect active and passive

This exercise focuses on nouns and verbs from the vocabulary lists for Chapters 8–10.

Underline the words in English that make up the verb and choose the correct form of the verb from the options below.

1. We were being invited by the noble women. (invītābāmur / invītābāmus)
2. The old men were approaching the ships. (appropinquābat /appropinquābant)
3. The soldier was holding his shield bravely. (tenēbātur / tenēbat)
4. The enemy were being killed by the inhabitants. (occīdēbantur / occīdēbant)
5. You (sg) were killing many fierce soldiers. (necābāris / necābās)
6. The leader and his sailors were gathering. (conveniēbāmus / conveniēbant)
7. The letters for their husbands were being written by their wives.
   (scrībēbant / scrībēbantur)
8. The soldiers were being sent around the town. (mittēbantur / mittēbant)
9. We were reading books written by the inhabitants. (legēbāmus / legēbāntur)
10. A famous sailor was being injured near the ships. (vulnerābat / vulnerābātur)

Exercise B10.5: Imperfect active, imperfect passive and perfect passive

This exercise practises verbs from the vocabulary lists for Chapter 9 and Chapter 10.

Identify the voice, person and tense of the verbs below and translate each one.

		voice	person	tense	translation
1	fugiēbant				
2	inveniēbantur				
3	doctī sunt				
4	nāvigābam				
5	quaerēbar				
6	superāta es				
7	gestum est				
8	oppugnābāmus				
9	incendēbātur				
10	vulnerābāris				

Exercise B10.6 Mixed verbs

This exercise practises verbs from the vocabulary lists for Chapter 9 and Chapter 10.

Translate each of these verbs into Latin.

1. they were killing, they were killed, they were being killed
2. you (sg) overpowered, you (sg) were overpowered,
   you (sg) were being overpowered
3. it was handed over, it was being handed over, he was handing over
4. we were inviting, we were being invited, we invited
5. I was wounding, I was being wounded, I was wounded
6. it was guarded, it was being guarded, he guarded
7. she was sent, she was sending, she was being sent
8. you (pl) were seizing, you (pl) were seized, you (pl) seized
9. I was being taught, I was teaching, I was taught
10. it was found, she found, she was finding

SECTION C10: ENGLISH TO LATIN SENTENCES

Exercise C10.1: Imperfect active, imperfect passive and perfect passive

Identify the tense and voice of the verbs in **purple** in the sentences below and translate them into Latin.

1. The leader of the Romans **was chosen** by the citizens.
2. Famous letters **used to be written** by the senator to his friend.
3. Often **we used to invite** the sailors to dinner.
4. Suddenly our town **was destroyed** by the cruel enemy.
5. The wife **began to lead** her husband through the large crowd.
6. A letter **was sent** to the king in which he was ordered to flee.
7. Water **was being carried** from the river by the slave.
8. For a long time the extraordinary light **was seen** by the crowd.
9. **You were holding** the letter sent by your husband.
10. 'Our ship **has been found**!' shouted the sailors.

Exercise C10.2: Sentences to translate into Latin

1. It was necessary for us to flee, because our town was being burned.
2. I used to have a book written by a very famous Roman named Caesar.
3. 'O slave, bring me more wine!' said the master, while eating dinner.
4. The soldier wounded by the savage enemy asked for more water.
5. When the enemy were attacking, our men were the first to burn the houses.
6. Although his men fought very bravely, the leader was overpowered, captured and killed.
7. It was not safe to flee, because the town was being guarded by a savage, cruel enemy.
8. Because the soldiers did not have enough weapons, they were overpowered by the inhabitants of the town.
9. Surely the children who were taught by the good teacher were praised by their parents?
10. Some men want to have more gold, but others want bigger swords.

SECTION D: CONSOLIDATION

Exercises for Additional Language Section D are available on the companion website. Exercises are structured by grammatical category, and cover all Core Vocabulary met so far within each category. For Chapter 10, these exercises are as follows:

- Exercise D10.1: Neuter nouns in the 2nd and 3rd declensions
- Exercise D10.2: 4th conjugation and mixed conjugation verbs

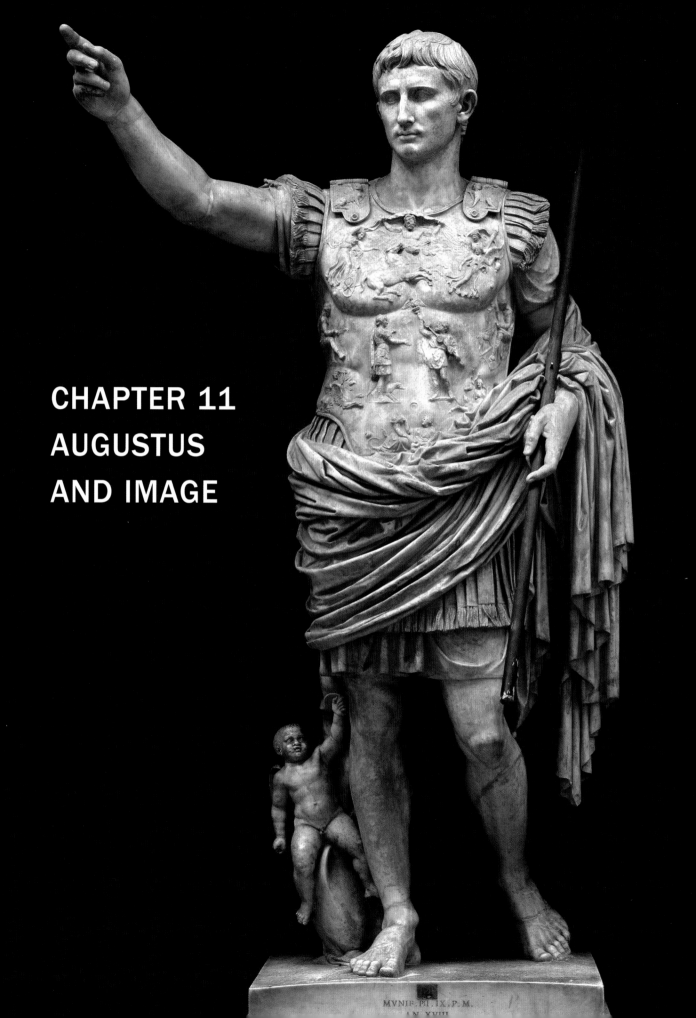

CHAPTER 11
AUGUSTUS
AND IMAGE

Chapter 11: Introduction

Octavian / Augustus and a new era for Rome

Augustus is the name given to Octavian, the man we have already met in Chapters 8–10 as Julius Caesar's heir and the winner of the civil war against Mark Antony. He became known as Augustus in his role as Rome's first emperor. As discussed in Chapters 8–10, Octavian's rise to power came at the end of the bitter and bloody civil wars that ravaged the Roman Republic in the 1st century BC. Octavian used his power to establish a new political system at Rome and he achieved a long-lasting peace. He was celebrated by the Romans as the man who ushered in a new and more successful era for Rome. By the time of Augustus' death in AD 14, the Roman world was wealthier than it had ever been before: Augustus had extended the territory controlled by Rome in almost every direction, gaining land in modern-day Spain, Switzerland, the Balkans and Turkey, as well as bringing Egypt under Roman control. An extensive programme of land distribution and building construction helped to heal the wounds caused by repeated civil wars. For the first time in many years, people could get on with their lives in the stability of peace.

Julius Caesar's death and the beginnings of Octavian's power

Octavian was the great-nephew of Julius Caesar. As Caesar had no legitimate male heirs, he had adopted Octavian as his son when he was 17 years old. This meant that when Caesar was killed in 44 BC, Octavian was suddenly thrust into the limelight as the owner of a vast personal fortune. As you will read in Exercise 11.2, at the time of Caesar's death Octavian was in the Roman territory known as Illyria. He wasted no time in travelling to Rome to demand his inheritance. Knowing that he was young and unlikely to be taken seriously, Octavian used Caesar's wealth to gather an army to support him.

In the aftermath of Caesar's death there was conflict in Rome between the Liberators who had supported the assassination of Caesar and those who sought to avenge him. Mark Antony was the leader of Caesar's supporters and he had succeeded in driving out many of the Liberators. Octavian seized the initiative by using his new-found wealth to bribe Antony's soldiers to betray their general and join his own private army.

In the fighting that followed, the consuls for that year were killed. The power-hungry Octavian sent soldiers to Rome to demand one of the vacant consulships for himself. Suetonius, a Roman biographer from the end of the 1st century AD, tells us that the senate

FIGURE 11.1   The Prima Porta statue of Augustus

This statue is over 2m tall and is one of the most well-known images of Augustus. The version here is a marble copy of a bronze original and dates from early in the 1st century AD. It takes its name from the Italian district of Prima Porta, where this statue was found, in a villa that belonged to Augustus' wife. It is now part of the collection in the Vatican Museums in Rome. Like many representations of Augustus, it presents a carefully constructed image: depicted on his breastplate are the gods of the sky, sun and earth. A young child, who may be Venus' son Cupid, sits at his feet. Augustus is shown to be a powerful general, whose victories reach across the expanse of the world and bring with them the promise of a bright future.

FIGURE 11.2   Modern copy of the Prima Porta statue

This painted plaster cast is part of the collection in the Ashmolean Museum in Oxford. The gleaming white marble image in Figure 11.1 is the version of the statue which is most familiar to a modern audience, but traces of paint were found on its surface: this suggests that, like most ancient statues, it used to be painted. This reconstruction is a suggestion of what the statue might have looked like to its original audience.

refused to make the young man consul. At this, one of Octavian's centurions threw back his cloak to reveal his sword, saying, 'This will make him consul, if you do not.' When the senate refused to support him, Octavian decided to follow the example of Sulla (see Chapter 9, p78), and he marched eight legions into Rome to take what he wanted. He was duly elected consul in 43 BC, aged only 19.

The triumvirate

Octavian and Mark Antony soon realized that they had more to gain by cooperation than conflict. At the end of 43 BC Antony, Octavian and Lepidus had formed the alliance which was called the triumvirate. Between them, they ended the Liberators' civil war at the Battle of Philippi in 42 BC. As you will read in Exercise 11.4, Octavian took great pleasure in avenging the murder of his adopted father and treated Marcus Brutus, one of the leaders of the Liberators, horrendously. In Rome, the triumvirate then dealt with their political enemies and raised funds by ordering the deaths of hundreds of wealthy Romans and confiscating their property. They published the names of these enemies on a list known as a proscription. You can read more about this in Source 11.1.

The Battle of Actium

In time the triumvirate broke apart: Octavian held power in the west and Mark Antony in the east. Antony and Octavian eventually declared war on one another in 32 BC. As discussed in Chapter 10, and as you will read in Exercise 11.6, the definitive moment in this conflict came in 31 BC in a sea battle fought near Actium on the coast of western Greece. The Battle of Actium was seen by the Romans as a turning point in Roman history, and many writers were fascinated by the clash between east and west, and the prize of uncontested power that Octavian's victory brought with it. After the death of Antony in 30 BC, Octavian ruled the Roman world alone. Rome had been in a state of civil war on and off for almost 100 years, but now Octavian had control of a larger empire than any Roman before him.

FIGURE 11.3 Panel from the Ara Pacis

The Ara Pacis (Altar of Peace) was dedicated in 13 BC as a gift to Augustus in celebration of the peace he had established. It can be seen today in the Museo dell'Ara Pacis in Rome. The section shown above is known as the Tellus panel, because it is thought to show Tellus, the goddess of the earth. To the left and the right are personifications of the land and the sea. These figures are thought to symbolize the far-reaching extent of Augustus' peace.

Peace and a new beginning

In 30 BC, Octavian faced two problems. The first was that Rome and its provinces had been neglected and devastated by war and they were in need of the benefits of a long-lasting peace and a steady government. Here lay Octavian's second, more complicated problem: what form could this government take? The power-sharing days of the Roman Republic were over: Octavian did not share equal power with another consul and he was clearly the most powerful man in Rome, without any rivals. In Chapter 7 we discussed how the memory of kings was detested in Rome, and in Chapters 8 and 9 we saw how the behaviour of Julius Caesar had encouraged the Liberators to assassinate him in order to prevent one-man rule and preserve the Republic. Octavian knew that he needed to tread carefully.

Octavian continued to be elected consul every year until 23 BC, beating even Marius' impressive record (see Chapter 9, p76). As you will read in Exercise 11.8, during this time Octavian adopted an important title: *princeps* (first citizen). This echoed the Republican title *princeps senatus* (first in the senate) which had been awarded to revered men, such as Quintus Fabius Maximus in the 3rd century BC. The title denoted a senator's status as the most senior within the senate. It did not bring with it any official power – *imperium* – in the way that an elected position such as consul did, but it guaranteed that the *princeps senatus'* opinions would carry a great deal of weight. When Octavian adopted the title of *princeps* it was a shrewd move: it acknowledged the primacy of his position, but he avoided the more toxic associations that the absolute *imperium* of the permanent position of dictator had brought to Julius Caesar.

Augustus, the first Roman emperor

In 27 BC, Octavian handed back all of the emergency powers he had been granted in the civil war and officially declared a return to the rule of the elected magistrates of the Roman Republic. In return, the senate granted him another title, the name *Augustus,* which roughly translates as venerable or revered. It is this second name that we use to refer to Octavian in his role as the first Roman emperor.

27 BC is where most people mark the end of the Roman Republic and the start of the Roman Empire. This is because, despite Augustus' claims that the Republic had been restored, in reality this was far from the truth. As *princeps*, Augustus was entitled to speak in the senate first and order its business. This, together with his considerable *auctoritas*, gave him a significant influence in any discussion. In addition, he held a number of different offices, the combination of which gave him an unprecedented quantity of *imperium.* Moreover, all 25 legions of the army swore an oath of loyalty to Augustus and he maintained direct control of the most important provinces in the empire for the next 10 years.

In 23 BC Augustus became seriously ill, so ill that he thought he was going to die. It is hard for us to say whether the Roman Empire would have lasted as long as it did if he had. Perhaps Rome would have descended into yet another civil war between another generation of generals and politicians struggling for power. Augustus soon recovered, however, and went on to live for more than thirty years. Without a doubt, one reason for Augustus' success was his longevity. He died in AD 14, after ruling for 44 years.

Augustus' successor was his adopted son, Tiberius, who became the new *princeps*. From this point on the precedent had been established that this was a hereditary role, to be passed down within the family. The first five emperors were all part of Augustus' extended family and collectively they are known as the Julio-Claudians. Other family dynasties followed. From the reign of Augustus until the death of Marcus Aurelius in AD 180, Rome enjoyed a period of stability known as the *Pax Romana* under the rule of its emperors, but the Roman Republic was long gone. As later historians such as Tacitus noted, 500 years after the kings were overthrown, Rome was effectively under the rule of kings once again.

FIGURE 11.4 Livia, Augustus' third wife

Women had no formal political power in Rome, but there are many stories of their influence behind the scenes. Roman historians presented Livia as manipulative and ambitious: Tacitus even suggests that she may have murdered Augustus in an attempt to ensure that her son Tiberius, who had been adopted by Augustus, would go on to rule in his place. This marble bust dates from the 1st century AD, and it is currently held in the Hermitage Museum in St Petersburg, Russia.

Propaganda

A new start required a new image and Augustus did much to spread the message that he was responsible for a glorious and prosperous era at Rome. Suetonius records that, towards the end of his life, Augustus said, 'I found Rome as a city of brick, but left it a city of marble.' The Augustan period saw vast building programmes not just in Rome but across the whole empire. Augustus completely transformed the Roman forum and built or restored more than 80 temples. New buildings were one way Augustus tried to show a break with the past and get the Romans to look forward to a bright future rather than back at the bloodshed of their recent history.

FIGURE 11.5   **Temple to Mars Ultor**

Very little remains of the Augustan forum, one of Augustus' most impressive building projects. This image shows the remains of the temple to Mars Ultor (Mars the Avenger), which was built as part of the forum and dedicated in 2 BC. Octavian had promised to build the temple during his campaign of vengeance against Julius Caesar's assassins.

Augustus also made good use of the images he put on coins to influence the way people saw him. Coins were an excellent way to communicate ideas to the masses, as they were used and seen by many people nearly every day. As you can see in Source 11.2, some of these coins showed his victory over Mark Antony and Egypt. He also often put the goddess *Pax* (Peace) on his coins. It was a simple but effective message.

Augustus made much of his religious devotion and his personal connection to the gods. Through Julius Caesar's ancestry, Augustus could claim to be connected to Aeneas and Venus. In 44 BC, a comet had been seen in Rome, which many believed to be the soul of Caesar ascending into heaven. Back then, Octavian had made the most of the opportunity and joined Antony in declaring his adopted father to be a god, the *Divus Julius*. Technically this made Augustus the son of a god and he went to great lengths to remind people of it. The comet or Julian star appears on many of Augustus' coins. This was a clever use of imagery and propaganda. After all, who would wish to overthrow the son of a god?

Augustus and the poets

As we discussed in Chapter 7, wealthy Romans could act as patrons, and offer financial assistance to their clients in return for support from them. As you will read in Exercise 11.9, Augustus' friend Maecenas was a patron to several poets, including Horace and Virgil, and many scholars have thought that Maecenas asked these poets to celebrate the achievements of Augustus. Chapter 10 contained an example of one of these poems: Source 10.4 was a translation of Horace's ode about Octavian's success in the Battle of Actium. Virgil's most famous poem is the *Aeneid*: this great epic tells the history of Rome through the story of its founding father Aeneas. In Book 1 you met several of its stories. Although the main plot of the *Aeneid* is set at the very beginning of Roman history, Virgil uses prophecy to look forward to the future. Augustus' rule is presented as the climax in Roman achievement and the golden age that will make all Aeneas' toils and hardship worthwhile. Halfway through the poem, Aeneas travels down to the Underworld to visit the soul of his dead father Anchises. His father describes to Aeneas the future span of Rome's history, a future which is to reach its peak in the age of Augustus. Anchises tells Aeneas that people all over the world will tremble at the divine prophecies of Augustus' arrival. In addition to this, at the centre of Aeneas' shield, made for him by the god Vulcan, Augustus is shown winning the battle of Actium.

At first glance, it appears that the *Aeneid* portrays the rule of Augustus as a golden age and glorifies Augustus himself. A closer look, however, reveals that it is not quite as simple as this. The poem is acutely aware that victory through war always comes at the cost of human suffering, the consequences of which are not easy to ignore. Augustus took a great interest in Virgil's work and on more than one occasion the poet read extracts to him personally. As Virgil lay dying in 19 BC, his final wish was that the *Aeneid*, which he had not finished editing, be burnt or at least never published. As soon as Virgil was dead, however, Augustus ordered it to be

FIGURE 11.6   **The Via Labicana Augustus**

This marble statue dates from 12 BC, the year that Augustus was appointed Rome's Chief Priest. It shows a different side to the emperor. Augustus' head is veiled in the manner of a priest preparing for sacrifice and showing due respect to the gods. Augustus would have been over 50 years old when this statue was made, but, as with many of his statues, it portrays a younger, idealized image. It is now part of the collection in the Palazzo Massimo alle Terme in Rome.

published with minimal changes. Regardless of the mixed messages within the *Aeneid*, Augustus himself clearly believed that the propaganda opportunities offered by such a poem were too good to miss.

CHAPTER 11: SOURCES TO STUDY

Source 11.1: The women of Rome oppose the triumvirate

In 43–42 BC Octavian, Antony and Lepidus published a list of their enemies and ordered that they be killed and their property confiscated. This list was called a proscription. To raise further funds, the triumvirs then decided to take money from the wealthiest women in Rome. The wealth of Roman women was inherited or given to them by their families. In the event of divorce, a woman typically retained the wealth she had brought with her to the marriage.

This source is from a history of Rome, written by Appian. Appian was born at the end of the 1st century AD: he was Greek by birth, but he moved to Rome and became a Roman citizen. Like many Greek historians, he was interested in the great speeches of the past: below is an extract from his version of what Hortensia, a wealthy Roman woman, said in response to the triumvirs' plan to take money from the wealthy women of Rome.

> A **tribunal** was a raised platform used for public speeches.

The triumvirs posted a list of 1,400 particularly wealthy women, who had to have their property valued and contribute to the war expenses an amount individually assessed by the triumvirs. Penalties were imposed for undervaluation or concealing any assets, and rewards were offered for information passed on by free persons and by slaves. The women decided to appeal to the female relatives of the triumvirs. They succeeded in winning support from Octavian's sister and Antony's mother, but were turned away from the door of Fulvia, Antony's wife. Resentful at her rudeness, they pushed their way to the magistrates' **tribunal** in the forum, where the people and the military guard parted for them, and their chosen spokeswoman Hortensia spoke for them as follows:

'As was appropriate for women of our rank who wished to make an appeal to you, we went to your womenfolk; but the treatment we have received from Fulvia has been inappropriate, and we have been driven by her to the forum. You have already taken our fathers, sons, husbands and brothers from us on the pretext that you have been wronged by them. If you also take our property, you will reduce us to squalor unworthy of our family, character and feminine nature. Do you allege that we, like our menfolk, have wronged you? If so, proscribe us too, as you have proscribed them. But if we women have voted none of you an enemy of the state, nor torn down your houses, nor destroyed your army or put another in the field of battle against you, why do we share the punishment when we have not collaborated in the crime? Why should we pay tax, when we have no share in magistracies, or military commands, or in public affairs at all, where your conflicts have brought us to this terrible state?

After these words of Hortensia's, the triumvirs were annoyed that when men were submissive women were standing up to them, making public speeches, and questioning their actions. They instructed their attendants to clear the women away from the tribunal, but when the crowd began to boo the attendants stopped and the triumvirs said that they were deferring the question to the following day. The next day they posted a notice that 400 women instead of 1,400 were to have their property valued.

Appian, The Civil Wars, IV.32–34 (with omissions, trans. slightly adapted)

Source 11.1: Questions

1 Whom do the women appeal to first? Why do they then go into the forum?
2 Explain in your own words why the women do not think it is appropriate for the triumvirs to take their money.
3 Why were the triumvirs angry with the women?
4 What does this source show us about the role of women in Rome at this time in relation to

    a. their families and husbands
    b. men not in their families
    c. other women
    d. public affairs such as politics and warfare?

5 What does this source make you think about the way the triumvirs behaved?
6 Appian's version of Hortensia's speech was written more than 100 years later and it is likely to be partly a work of his imagination rather than a fully accurate record of what she said: do you think this reduces its value to us as a historical source?

Source 11.2: Augustan coins

Coins were a very effective way for Roman rulers to project their image because the coins would have been used by many people on a daily basis across the empire. A clever ruler could use coins to make sure that as many people as possible were exposed to the right images, ideas and propaganda.

In 30 BC, Egypt became a Roman province, and in 28 BC a coin was minted which celebrated this. On one side is a picture of a crocodile, with the words AEGYPTO CAPTA *('After the conquest of Egypt'). On the other side is an image of Augustus, bearing the name of his adopted father, Caesar. This example of the coin is now in the British Museum.*

FIGURE 11.7   **Aegypto capta denarius**

The denarius below dates from just after the Battle of Actium and highlights the peace that Augustus brought to Rome. On one side of the coin, we can see the profile of Augustus. The other side shows Pax, the personification of the goddess of peace, and the words CAESAR DIVI F: *'Caesar son of a god'. Pax holds an olive branch, a symbol of peace. In her other hand, she cradles a cornucopia (horn of plenty) to symbolize the prosperity that comes with peace. This example of the coin is now in the British Museum.*

FIGURE 11.8   *Pax denarius*

Source 11.2: Questions

1 A crocodile is depicted on the coin in figure 11.7. Why do you think think this image was chosen? What do you think people would have thought when they saw it?

2 The first coin celebrates conquest, the second coin peace. Which concept do you think the Roman people would have been more glad to see, and why?

3 The first coin reminds people that Augustus was a victorious military leader, and the second coin that he was the son of a god. Which coin do you think is a more impressive reminder of Augustus' power? Explain your answer.

4 Which of these two coins do you find most memorable, and why?

Source 11.3: Augustus' achievements

This extract is from the Res Gestae Divi Augusti (The deeds of the Divine Augustus)*, and it was written by Augustus himself. It was used as a funerary inscription and put up in different languages in various locations throughout the empire after his death in AD 14. The* Res Gestae *gives us a fascinating insight into how Augustus wanted his legacy to be remembered. The following section comes from the very end of the text.*

In my **sixth and seventh consulships**, after I had put an end to civil wars, although by everyone's agreement I had power over everything, I transferred the state from my power into the control of the Roman senate and people. For this service, I was named Augustus by senatorial decree, and the doorposts of my house were publicly clothed with laurels, and a civic crown was fastened above my doorway, and a golden shield was set up in the Julian senate house; through an inscription on this shield the fact was declared that the Roman senate and people were giving it to me because of my valour, clemency, justice and piety. After this time I excelled everyone in influence, but I had no more power than the others who were my colleagues in each magistracy.

> Augustus' **sixth and seventh consulships** were in 28–27 BC.

When I was holding my **thirteenth consulship**, the senate and equestrian order and people of Rome all together hailed me as father of the fatherland, and decreed that this title should be inscribed in the forecourt of my house and in the Julian senate house and in the Augustan forum under the chariot, which was set up in my honour by senatorial decree. When I wrote this I was in my seventy-sixth year.

> Augustus' **thirteenth consulship** was in 2 BC.

Res Gestae Divi Augusti, 34–35

Source 11.3: Questions

1 How does Augustus make it seem that he did not wish to have control of the Roman state after the civil wars?
2 What honours did Augustus receive in his sixth and seventh consulships?
3 The civic crown was one of Rome's most prestigious awards. What can you find out about it?
4 Augustus wrote that he was awarded a golden shield because of his 'valour, clemency, justice and piety'. What do these words mean?
5 Augustus tells us that he was awarded the title *pater patriae* – father of the fatherland. Why do you think he ends his text with this? What image is he presenting here?
6 Augustus requested that the *Res Gestae* be inscribed on bronze and displayed in front of his tomb. What messages do you think he was aiming to send to the Roman people by choosing to publish the text in this way?

Source 11.4: Tacitus summarizes Augustus' rise to power

The Roman historian Tacitus was born in AD 56. One of his main works was the Annals, *a history of Rome under its first emperors. At the start of the* Annals *he offers a summary of Octavian's rise to power and, in a sweeping overview, he lists the chain of events from the deaths of Brutus and Cassius (who had led the assassination of Julius Caesar), to the defeat of Pompey and then the collapse of the triumvirate. With his typically acerbic tone, Tacitus is keen to explore the gap between propaganda and truth, and the reasons why the citizens and provinces of Rome were ready to accept rule by one man.*

> By **Julian faction leader**, Tacitus means the leaders of those who had fought to avenge Julius Caesar's death.

> **Tribunician authority** is a reference to the power which the office of *tribunus plebis* brought with it. There were 10 tribunes of the people each year, and their role was partly to protect the interests of the common people of Rome.

After Brutus and Cassius were killed, the state was no longer armed. Pompey was crushed in Sicily and, with Lepidus discarded and Antony dead, the only **Julian faction leader** left was Octavian, who then dropped the triumvir title. *I am a consul*, he proclaimed, *content with **tribunician authority** for protecting the people*. When he had enticed the army with gifts, the people with subsidised food and everyone with the sweetness of leisure, he rose up gradually and absorbed the functions of senate, magistrates and laws, without opposition: the most spirited men had perished in battle or through proscription, and the rest of the elite were exalted with wealth and office to the extent to which each man showed he was ready for servitude. The men who had profited from revolution now preferred a safe present to former perils. Nor did the provinces protest this state of affairs: the rule of senate and people was feared because of powerful men's rivalries and magistrates' greed, and the protection of the laws was feeble, given their constant disruption by violence, self-interest and finally cash.

Tacitus, *Annals* 1.2 (trans. adapted)

Source 11.4: Questions

1 Tacitus claims that after Octavian had won the civil war he said that he was content to be consul rather than retain the exceptional powers he had held during the fighting. Do you think that Tacitus wants us to believe this was true? Explain your answer.

2 Tacitus writes that Octavian 'enticed' the army and the people: what does this mean, and how did Octavian do it?

3 Tacitus describes the noble elite as ready for 'servitude': based on your understanding of Roman society and the Republican principle of *libertas*, what judgement do you think Tacitus is making about Roman society at this point?

4 What does this source tell us about the relationship between Rome and her provinces at this time?

5 Tacitus suggests that everyone was only too willing to accept rule by one man: do you think that the Romans were weak and foolish to do this, or do you think it was understandable in the context of the years of civil war?

6 Tacitus' view of the emperors was probably coloured by his experience of Rome's rulers during his own lifetime. He lived through the cruelties of the reign of the emperor Domitian: what can you find out about this emperor?

CHAPTER 11: QUESTIONS FOR DISCUSSION

1 Augustus was ruthlessly ambitious and responsible for thousands of deaths, but he also restored peace and prosperity to the Roman state. From a 21st-century viewpoint, how do you think we should judge him?
You might like to consider
- his use of force
- his relationships with other nobles such as Mark Antony
- his actions after the civil war
- the values he promoted through his own image

2 What challenges do you think might have faced the Roman people after Augustus' death?
You might like to consider
- the length of Augustus' rule
- the ambition of Rome's leading nobles
- the memory of civil war
- the reputation of Augustus
- the size of the empire

3 Take Augustus as a case-study: do you think we need to be concerned about the extent to which political image and propaganda is based on truth or not?
You might like to consider
- the values Augustus promoted
- the needs of the war-torn Roman state
- the attitudes of the Roman people
- the relationship between Rome and her provinces
- our current attitude to truth and image within modern-day media

ⓒⓦ Chapter 11: Core Language Vocabulary List

putō	putāre, putāvī, putātum	think
stō	stāre, stetī, statum	stand
intrō	intrāre, intrāvī, intrātum	enter
nūntiō	nūntiāre, nūntiāvī, nūntiātum	announce; report
servō	servāre, servāvī, servātum	save; protect; keep
dēbeō	dēbēre, dēbuī, dēbitum	owe; ought; should; must
taceō	tacēre, tacuī, tacitum	be silent; be quiet
discēdō	discēdere, discessī, discessum	depart; leave
intellegō	intellegere, intellēxī, intellēctum	understand; realize
redūcō	redūcere, redūxī, reductum	lead back; bring back
relinquō	relinquere, relīquī, relictum	leave; leave behind
accipiō	accipere, accēpī, acceptum	receive; accept; take in
adveniō	advenīre, advēnī, adventum	arrive
poēta	poētae, m	poet
porta	portae, f	gate
unda	undae, f	wave
cōnsilium	cōnsiliī, n	plan; idea; advice
socius	sociī, m	ally
pāx	pācis, f	peace
tempus	temporis, n	time
cārus	cāra, cārum	dear; beloved
validus	valida, validum	strong
prō	+ ablative	in front of; for; on behalf of
propter	+ accusative	on account of; because of
quō?		to where?
unde?		from where?
posteā		afterwards
autem		but; however
neque, nec		and not; nor; neither
ecce!		look!

People and places

Octāviānus, Octāviānī, m **Augustus, Augustī, m** 63 BC–AD 14	**Octavian**, later known as **Augustus**, became the first Roman emperor.
Caesar, Caesaris, m 100–44 BC	Octavian's meteoric rise to power started in 45 BC when he was adopted by his great-uncle, **Julius Caesar**, and became the heir to most of his vast personal fortune.
Lepidus, Lepidī, m 89–13 BC **Marcus Antōnius,** **Marcī Antōniī, m** 83–30 BC	In the aftermath of Caesar's death, Octavian joined with **Lepidus** and **Mark Antony** to form a powerful alliance, known as the triumvirate. Several years later, this alliance started to fracture, culminating in civil war between Octavian and Antony.
Actium, Actiī, n	**Actium** was a town on the west coast of Greece. The famous sea battle fought by Octavian against Antony and Cleopatra took place near here in 31 BC.
Vergilius, Vergiliī, m 70–19 BC	**Virgil** was one of the most highly regarded Roman poets in the Augustan era. In Chapters 1–6 you read several stories from his great epic poem, the *Aeneid*. This poem has been seen by many as a piece of Augustan propaganda in celebration of Augustus as a new founder of Rome.

Consolidation: adverbs

You have met many different **adverbs** along with their **comparative** and **superlative** forms. Here are some examples:

	comparative	superlative
diū	diūtius	diūtissimē
celeriter	celerius	celerrimē
saevē	saevius	saevissimē

Each adverb does not change its ending.

It is possible to create adverbs from adjectives; Latin does this in two main ways.

adjective	adverb
laetus, laeta, laetum	laetē
crūdēlis, crūdēle	crūdēli**ter**

Within usual Latin **word order**, adverbs are either placed at the start of the sentence (if they relate to the whole sentence), or just before the word they qualify. Adverbs are most often used with a **verb**.

diū contrā Carthāginiensēs Rōmānī pugnābant.

in forum nūntius **celeriter** cucurrit.

For a long time, against the Carthaginians, the Romans fought bravely.

Into the forum, the messenger ran **quickly**.

TEST YOURSELF!

Can you remember the meaning of the following adverbs?

1. saepe
2. fortiter
3. diū
4. ōlim
5. subitō
6. semper
7. iterum
8. magnopere
9. mox
10. nunc
11. hīc
12. iam
13. ibi
14. numquam
15. sīc
16. frūstrā
17. bene
18. deinde
19. forte
20. statim

Consolidation: adverbs and idiom

In the Latin sentences and stories so far you have met various examples of **idiom** relating to **adverbs**.

- ***quam*** can be used with a superlative adverb to mean *as . . . as possible.*

  fīlius **quam celerrimē** cucurrit.   The son ran **as quickly as possible**.

- **nominative** adjectives can be sometimes be used instead of an adverb.

  māter **īrāta** fīliōs pūnīvit.   The mother punished her son **angrily**.

- ***prīmus*** can be used to mean *the first to do something.*

  līberī **prīmī** fūgērunt.   The children **were the first to** flee.

- in the ablative case, ***prīmō*** can also be used as an **adverb of time** to mean *at first.*

  prīmō rēgēs bene regēbant.   **At first** the kings ruled well.

- ***multus*** is often used in the **ablative case** as an **adverb of extent** to mean *by much* or *much*.

  līberī **multō** laetiōrēs erant.   The children were **much** happier.

EXERCISE 11.1

1. diū sed frūstrā senātor dē cōnsiliō tacēbat.

2. posteā multī cīvēs in mediō forō stābant.

3. cūr senī quam ferōcissimē respondistī?

4. hī nautae multō miserius perībant quam illī.

5. prīmō sociī pugnāre volēbant sed tum ē proeliō celerrimē discessērunt.

6. ecce! in undīs haec nāvis prīma subitō dēlēta est!

7. iterum propter lūcem fīlia parva nōn dormīre poterat.

8. mīlitēs, prō patriā audācter et fortiter bellum gerentēs, vulnerātī sunt.

9. 'bene mē audīvistī,' laetus inquit magister, 'et nunc tempus est discēdere.'

10. forte līberī fēlīcēs pecūniam prope viam invēnērunt.

EXERCISE 11.2: OCTAVIAN BECOMES JULIUS CAESAR'S HEIR

Julius Caesar chose to make his great-nephew, Octavian, his heir. After Caesar's death, Octavian used the enormous wealth he had inherited from Caesar to fund a private army and take vengeance on those who had killed Caesar. The story below is taken from Suetonius' biography of Octavian; it shows that from an early age Octavian understood only too well the relationship between money, military strength and power.

ubi Caesar in <u>Hispāniā</u> cum fīliīs <u>Pompēiī</u> pugnābat, Octāviānus, quamquam eō tempore iuvenis erat, auxilium <u>avunculō magnō</u> ferre volēbat. itaque cum mīlitibus paucīs ad Caesarem iter difficile et longum fēcit. per perīculum maximum, per viās, ubi multī hostēs aderant, et trāns mare, ubi <u>tempestātēs</u> magnae nāvēs dēlēvērunt, suōs dūxit. Caesar, ubi Octāviānus advēnit, 5 magnopere eum laudābat: 'tū es fortis et audācissimus,' inquit Caesar, 'et nunc mihī cārissimus es. nunc <u>sīcut</u> parēns tibī erō.'

Caesar, ubi fīliōs Pompēiī vīcit, Octāviānum in <u>Illyriam</u> mīsit: 'tū es mīles bonus,' inquit Caesar, 'sed necesse est tibī aliōs dūcere, nōn <u>sōlum</u> pugnāre. nunc necesse est tibī in Illyriam īre; ibi multōs librōs Graecōs legēs et tum multa 10 intellegēs. ubi doctus eris, aliōs bene dūcēs.'

post mortem Caesaris, nūntiī in Illyriam ad Octāviānum advēnērunt. 'Caesar,' nūntiāvērunt, 'interfectus est. tū es Caesaris <u>hērēs</u>.' prīmō Octāviānus <u>ānxius</u> erat: 'hīc tūtus sum,' putābat, 'sed Rōmae multī <u>inimīcī</u> erunt: eī, quī Caesarem interficere volēbant, <u>fortasse</u> etiam mē interficere volunt. pecūnia tamen 15 Caesaris mihī relicta est. dēbeō hanc pecūniam accipere.' itaque ex Illyriā discessit et Rōmam redībat.

Octāviānus, ubi pecūnia accepta est, multa facere poterat. 'plurimīs mīlitibus pecūniam dabō,' laetus inquit, 'et illī mīlitēs auxilium mihī dabunt. ego et mīlitēs meī cum eīs quī Caesarem interfēcērunt pugnābimus et saevissimē eōs 20 pūniēmus.'

mox Octāviānus etiam <u>cōnsul</u> esse magnopere cupiēbat: multī tamen senātōrēs hoc nōlēbant. 'Octāviānus iuvenis est,' īrātī clāmantēs inquiunt. '<u>mōs</u> Rōmānōrum nōn est iuvenēs cōnsulēs facere.' Octāviānus, tamen, nunc plūrimōs mīlitēs habēbat. 'mē cōnsulem facite!' inquit Octāviānus. ubi senātōrēs 25 hoc facere nōlēbant, <u>centuriō</u> Octāviānī, <u>Cornēlius</u> nōmine, subitō inter senātōrēs gladium ostendit: 'quamquam hoc nōn vultis,' fortiter clāmāvit, 'hic gladius Octāviānum cōnsulem faciet.' ubi etiam tum senātōrēs eum cōnsulem facere nōlēbant, Octāviānus mīlitēs suōs Rōmam celeriter dūxit. iam senātōrēs perterritī erant: Octāviānus cōnsul factus est. 30

Octāviānus pecūniam multam et plūrimōs mīlitēs habēbat. 'nunc id quod volō faciam!' laetissimus sibi inquit.

Hispānia, Hispāniae, f	Hispania, a Roman province which included the territory of modern-day Spain
Pompēius, Pompēiī, m	Pompey, the noble whom Caesar fought against in the civil war in 49 BC
avunculus magnus, avunculī magnī, m	great-uncle
tempestās, tempestātis, f	storm
sīcut	just as
Illyria, Illyriae, f	Illyria, an area of territory to the north of the Balkan peninsula
sōlum	only
hērēs, hērēdis, m	heir
ānxius, ānxia, ānxium	anxious
inimīcus, inimīcī, m	(personal) enemy
fortasse	perhaps
cōnsul, cōnsulis, m	consul
mōs, mōris, m	custom
centuriō, centuriōnis, m	centurion
Cornēlius, Cornēliī, m	Cornelius

Consolidation: the infinitive

You have met three different ways of using an infinitive.

- with a **neuter adjective**

    bonum est prō patriā **pugnāre**.   It is good **to fight** for one's country.

- with **another verb**

    fugere volō.   I want **to flee**.
    ambulāre nōn possum.   I am not able **to walk**.

- with a **noun**

    tempus erat **fugere**.   It was time **to flee**.

Notice that an **accusative noun** is often used with an infinitive.

    eum fugere iubeō.   I order **him** to flee.
    līberōs laetōs esse volō.   I want **my children** to be **happy**.

EXERCISE 11.3

1. ō servī, cēnam celerius parāre dēbētis; nunc tempus est cibum cōnsūmere!

2. ducī difficile erat cōnsilium novum capere.

3. dux suōs iūssit nāvēs custōdīre.

4. volō in mediō forō stāre et senātōrem audīre.

5. necesse erat parentibus līberōs in vīllā relinquere.

6. nōlēbāmus sociōs auxilium hostibus trādere.

7. facile erat mulierī virum alium invenīre.

8. diūtissimē tacēre dēbēs.

9. mox verba poētae doctissimī audīre poteris.

10. rēx suōs nāvem validam statim aedificāre iūssit.

EXERCISE 11.4: OCTAVIAN, MARK ANTONY AND LEPIDUS

After Julius Caesar's death, Octavian formed a power alliance with two of Rome's foremost citizens: Mark Antony and Lepidus. This alliance was known as the triumvirate, and together they pursued a brutal campaign of vengeance against Caesar's murderers. Octavian, in his own memoirs, presented this campaign as an act of liberation for his homeland. The details of the campaign recorded by the historian Suetonius, such as the harsh treatment of Brutus, give a rather different colour to the picture.

Caesar ā multīs senātōribus necātus erat: inter hōs erant <u>Brūtus</u> et <u>Cassius</u>. 'Caesar,' clāmantes inquiunt, 'rēx esse omnium Rōmānōrum volēbat; Caesar dominus cīvium esse cupiēbat. itaque Caesarem interfēcimus et <u>rem pūblicam</u> līberāvimus.'

5　Octāviānus, tamen, post mortem Caesaris, īrātissimus erat: eōs, quī parentem necāverant, occīdere volēbat. 'Caesar,' inquit, 'clārissimus et optimus erat; Caesar prō patriā multa bella fortissimē gessit. illī cīvēs, quī Caesarem interfēcērunt, mihī patriaeque hostēs sunt et illī, quī patriam amant, nunc mihī auxilium dare dēbent.' inter Rōmānōs, duo senātōrēs, Lepidus et Antōnius
10　nōmine, <u>potentissimī</u> erant. 'sociī tibī erimus,' inquiunt, 'et cum eīs quī Caesarem necāvērunt pugnābimus.'

Brūtus, Brūtī, m	Brutus
Cassius, Cassiī, m	Cassius
rem pūblicam (accusative)	'the Republic'
potēns, potentis	powerful

Philippīs erat proelium maximum: multī occīsī sunt. inter mortuōs erat Brūtus. 'mihī caput Brūtī date!' saevissimē clāmāvit Octāviānus, 'et ego caput Brūtī Rōmam mittam. prope statuam Caesaris caput Brūtī pōnam. caput Brūtī omnibus cīvibus ostendam. Brūtus parentem meum interfēcit et nunc Brūtus 15 ipse quoque interfectus est.'

decem annōs Octāviānus et Lepidus et Antōnius sociī erant. amīcōs illōrum, quī Caesarem interfēcērunt, quoque saevissimē pūnīvērunt. 'propter mortem Caesaris vīllās dēlēbō, pecūniam capiam, fīliōs et patrēs interficiam,' clāmāvit Octāviānus; 'propter mortem Caesaris multī perībunt.' plūrimī cīvēs crūdēliter 20 et saevissimē occīsī sunt: inter hōs erat Cicerō.

multī cīvēs lacrimābant et haec putābant: 'Rōmae nōn tūtī sumus. saepius cīvēs ā cīvibus interfectī sunt.' Octāviānus, tamen, gaudēbat: 'eī, quī Caesarem interfēcērunt, potestātem sibi cupiēbant. patriam nōn amābant: volēbant dominī patriae esse, nōn cīvēs. inimīcōs pūnīvī et patriam līberāvī.' 25

Philippīs	'at Philippi' (a city in Macedonia to the north of Greece)
caput, capitis, n	head
statua, statuae, f	statue
ipse (nominative masculine sg)	'himself'
Cicerō, Cicerōnis, m	Cicero
gaudeō, gaudēre	rejoice
potestās, potestātis, f	power
inimīcus, inimīcī, m	(personal) enemy

Indirect statement

An **accusative** noun and an **infinitive** often follow a verb of **saying**, **knowing**, **thinking**, etc. This is known as an **indirect statement**.

> dīcō **tē** laetum **esse**.   I say **you to be** happy.

It would be very unusual, however, to translate the Latin this way: in English a **subordinate clause** is used instead, and it is usual to start this subordinate clause with the word **_that_**.

> dīcō **tē** laetum **esse**.   I say **that you are happy**.

Notice how the tense of the verb in the indirect statement changes in English if the main verb of the sentence is in a **past tense**.

> **dīcō** Rōmānōs pugnāre.   **I say** that the Romans **are fighting**.
> **dīxī** Rōmānōs pugnāre.   **I said** that the Romans **were fighting**.

If the infinitive has an **object**, it will also be **accusative**. Word order and sense shows which accusative noun is the infinitive's subject and which is its object.

> **puerum equum** vulnerāre vīdī.   I saw that the **boy** was wounding the **horse**.

EXERCISE 11.5

1. cūr putābās sociōs fugere?

2. in forō audīvit senātōrēs iam prope portam stāre.

3. nunc, quod mātrem tuam servāvimus, intellegis nōs amīcōs tuōs esse.

4. quandō nūntiāvit nāvēs discēdere?

5. rēx dīcit sē omnēs cīvēs amāre.

6. puella misera nōlēbat audīre mātrem īrātam esse.

7. amīcīs dīxī mē perterritam esse.

8. nōnne intellegitis Caesarem mortuum esse?

9. forte agricola equōs ex agrō fugere audīvit.

10. nec pater nec māter vīdit servōs līberōs parvōs redūcere.

EXERCISE 11.6: ACTIUM

Over time, the alliance between Octavian, Lepidus and Mark Antony fractured and disintegrated. Antony held power in the east and joined forces with Cleopatra; Octavian held power in the west. The Battle of Actium was seen by the Romans as one of the turning points in their history: Octavian's victory over Antony and the forces of the east left him without any significant rival. From this point on, he was indisputably more powerful than any other Roman alive at that time.

nunc Octāviānus et Antōnius <u>inimīcī</u> erant. 'tempus est,' nūntiāvit Octāviānus, 'cum Antōniō pugnāre. mihī <u>Agrippa</u> dux nāvium erit, quod Agrippa comes optimus est.'

Antōnius <u>Cleopātram</u> sociam habēbat. 'plūrēs et maiōrēs nāvēs habeō quam
5 Octāviānus,' inquit Antōnius, 'quod Cleopātra pecūniam plūrimam habet. Octāviānum vincam!' nāvēs Octāviānī minōrēs erant, sed facilius erat hās nāvēs movēre. in proeliō <u>Actiacō</u> Agrippa nāvēs celeriter mōvit: nautae circum nāvēs Antōniī nāvigāre poterant; itaque nautae nāvēs Antōniī incendere et dēlēre poterant. Cleopātra, ubi cōnspexit nautās Agrippae nāvēs incendere, perterrita
10 erat. 'quō fugiam?' inquit Cleopātra. 'hīc maximum est perīculum.'

inimīcus, inimīcī, m	(personal) enemy
Agrippa, Agrippae, m	Agrippa
Cleopātra, Cleopātrae, f	Cleopatra
Actiacus, Actiaca, Actiacum	at Actium

deinde Cleopātra nāvēs suās per undās dūcēns fūgit. tum nautae Antōniī quoque, ubi vīdērunt Cleopātram fugere, perterritī erant. 'ecce!' clāmāvērunt, 'Cleopātra et nautae per undās fugiunt! nunc vincere nōn possumus.' deinde nautae Antōniī quoque fugiēbant. Antōnius nautās fugere vīdit; deinde Antōnius magnopere <u>dēspērābat</u>: 'multae nāvēs incēnsae sunt; multae nāvēs dēlētae   15
sunt; multī nautae perterritī sunt. neque satis nāvium, neque satis nautārum habeō. relictus sum. nunc vincere nōn possum.'

Antōnius quoque fūgit: '<u>fortasse</u> terrā, nōn marī, cum Octāviānō pugnābō,' putāvit. posteā autem, ubi mīlitēs suōs pugnāre nōlle intellēxit, miserrimus erat. 'Octāviānus,' sibi inquit, 'mē vīcit.' deinde audīvit Cleopātram mortuam   20
esse. 'neque mīlitēs neque comitēs habeō,' inquit Antōnius magnopere lacrimāns. Antōnius maximē dēspērāns gladiō suō sē vulnerāvit. 'nunc tempus est perīre,' inquit miserrimē. subitō tamen audīvit Cleopātram nōn mortuam esse. 'ad Cleopātram mē ferte!' clāmāvit. Antōnius magnopere vulnerātus ad Cleopātram advēnit. nōn multō posteā <u>in sinū</u> Cleopātrae periit.   25

Octāviānus laetissimus erat. 'quis nunc contrā mē pugnābit?' sē rogāvit. 'unde inimīcī venient? Antōnium Cleopātramque vīcī. itaque omnēs inimīcōs vīcī. nunc omnibus Rōmānīs pāx erit.'

dēspērō, dēspērāre, dēspērāvī, dēspērātum	despair
fortasse	perhaps
in sinū	'in the embrace'

Present passive

The **present passive** can be translated as follows.

regor   I **am being** ruled
             I **am** ruled

As with the imperfect tense, the **present passive** is very similar in form to the present active: the main difference is the **person ending**.

The **present passive** uses the **present stem**, and so the **vowels** used vary across the conjugations.

	1st conjugation	2nd conjugation	3rd conjugation	4th conjugation
I	am**or**	terr**eor**	reg**or**	aud**ior**
you (sg)	am**āris**	terr**ēris**	reg**eris**	aud**īris**
he / she / it	am**ātur**	terr**ētur**	reg**itur**	aud**ītur**
we	am**āmur**	terr**ēmur**	reg**imur**	aud**īmur**
you (pl)	am**āminī**	terr**ēminī**	reg**iminī**	aud**īminī**
they	am**antur**	terr**entur**	reg**untur**	aud**iuntur**

> **Look it up!** For the endings in the mixed conjugation see p238.

EXERCISE 11.7

1. sociī nostrī ab hostibus terrentur.

2. 'audior,' inquit poēta laetus, 'ab omnibus quī in mediō forō sunt.'

3. patria ā mīlitibus fortibus nunc servātur!

4. omnēs ā duce ad urbem redūcimur.

5. ecce! ab illō nautā gladiō tuō vulnerāris.

6. cūr hī nautae prope mare relinquuntur? illī nautae nāvēs celerius nōn nāvigābunt!

7. quam celerrimē festīnāte! in forō pāx nūntiātur!

8. ō līberī, saevius pūnīminī.

9. urbs nostra ab hostibus occupātur et nunc perterritī sumus.

10. hic liber ab illō puerō legitur: magister laetissimus erit!

EXERCISE 11.8: AUGUSTUS AS *PRINCEPS*

After the Battle of Actium, Octavian returned to Rome where he was praised as a great victor, but his political manoeuvrings in Rome were possibly more significant for the history of Rome than his military success. Octavian managed his political image carefully and, through buildings, statues, coins and written texts, he presented himself as the bringer of peace, the son of a god, and the greatest of the Romans.

Octavian understood that his power had to sit within the structure of the Republic: he refused to be elected dictator, or do anything which might look like he wanted to be king. Instead he preferred the title of princeps. *This title was a mark of respect: it acknowledged his primacy within Rome, but, on the surface at least, it did not go against the republican principle that no one man should have more official power on a permanent basis than everyone else.*

As the years passed, the Romans heaped more honours upon him: he was given a new name, Augustus, and in 2 BC *he was awarded the honorific title* pater patriae.

Octāviānus, postquam Antōnium et comitēs superāvit, Rōmam intrāvit. 'Antōnius Cleopātraque Rōmānīs hostēs erant,' senātōribus nūntiāvit, 'et nunc victī sunt. prō patriā fortiter pugnāvī et nunc ē perīculō patriam līberāvī. nunc <u>ubique</u> pāx est. nunc portās bellī <u>claudere</u> possumus. nunc cīvis sum, nōn mīlitum <u>imperātor</u>.' senātōrēs laetiōrēs erant: 'bellum longissimum erat,' 5
clāmāvērunt, 'et nunc pāx est. prō patriā tū <u>victor</u> es et nunc ab omnibus laudāris.'

Octāviānus laetissimus erat: 'multōs annōs bellum habuimus,' inquit, 'sed nunc pāx est. Rōmam validam pulchramque faciam: multa templa aedificābō quod fīlius <u>dīvī</u> Caesaris sum et quod multī deī auxilium mihī dedērunt. multī hominēs 10
vidēbunt Rōmam pulcherrimam esse. multī hominēs intellegent deōs Rōmam amāre et Rōmam validam esse. in aliīs locīs quoque templa et <u>statuās</u> pōnam: haec templa et hae statuae ostendent mē cīvem optimum esse.'

Octāviānus quoque <u>nummōs</u> fēcit: aliī nummī eum fīlium deī esse ostendērunt; aliī nummī pācem esse ostendērunt. 'hī nummī ā multīs videntur,' inquit 15
Octāviānus. 'itaque in multīs locīs sum nōtissimus et clārissimus. nunc omnēs hominēs intellegunt mē esse prīmum inter omnēs Rōmānōs.'

Romae Octāviānus volēbat cīvēs sē amāre: 'optimus sum omnium Rōmānōrum,' inquit Octāviānus, 'quod <u>rem pūblicam</u> servāvī: neque <u>dictātor</u> neque rēx erō quod nunc rēs pūblica valida est. <u>prīnceps</u> autem erō quod prīmus inter 20
senātōrēs sum.' Octāviānus ā cīvibus magnopere laudābātur. mox nōmen novum eī datum est: 'nunc,' inquiunt senātōrēs, 'tū ā nōbis Augustus vocāris.' Augustus laetissimus erat. 'nunc Augustus vocor,' inquit Augustus, 'nunc ab omnibus cīvibus etiam magis laudor.'

25   multōs annōs Rōmae pāx erat. itaque cīvēs et senātōrēs laetissimī erant. iterum Augustum maximē laudāvērunt: 'tū,' laetē inquiunt, 'optimus omnium Rōmānōrum es quod et patriam et rem pūblicam servāvistī. nunc tē patrem patriae vocābimus.'

ubique	everywhere
claudō, claudere, clausī, clausum	shut
imperātor, imperātōris, m	commander
vīctor, vīctōris, m	victor
dīvus, dīva, dīvum	divine
statua, statuae, f	statue
nummus, nummī, m	coin
rem pūblicam (accusative) / rēs pūblica (nominative)	'the Republic'
dictātor, dictātōris, m	dictator
prīnceps, prīncipis, m	*princeps* (first citizen)

The Augustan age brought with it several great writers. Two of the most famous of these were the poets Horace and Virgil. Many have believed that Horace and Virgil were part of Augustus' system of propaganda. Their patron, Maecenas, was a close friend of Augustus, and the Roman system of patronage expected that patrons would receive some return on the help they gave to their clients. It was not unusual therefore for writers to write in honour of their patrons, or their patrons' friends.

Virgil's most famous poem is the Aeneid. It has been seen by many as a work of Augustan propaganda. Beneath its surface, however, is a fraught account of the misery, deceit and failure suffered at multiple points in the poem. It is hard to believe that glory and success were all that Virgil saw in the new Augustan regime.

Augustus amīcum nōtissimum, <u>Maecēnātem</u> nōmine, habēbat. Maecēnās pecūniam plūrimam habēbat et saepe auxilium poētīs dedit. 'patrōnus sum,' inquit Maecēnās. 'auxilium ā mē poētīs datur et ā poētīs laudor.' inter hōs poētās erant duo poētae nōtissimī, Vergilius et <u>Horātius</u> nōmine. Horātius <u>carmina</u> multa et optima scrīpsit; Maecēnātem laudāvit quod <u>fundus</u> et pecūnia 5 sibī ā Maecēnāte datī erant. 'multōs annōs,' scrīpsit Horātius, 'bellum tristissimum erat. multī agrī dēlētī sunt et multī cīvēs necātī sunt. nunc fundum novum habeō et in hōc fundō habitāns laetissimus sum. in bellō <u>horror</u> magnus est sed magna <u>laetitia</u> in agrīs in pāce. nunc laetus in meō fundō habitāns multa carmina scrībō.' 10

Vergilius quoque erat poēta clārissimus quī carmina nōtissima scrīpsit. aliud carmen, <u>Geōrgica</u> nōmine, dē <u>rūre</u> scrīpsit, et scrīpsit dē Augustō aliud carmen, <u>Aenēida</u> nōmine, quod multī putābant Geōrgicīs multō melius esse. in hōc carmine Augustum laudāvit quod Augustus pācem omnibus Rōmānīs dederat. in hōc carmine <u>pietātem</u> quoque laudāvit, quod propter pietātem cīvēs patriam, 15 nōn sē, amant. Vergilius autem carmen suum nōn laudāvit et, ubi perībat, hoc carmen incendere volēbat. Augustus tamen hoc carmen servāvit, quod putābat optimum esse: 'hoc carmen mē laudat,' inquit Augustus, 'et mē ducem optimum esse ostendit. multī hoc carmen legere dēbent.'

<u>fortasse</u> Vergilius carmen suum incendere volēbat quod laetitia minima in 20 carmine est. <u>Aenēās</u>, <u>herōs</u> huius carminis, semper miserrimus est: aliī virī fēminaeque quoque miserrimī sunt. fortasse Vergilius putābat pietātem esse difficillimam et miserrimōs esse eōs quī semper ducibus <u>pārērent</u>.

Maecēnās, Maecēnātis, m	Maecenas
patrōnus, patrōnī, m	patron
Horātius, Horātiī, m	Horace
carmen, carminis, n	poem
fundus, fundī, m	farm
horror, horrōris, m	horror
laetitia, laetitiae, f	happiness
Geōrgica, Geōrgicōrum, n pl	the *Georgics*
rūs, rūris, n	countryside
Aenēida (accusative sg)	the *Aeneid*
pietās, pietātis, f	duty to one's community
fortasse	perhaps
Aenēās, Aenēae, m	Aeneas
hērōs, herōis, m	hero
pārērent (+ dative)	'they obey'

Chapter 11: Additional Language

SECTION A11: CHAPTER 11 VOCABULARY

Exercise A11.1: Derivations wordsearch

The table below contains words from Chapter 11. Next to each Latin word is an anagram of an English derivation, and an explanation of the English word's meaning.

Unscramble each anagram and then find the unscrambled derivation in the wordsearch.

	Latin word	anagram	unscrambled English derivation	explanation
1	dēbeō, dēbēre, dēbuī, dēbitum	tebid		to take money from an account because it is owed elsewhere
2	relinquō, relinquere, relīquī, relictum	querinhlis		to give something up or leave it for someone else
3	adveniō, advenīre, advēnī, adventum	tvande		in the Christian calendar, the time which prepares for the arrival of Christ
4	taceō, tacēre, tacuī, tacitum	attyicl		to do something silently
5	socius, sociī, m	yeticos		a group of individuals within a shared community
6	unda, undae, f	duunteal		to move with a rising and falling, like a wave
7	validus, valida, validum	teadavil		to strengthen an argument or idea by confirming it to be true
8	pāx, pācis, f	picyfa		to restore peace by subduing or appeasing something which is angry or aggressive
9	tempus, temporis, n	merryatop		for a time only, not permanent
10	putō, putāre, putāvī, putātum	tapteuvi		supposed, generally thought or considered to be so

Y	D	Q	N	P	J	O	D	T	B	M	W	K	T	Y
A	R	P	J	V	O	S	F	F	I	C	K	K	R	O
K	I	A	Y	F	I	C	A	P	H	B	V	T	F	K
K	E	M	R	P	U	T	A	T	I	V	E	Z	A	I
J	T	V	L	O	O	U	A	F	T	Y	E	D	Q	V
N	A	E	S	O	P	X	T	C	G	Q	V	X	F	Q
E	L	I	A	I	G	M	B	G	I	E	K	E	T	L
W	U	T	P	S	U	Y	E	D	N	T	T	Y	S	Q
Z	D	S	E	D	X	Q	P	T	P	A	L	R	O	G
G	N	T	M	I	R	N	D	V	D	H	S	Y	C	S
Q	U	K	B	S	T	A	L	I	A	T	O	L	I	M
H	S	I	U	Q	N	I	L	E	R	I	Z	A	E	R
G	Z	R	R	N	W	A	R	K	P	Z	K	B	T	G
E	J	U	L	W	V	B	R	E	S	H	W	I	Y	M
Q	C	Y	A	H	K	F	S	B	C	S	X	N	T	S

Exercise A11.2: Case endings (nouns and participles)

Circle the stem, give the meaning, and identify the declension of the following nouns and participles from Chapter 11. Then give the case requested.

	Latin	meaning	declension	
1	porta, portae, f			genitive sg =
2	tempus, temporis, n			nominative pl =
3	cōnsilium, cōnsiliī, n			dative pl =
4	pāx, pācis, f			ablative sg =
5	unda, undae, f			ablative pl =
6	socius, sociī, m			accusative pl =
7	poēta, poētae, m			dative pl =
8	putāns, putantis			accusative masculine sg =
9	intellegēns, intellegentis			genitive feminine pl =
10	acceptus, accepta, acceptum			accusative neuter pl =
11	reductus, reducta, reductum			ablative masculine pl =
12	adveniēns, advenientis			dative feminine sg =

Exercise A11.3: Adjectives

The table below contains nouns, adjectives and participles from Chapter 11.

Identify the case, gender and number of each noun and then circle the correct form of the adjective or participle to agree with the noun. Then translate each phrase.

	noun	case, gender, number	adjective / participle	translation
1	poētīs		intrantēs / intrantibus	
2	cōnsiliō		intellēctō / intellēcta	
3	tempus		cāram / cārum	
4	sociōs		stantēs / stantis	
5	undārum		tacentium / tacentibus	
6	portam		validam / validās	
7	pāce		servātā / servātō	
8	poētae		relictae / relictī	
9	cōnsiliīs		acceptīs / acceptōs	
10	socium		reductam / reductum	

Exercise A11.4: Verbs

Identify the tense of the Chapter 11 verbs in the table below and translate each one. Then change the form from singular to plural, or plural to singular, keeping the tense and person the same.

Remember that you need to look at the stem as well as the ending. Here are the principal parts for each verb so that you can see their different stems.

stō, stāre, stetī, statum
redūcō, redūcere, redūxī, reductum
taceō, tacēre, tacuī, tacitum
intellegō, intellegere, intellēxī, intellectum
accipiō, accipere, accēpī, acceptum

	Latin	tense	translation	new form
1	stetit			
2	stat			
3	stabat			
4	redūcunt			
5	redūxērunt			
6	redūcitur			
7	tacuistis			
8	tacēs			
9	tacuerat			
10	intellegēs			
11	intellegis			
12	intellectum est			
13	accipimus			
14	accēpimus			
15	accepta erat			

SECTION B11: GRAMMAR

Exercise B11.1: Identifying the passive voice and participles

This exercise focuses on nouns and verbs from the vocabulary lists for Chapters 9–11.

In the following sentences, underline all the words that make up the main verb, and say whether it is active or passive, and what tense it is. Then identify the case of the nouns in **purple**.

Each sentence also contains something which could be translated into Latin as a participle. Circle this and identify the tense, voice and case of participle needed.

1. The ally understands the **plan**, announced by the sailor.
2. The **plan**, announced by the sailor, is being understood by that man.
3. Who is saving the fleeing **parents**?
4. The **wives**, entering the town, are being saved by the inhabitants.
5. The husband is **leaving** his **wife** standing near the gate.
6. The **crowd**, while **leaving**, is being silent.
7. The wounded **enemy** are being overpowered by the huge waves.
8. The **poet**, having been defended by these forces, is happy.
9. The general is guarding the killed **soldiers**.
10. Are the **comrades** being taken in by the sailors left behind on the boat?

> Do not confuse **discēdō** (*I leave, go away from*) with **relinquō** (*I leave [somebody / something] behind*).

Exercise B11.2: Present passive

This exercise practises verbs from the vocabulary lists for Chapters 9–11.

Translate the following present passive verbs.

	Latin	translation
1	accipitur	
2	mittuntur	
3	redūcor	
4	nūntiātur	
5	tenēris	
6	inveniuntur	
7	custōdīmur	
8	vulnerāminī	
9	servor	
10	invenītur	

Exercise B11.3: Present passive by conjugation

This exercise practises verbs from the vocabulary lists for Chapters 9–11.

Here are all 4 conjugations of the present passive. The endings for the mixed conjugation are on p238.

	1st conjugation	2nd conjugation	3rd conjugation	4th conjugation
I	am**or**	terr**eor**	reg**or**	aud**ior**
you (sg)	am**āris**	terr**ēris**	reg**eris**	aud**īris**
he / she /it	am**ātur**	terr**ētur**	reg**itur**	aud**ītur**
we	am**āmur**	terr**ēmur**	reg**imur**	aud**īmur**
you (pl)	am**āminī**	terr**ēminī**	reg**iminī**	aud**īminī**
they	am**antur**	terr**entur**	reg**untur**	aud**iuntur**

Identify the conjugation of each of the following verbs and give the form requested.

	Latin verb	conjugation	
1	servō, servāre, servāvī, servātum		I am being protected =
2	relinquō, relinquere, relīquī, relictum		he is being left =
3	nūntiō, nūntiāre, nūntiāvī, nūntiātum		it is being announced =
4	intellegō, intellegere, intellēxī, intellēctum		it is being understood =
5	redūcō, redūcere, redūxī, reductum		they are being led back =
6	accipiō, accipere, accēpī, acceptum		it is being received =
7	rapiō, rapere, rapuī, raptum		you (pl) are being seized =
8	moveō, movēre, mōvī, mōtum		I am being moved =
9	dēleō, dēlēre, dēlēvī, dēlētum		we are being destroyed =
10	inveniō, invenīre, invēnī, inventum		you (sg) are being found =

Exercise B11.4: Mixed tense passives

This exercise focuses on verbs from the vocabulary lists for Chapters 9–11.

The following sentences contain verbs in the present passive, imperfect passive or perfect passive. Choose the correct Latin verb from the options given.

1. A gift was received by the senator.
   (accipitur / accipiēbātur / accēptum est)
2. The town was being guarded by our soldiers.
   (custōdītur / custōdiēbātur / custōdītum est)
3. Wounded men are being moved from the battle.
   (moventur / movēbantur / mōtī sunt)
4. The body was left near the river.
   (relinquitur / relinquēbātur / relictum est)
5. Many words were being announced by the messenger.
   (nūntiantur / nūntiābantur / nūntiāta sunt)
6. The boy was taught by the cruel teacher.
   (docētur / docēbātur / doctus est)
7. Good people were being overpowered by a bad king.
   (superantur / superābantur / superātī sunt)
8. Is the town being destroyed?
   (dēlētur / dēlēbātur / dēlētum est)
9. The gold was seized by the daring young man.
   (rapitur / rapiēbātur / raptum est)
10. The tired slaves, while working, were killed by the cruel master.
    (occīduntur / occīdēbantur / occīsī sunt)

Exercise B11.5: Adverbs

This exercise focuses on adverbs you have met throughout this course, including comparative and superlative adverbs.

Translate each of the following adverbs.

1. diū
2. saepius
3. celerrimē
4. crūdēliter
5. magis
6. pessimē
7. fortissimē
8. melius
9. optimē
10. bene

SECTION C11: ENGLISH TO LATIN SENTENCES

Exercise C11.1: Indirect statements

Each of the following sentences contains an indirect statement. Highlight the words that make up the indirect statement in English, and then give the Latin accusative and infinitive translation for the subject and the verb within each indirect statement.

1. The messengers announce that the enemy are approaching!
2. I hear that you love books.
3. O children, you think that all teachers are cruel.
4. We believe that the gods are punishing the citizens.
5. **They said** that they were looking for the enemy.
6. He announced that the senator was arriving in the forum.
7. You heard that our allies were defending the town.
8. We thought that the sailor was preparing his ship.
9. He believed that his father wanted to flee from danger.
10. The mistress said that the slaves were able to return from the town.

> *inquit / inquiunt* is only used with direct speech; to introduce an indirect statement, ***dīxērunt*** should be used for ***they said***.

Exercise C11.2: Sentences to translate into Latin

1. The soldiers ought to fight boldly although it will be difficult to overpower the enemy.
2. At first the sailors did not want to depart because it was not safe to sail.
3. When those children were being praised, these parents were smiling most happily.
4. That fortunate slave, having been called into the house, was set free by his master.
5. Who is being punished because our town was destroyed?
6. Is that woman, who goes to the temple rather often, loved by the goddess?
7. He said that the boat was strong but the journey was difficult.
8. The leader of the soldiers ordered his men to flee quickly. However, soon they were being overpowered.
9. The captured children are being fiercely guarded by their captured mothers.
10. Having been saved by their mothers, the boys and girls at last ran from the conquered town.

SECTION D: CONSOLIDATION

Exercises for Additional Language Section D are available on the companion website. Exercises are structured by grammatical category, and cover all Core Vocabulary met so far within each category. For Chapter 11, these exercises are as follows:

- Exercise D11.1: Prepositions
- Exercise D11.2: Pronouns
- Exercise D11.3: Irregular verbs

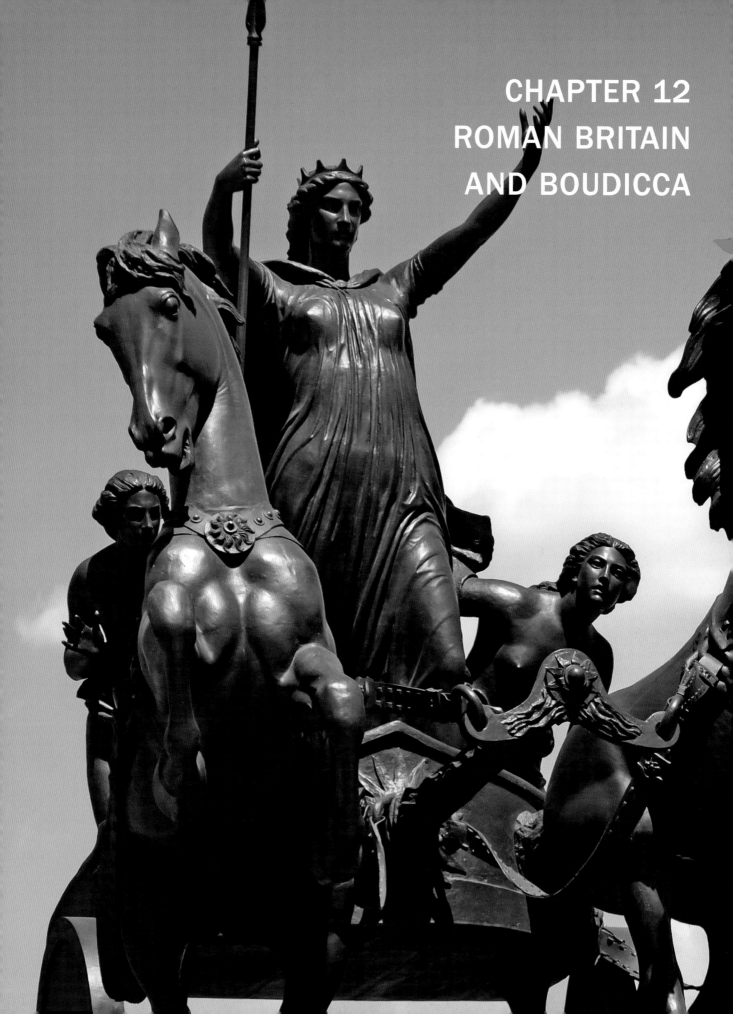

ⓒⓦ Chapter 12: Introduction

The Roman empire

As we discussed in Chapter 11, Augustus ushered in a new period of Roman history. For roughly 500 years, western Europe was under the control of the Roman empire. At its greatest size in the 2nd century AD under the emperor Trajan, the empire stretched from Britain in the north to Egypt in the south and from Portugal in the west all the way to the Persian Gulf in the east. The empire had an estimated population of 50–60 million people spread over approximately 5 million sq km.

Britannia

The Roman province of Britannia was not established until AD 43, but Britain had been known to the Greeks and the Romans for hundreds of years. The Greek geographer Strabo records the expedition of Pytheas, a Greek who sailed to Britain in the 4th century BC, and in Source 12.1

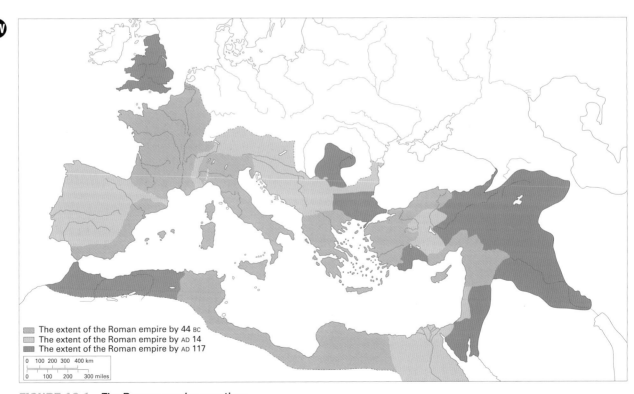

The extent of the Roman empire by 44 BC
The extent of the Roman empire by AD 14
The extent of the Roman empire by AD 117

0 100 200 300 400 km

0   100   200   300 miles

FIGURE 12.1 The Roman empire over time.

you can read Strabo's own description of Britain and its tribes. There is a chance that the peoples of the Mediterranean discovered Britain even earlier than this. Pliny the Elder refers to the voyage of a Carthaginian explorer named Himilco who supposedly sailed through the straits of Gibraltar all the way to Britain in the 5th or possibly even 6th century BC.

The tribes of Britain

Britain was inhabited by numerous tribes. Although they referred to themselves by all sorts of different names, from the Dumnonii in Cornwall to the Iceni in Norfolk, many of their societies, languages and beliefs were very similar. To reflect these similarities, we often refer to these groups of people as Celts and their cultures as Celtic.

One aspect of British culture that multiple Roman authors commented on was their religion. The British tribes worshipped local deities often connected with nature. Many Celtic societies left religion in the hands of a group of priest-like figures known as the druids. Although the druids were found elsewhere in Europe, particularly in Gaul, Julius Caesar wrote that he believed that they originated from Britain. He tells us that young men who wished to learn the ways of the druids would travel to Britain to study, sometimes for up to twenty years.

Sacrifice was a significant part of Celtic religion. Caesar claimed that the druids did not just sacrifice animals like the Greeks and Romans: they also sacrificed humans. When Caesar first encountered this practice in Gaul, he was horrified. He said that the druids would build huge wicker-men, woven from wood, and fill them with living people. The wicker men would then be set on fire. We should hesitate, however, before taking this story at face value. Modern archaeological evidence does not necessarily support such claims and the Romans were often eager to demonise their enemies by making outrageous accusations like these.

Caesar's invasions of Britain

As we saw in Chapter 9, when Julius Caesar was in Gaul, he invaded Britain twice, first in 55 BC, then again in 54 BC. The Romans knew that the island of Britain was rich in metals such as tin and lead. These metals would have been a useful source of wealth for Rome. When Caesar found out that the Britons had been helping the Gauls fight against him, he had yet another reason to attack them.

As we saw in the Sources for Chapter 9, Caesar himself wrote that his first landing in 55 BC did not go to plan. As the Romans sailed towards Dover, a huge army of Britons, who had found out about the invasion, watched them from the white cliffs. When Caesar tried to land on a nearby beach instead, his soldiers were forced to jump from their boats, which could not make it the whole way, and wade the final distance whilst being attacked by the Britons the whole time. It was not until the catapults on the ships started firing that the Romans were able to drive off the Britons and land properly. After a short and relatively unsuccessful campaign, Caesar was forced to return to Gaul before winter made a channel crossing impossible and cut him off completely from reinforcements and supplies.

Although the Britons may have felt safe now that they had driven away the foreign invaders, they did not yet know how stubborn Caesar was, nor how quickly the Romans learnt from their mistakes. Caesar spent the winter redesigning his ships to have flatter bottoms so that they would be more suitable for beach landings. He also made sure he took a much larger army with him, including plenty of cavalry. In 54 BC his invasion was more successful. Caesar made alliances and deals with the leaders of different tribes, and he might well have established a permanent Roman settlement in Britain had he not been called away to deal with unrest back in Gaul. After he left, Roman soldiers did not set foot in Britain again for almost 100 years.

An image of Claudius defeating Britannia

This carved marble relief was made in the 1st century AD and it shows the emperor Claudius standing over a woman who is the personification of Britannia. Interestingly, it was found on the side of a temple in Aphrodisias, a Greek city situated in modern-day southwest Turkey, and it shows that the Romans were keen to convey this success even on the opposite side of the empire. The relief is now in the Aphrodisias Museum in Turkey.

Claudius' invasion of Britain

Caesar had not conquered Britain, but he had established contact, as well as many long-lasting friendships between the Romans and some of the tribes, which were maintained throughout the next century. Indeed, two British kings fled to Augustus to seek help when they were driven out by their tribes. The geographer Strabo believed that at this time the Britons paid so much money in trade taxes and gifts to Augustus that there would have been little financial gain from an invasion: the cost of funding the expedition would have outweighed the immediate profit from conquest.

In AD 43, however, when a pro-Roman king was driven out by his tribe and appealed to the Romans for help, the emperor Claudius seized the opportunity and gave the order to invade. At this point, Claudius had only been emperor for two years. As you will see in Exercise 12.2, Claudius had suffered from illness and physical disability for much of his life. His family had responded to this with scorn and ridicule and, according to some writers, refused even to let him be seen in public. Claudius must have felt that he needed to establish his reputation and that military success was a good way to do this. He sent four legions to Britain under the command of Aulus Plautius, who quickly subdued the rebellious Britons. When everything was calm, Plautius sent word to Claudius, who arrived with reinforcements just in time to receive the official surrender of eleven British kings, winning all the glory for none of the work. After just 16 days in Britain, Claudius left. The senate granted him a triumph for the conquest as well as the honorary title Britannicus.

The Iceni and Boudicca's revolt

Unlike many other tribes, the Iceni did not try to fight the Romans when they invaded, but instead made an alliance with them. When Claudius died in AD 54, Nero became the fifth Roman emperor, and a few years later Prasutagus, the king of the Iceni, made him an heir to his throne along with Prasutagus' two daughters. The king hoped that in recognition of this gift, the Romans would continue to cooperate with the royal family peacefully. This hope was a mistake: the Romans stationed near the lands of the Iceni now saw the territory as their own. They treated the Iceni appallingly: Prasutagus' wife Boudicca was beaten and her two daughters were raped by Roman soldiers. The tribal chiefs of the Iceni were treated like slaves and much of their wealth was stolen. Boudicca was enraged. She gathered an army made up of the Iceni and other local tribes who had been wronged by the Romans, and declared war.

Under Roman rule, Britain, like many provinces of the empire, was run by a governor. The governor's role was to manage the province, settle any legal disputes, quell any uprisings or revolts and ensure that regular tax and revenue payments made their way back to Rome. At this time, the governor of Britannia was a man named Suetonius Paulinus. When Boudicca's revolt began, he was in Wales subduing the tribes there. In the time it took him to march his army east and prepare to fight, Boudicca achieved some significant victories over the Romans. First, she marched to Camulodunum, the Roman settlement at modern-day Colchester. Boudicca and her forces overwhelmed the Roman garrison stationed there and completely destroyed the city, including the temple that had been dedicated to Claudius. The reinforcement of the ninth legion arrived too late to save the city and Boudicca annihilated its soldiers, leaving only its leader and a few soldiers alive.

Suetonius realized that the threat posed by Boudicca was serious, but he had to wait until he could gather enough soldiers, particularly now that the ninth legion was gone. He decided not to try to save the town of Londinium (London), but instead to wait until he had amassed a stronger fighting force. When Boudicca arrived in Londinium she burnt it to the ground and killed anyone who had not fled the city beforehand. She then did the same to Verulamium (St Albans). By destroying these three settlements, she is believed to have killed 70–80,000 people. Tacitus tells us that the Iceni had no interest in taking prisoners and simply killed anyone they found.

The Battle of Watling Street

Once Suetonius had gathered enough soldiers from the fourteenth and twentieth legions he finally fought Boudicca and her rebels at the Battle of Watling Street. The precise location of this battle is unknown, but it takes its name from the Roman road which ran from the southeast corner of Britannia, up past Londinium to Verulamium and then westwards into Wales. The historian Cassius Dio says that Suetonius had just 10,000 men to face Boudicca's 230,000. Later historians have found these figures hard to believe, but it is generally agreed that the Romans were considerably outnumbered. Even so, the Romans won a decisive victory. Boudicca had numbers and the outrage of her followers on her side, but, as we saw in Chapter 9, the Roman army was a finely tuned machine that excelled at what it did. Boudicca had grown complacent, lulled into a false sense of security. So far, her army had

FIGURE 12.3 Bronze head, possibly of the emperor Claudius

This bronze head dates from the 1st century AD. It was found in the River Alde in Suffolk and it is now in the British Museum. Some think that it belonged to a statue of the emperor Nero or, more likely, the emperor Claudius. It has been suggested that it could be the head from the statue of Claudius that was placed next to his temple in Camulodunum, and that perhaps it was Boudicca and the Iceni who cut the head off when they attacked the town.

FIGURE 12.4 **Boudicca and her daughters**

This bronze statue of Boudicca was made in the late 1800s and it stands by Westminster Bridge in London. It was made during the reign of Queen Victoria. The statue's inscription reads 'Regions Caesar never knew, thy posterity shall sway.' It stands as a celebration of the reach of the British Empire into territory untouched by Julius Caesar. It is easy for later communities to take the past and twist it to serve their own ends: Boudicca, the queen who fought for the independence of her people, was used by the Victorians as an image for the celebration of their own world domination.

only fought elderly veterans left as a small garrison and the ninth legion, who were caught completely unawares. They were yet to face a fully equipped and prepared Roman army led by a general as experienced as Suetonius.

The Britons were so confident of their victory that they brought their women and children along to watch them fight, putting them on wagons which formed a barrier around one end of the battlefield. The Britons gathered into a huge mass, their chaotic organization in contrast to the ordered discipline of the Roman legions. The Romans made excellent use of their javelins and cavalry, and when the Britons tried to retreat, they were blocked in by their own wagons and families. The Romans charged forward and the slaughter began. The historian Tacitus claims that just 400 Romans died but 80,000 Britons were killed. It is said that Boudicca, defiant to the end, took her own life with poison. Like Cleopatra, she refused to become a prisoner paraded around at a Roman general's triumph. This marked the end of major opposition to Roman rule in Britain.

Roman Britain over time

The size of the province of Britannia grew over time. Following Boudicca's defeat, the successive governors of Britain pushed the border further and further north. The most famous of these governors, Gnaeus Julius Agricola, ruled Britannia for seven years from AD 77 to 84. He completed the conquest of Wales and England and even campaigned in the far north of Scotland. Here Agricola defeated the Caledonian chieftain Calgacus, as you will read in Exercise 12.9. The reason we know so much about Agricola is because the historian Tacitus was his son-in-law and he wrote a biography of him. Despite Tacitus' clear respect and admiration for his father-in-law, he was no fan of the emperors and one-man rule. As a result, Calgacus is presented by Tacitus as a freedom fighter and one of the last noble heroes to rally the independent tribes against the oppressive dominion of the mighty Roman empire. In his writing, Tacitus imagines Calgacus' speech before the battle with Agricola. The speech draws a moving contrast between the hired mercenaries of the Roman army and the Caledonians fighting through love for their country and their families.

In AD 122, the emperor Hadrian ordered the construction of a wall seemingly to mark the northern limit of Britannia. Hadrian's Wall was 73 miles long and was originally up to five or six metres high. It is the largest surviving Roman structure and it is estimated that it took about six years to construct. Soldiers from the Roman legions did most of the work. Forts were later added at regular intervals, both along the wall to house detachments of soldiers, and north of it where they could be used as observation posts. As you will read in Exercise 12.11, for many of these soldiers, life on the wall could be hard: they were far from home, not used to the cold weather and they were paid relatively little. Later emperors made attempts to build and occupy a wall even further north, but they were never completely successful in subduing the tribes of Caledonia; the Romans always found themselves returning to Hadrian's Wall.

It is not entirely clear why Hadrian ordered the construction of the wall. Although it offered numerous defensive benefits, we should not think that the wall was intended as an impenetrable barrier. If this was the case, then it would not have so many access points built into it to allow travel and free movement. Moreover, it would have been hugely expensive and inefficient to maintain a garrison big enough to cover all 73 miles of the wall if the aim was to repel invaders. It is more likely that the wall was intended just to control the flow of people and goods rather than separate the Romans of the empire from the peoples beyond.

The Romans had a remarkable influence on Britain. The presence of the army and the trade routes which the Roman empire opened up brought a multicultural dimension to the population of Britain. The army was manned by soldiers from all over the empire, including Spain, Romania, Belgium, Syria and North Africa. Trade links opened up the world even further: in 2016 two skeletons were found in London which are believed to be from the 2nd century AD and Chinese in origin. In Source 12.3 you can see evidence of other aspects of this multiculturalism.

By the time the Romans left Britain in AD 410, it had completely changed. Not only was it predominantly Christian like the rest of the empire, but the Romans had transformed it with their buildings. They constructed around 2,000 miles of roads, many of which are the basis for roads still used today, as well as systems that improved the supply of water, and sewers that improved hygiene in the cities. Many British place names such as Leicester, Manchester, Cirencester and Lancaster take their name from evolutions of the Latin word *castra,* meaning a camp. Many towns and cities still occupied in modern Britain were originally founded by the Romans, including York, Lincoln, Newcastle and London.

FIGURE 12.5 **Hadrian's Wall**

At every Roman mile along Hadrian's Wall there was a milecastle like the one pictured above. Between each milecastle were two smaller watchtowers known as turrets. This meant that soldiers could be spread along the wall so that threats were spotted quickly and reinforcements could be sent from larger forts nearby when needed. In this image is milecastle 39, close to the middle of the wall. Its location is a picturesque part of Northumberland, and also an area where plenty of the original wall still survives.

CHAPTER 12: SOURCES TO STUDY

Source 12.1: Britain and its inhabitants

Strabo, a Greek writer born in the 1st century BC, is most famous for his geographical text, the Geographica. *Like many other Greek intellectuals of the day, he spent time in Rome, and may have been granted Roman citizenship. In this extract he describes the riches of Britain, the peculiarities of the people themselves and the British weather. As Strabo is comparing the Britons with different Celtic tribes who lived elsewhere, in this text he uses the label Celts to refer to non-British tribes.*

Most of the island is flat and overgrown with forests, although many of its districts are hilly. It bears grain, cattle, gold, silver and iron. These things, accordingly, are exported from the island, as are also hides, and slaves, and dogs that are by nature suited to the purposes of the chase; the Celts, however, use both these and the native dogs for the purposes of war too.

The men of Britain are taller than the Celts, and not so yellow-haired, although their bodies are of looser build. The following is an indication of their size: I myself, in Rome, saw mere lads towering as much as half a foot above the tallest people in the city, although they were bandy-legged and presented no fair lines anywhere else in their figure.

Their habits are in part like those of the Celts, but in part more simple and barbaric – so much so that, on account of their inexperience, some of them, although well supplied with milk, make no cheese; and they have no experience in gardening or other agricultural pursuits. They have powerful chieftains in their country.

For the purposes of war they use chariots for the most part, just as some of the Celts do. The forests are their cities; for they fence in a spacious circular enclosure with trees which they have felled, and in that enclosure make huts for themselves and also pen up their cattle – not, however, with the purpose of staying a long time.

Their weather is more rainy than snowy; and on the days of clear sky fog prevails so long a time that throughout a whole day the sun is to be seen for only three or four hours round about midday.

Strabo, *Geography* Book 4.5 (trans. slightly adapted)

Source 12.1: Questions

1 What natural advantages did the Britons have?
2 For what reasons did Strabo think the Britons were more simple and barbaric than the Celts?
3 Strabo writes that he has seen Britons in Rome. Bearing in mind the century in which Strabo was writing, are you surprised by this? Why do you think the Britons might have been there?
4 Imagine you are reading this at the time that Strabo wrote it. What would you think of Britain? Would you want to visit it? Would you want to invade and conquer it?
5 Strabo himself never visited Britain. How reliable do you think this source is?

Source 12.2: The Battle of Watling Street

Tacitus was born in AD 56, so he would have been a small child at the time of Boudicca's rebellion in AD 61. The extract below is his recreation of the speeches before the Battle of Watling Street. He imagines Boudicca's outrage at the Roman treatment of herself, her family and her people. Tacitus follows Boudicca's speech with that of the Roman commander, Suetonius: he, too, encourages his men to have confidence despite the comparatively small size of the Roman force. In the battle that followed, the Romans won.

Boudicca drove round all the tribes in a chariot with her daughters in front of her. 'We British are used to woman commanders in war,' she cried. 'I am descended from mighty men! But now I am not fighting for my kingdom and wealth. I am fighting as an ordinary person for my lost freedom, my bruised body and my outraged daughters. Nowadays Roman rapacity does not even spare our bodies. Old people are killed, virgins raped. But the gods will grant us the vengeance we deserve! The Roman division which dared to fight is annihilated. The others cower in their camps, or watch for a chance to escape. They will never face even the din and roar of all our thousands, much less the shock of our onslaught. Consider how many of you are fighting – and why. Then you will win this battle, or perish. That is what I, a woman, plan to do! – let the men live in slavery if they will.'

Suetonius trusted his men's bravery. Yet he too, at this critical moment, offered encouragements and appeals. 'Disregard the clamours and empty threats of the natives!' he said. 'In their ranks, there are more women than fighting men. Unwarlike, unarmed, when they see the arms and courage of the conquerors who have routed them so often, they will break immediately. Even in the midst of many legions, it only takes a few men to win the battle: what special glory for your small numbers to win the renown of a whole army! Just keep in close order. Throw your javelins, and then carry on: use shield-bosses to fell them, swords to kill them. Do not think of plunder. When you have won, you will have everything.'

Tacitus, *Annals* 14.36–37 (trans. adapted)

Source 12.2: Questions

1 What does Boudicca say to fill her troops with the passion to fight? How would you feel if you were in her army?

2 What does Suetonius say to motivate his soldiers?

3 If you did not know what the outcome of the battle would be, which side would you prefer to be on?

4 What impression of Boudicca's character does Tacitus give in this extract? Do you think that he wanted his Roman readers to admire her?

Source 12.3: The inhabitants of Britain: Regina and Barates

This tombstone dates from the late 2nd century AD, and it was found in the Roman fort at South Shields, Newcastle. It shows a woman wearing a necklace, bracelets and a long-sleeved robe. In her lap is equipment for spinning wool, and at her feet is a basket of wool. Her right hand holds open the lid to what is probably a jewellery box.

The tombstone has two inscriptions. The first is in Latin and reads as follows:

> D(IS) M(ANIBUS) REGINA LIBERTA ET CONIUGE
> BARATES PALMYRENUS NATIONE
> CATUALLAUNA AN(NORUM) XXX

> TO THE SPIRITS OF THE DEPARTED (AND TO)
> REGINA, HIS FREEDWOMAN AND WIFE, A
> CATUVELLAUNIAN BY TRIBE, AGED 30, BARATES
> OF PALMYRA (SET THIS UP).

Underneath the first inscription is another, written in the Palmyrene script, which means 'Regina, the freedwoman of Barates, alas.'

FIGURE 12.6   Regina Tombstone

Source 12.3: Questions

1 What evidence can you see in this image that Barates and his wife were a reasonably wealthy couple?
2 Barates is from Palmyra, a town in modern-day Syria, but his wife was an ex-slave who had a Latin name: what do you make of this? In your answer you should also consider the meaning of her name.
3 What does this tombstone suggest about Regina's character?
4 Why do you think that some of the inscription is in the Palmyrene script?
5 What does this tombstone show us about the impact of the Roman empire on the people(s) living in Britain?

Source 12.4: Hadrian's Wall: Vindolanda tablet 346

The Vindolanda tablets are a collection of hundreds of short notes, written in ink on small pieces of wood. They were discovered near Vindolanda, a Roman fort near Hadrian's Wall. It is believed that they date from the 2nd century AD. The collection of tablets includes requests for items of clothing or food, invitations, and comments on the local Britons. The text of one of the most famous tablets, now in the British Museum, is printed here. It contains traces of a message received by one of the soldiers who garrisoned the wall.

. . . I have sent (?) you . . . pairs of socks from Sattua, two pairs of sandals and two pairs of underpants, two pairs of sandals . . . Greet . . .ndes, Elpis, Iu. . ., . . .enus, Tetricus and all your messmates with whom I pray that you live in the greatest good fortune.

Tab. Vindol. 346.

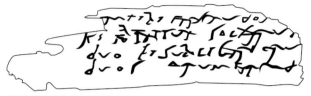

FIGURE 12.7 Vindolanda tablet 346.

Source 12.4: Questions

1 Why do you think the sender of this note was sending socks, sandals and underpants to this soldier?

2 What can you tell about the relationship between the sender and recipient of this note? Who do you think the sender might have been?

3 Imagine you are the soldier posted at Hadrian's wall. Write a letter replying to the sender of this note.

CHAPTER 12: QUESTIONS FOR DISCUSSION

1 This chapter discusses the Romans from the viewpoint of a province. Has it changed your opinion of the Romans?
You might like to consider
- the benefits that Roman infrastructure brought to Britain
- the impact of Roman rule upon local identity
- the treatment of local people by the Roman army
- the clash or the interaction between the different communities of soldiers and local inhabitants

2 The size of the empire changed the nature of the Roman army: its soldiers came from many different communities and they could end up far from home. How do you think this changed attitudes within the army?
You might like to consider
- who or what the soldiers were fighting for
- how far from home the soldiers may have been stationed
- the experience of daily life in a military camp

3 What do you think Boudicca's legacy is for us today?
You might like to consider
- the reasons she fought
- her actions in battle, including the numbers she killed and her tactics
- how she was viewed by later writers such as Tacitus and Cassius Dio
- the role of her statue near the Houses of Parliament

Ⓒⓦ Chapter 12: Core Language Vocabulary List

portō	portāre, portāvī, portātum	carry; bear; take
errō	errāre, errāvī, errātum	stray; make a mistake
nārrō	nārrāre, nārrāvī, nārrātum	tell; relate
dēspērō	dēspērāre, dēspērāvī, dēspērātum	despair
sedeō	sedēre, sēdī, sessum	sit
cōnstituō	cōnstituere, cōnstituī, cōnstitūtum	decide
colligō	colligere, collēgī, collēctum	gather together; collect
cadō	cadere, cecidī, cāsum	fall
trahō	trahere, trāxī, tractum	drag
contendō	contendere, contendī, contentum	hasten; march; compete
vēndō	vēndere, vēndidī, vēnditum	sell
effugiō	effugere, effūgī	escape
īnsula	īnsulae, f	island
ventus	ventī, m	wind
rēgnum	rēgnī, n	kingdom
nox	noctis, f	night
gēns	gentis, f	family; tribe; people
frāter	frātris, m	brother
soror	sorōris, f	sister
caput	capitis, n	head
nēmō	nūllīus	no one; nobody
celer	celeris, celere	quick; fast
gravis	grave	heavy; serious
nūllus	nūlla, nūllum	not any; no
crās		tomorrow
herī		yesterday
hodiē		today
fortasse		perhaps
igitur		therefore; and so
nam		for

nēmō has slightly unusual endings; see p251.

celer has slightly unusual endings; see p230.

nūllus has slightly unusual endings; see p251.

People and places

Britannia, Britanniae, f
Britannī, Britannōrum, m pl

The Roman province of **Britannia** was established by the emperor Claudius in AD 43. The **Britons** who lived there were a collection of Celtic tribes.

Claudius, Claudiī, m
10 BC–AD 54

Claudius was the fourth emperor of Rome and the great-nephew of Augustus; he was not expected to be a good ruler, but among his successes was the conquest of Britain in AD 43.

Icēnī, Icēnōrum, m pl
Prāsutāgus, Prāsutāgī, m
Boudicca, Boudiccae, f
1st century AD

The **Iceni** were a tribe in Norfolk who were grossly mistreated by the Romans following the death of their king **Prasutagus**. His wife, **Boudicca**, led a wide-reaching revolt against the Romans in the 60s AD.

Suētōnius Paulīnus,
Suētōniī Paulīnī, m
1st century AD

Suetonius Paulinus was the governor of Britain during Boudicca's revolt.

Calgacus, Calgacī, m
1st century AD

Calgacus was the leader of the Caledonian tribes who fought against the Roman governor Agricola in AD 83 or 84.

Hadriānus, Hadriānī, m
AD 76–138

Hadrian was the thirteenth emperor of Rome. He ordered the construction of a wall in the north of Britain in AD 122.

Future passive

The future passive can be translated as follows:

regar   I **shall be** ruled

As with the present and imperfect tenses, the **future passive** is very similar in form to the **future active**: the main difference is the **person ending.**

The future passive uses the **present stem** and, as with the future active, there are two main sets of endings; the vowels used before these endings vary across the different conjugations.

Look it up! For the endings in the mixed conjugation see p240.

	1st conjugation	2nd conjugation	3rd conjugation	4th conjugation
I	am**ābor**	terr**ēbor**	reg**ar**	aud**iar**
you (sg)	am**āberis**	terr**ēberis**	reg**ēris**	aud**iēris**
he / she / it	am**ābitur**	terr**ēbitur**	reg**ētur**	aud**iētur**
we	am**ābimur**	terr**ēbimur**	reg**ēmur**	aud**iēmur**
you (pl)	am**ābiminī**	terr**ēbiminī**	reg**ēminī**	aud**iēminī**
they	am**ābuntur**	terr**ēbuntur**	reg**entur**	aud**ientur**

EXERCISE 12.1

1. servus sum et mox ā dominō vēndar.

2. haec īnsula ā cōpiīs ferōcibus occupābitur.

3. quō effugimus? ibi servābimur?

4. cūr hic senex ā tē vulnerābitur?

5. quamquam nunc in hōc locō manēre vīs, crās ex hīs silvīs trahēris.

6. quod eōs magnopere amātis, ō sorōrēs, līberī ā vōbis colligentur.

7. haec verba mox ab illō nūntiō narrābuntur.

8. nōnne ille incola ventīs magnīs terrēbitur?

9. monēbiminīne, ō mīlitēs, ā duce vestrō?

10. quod magnopere errāvērunt, crās puerī ā patribus custōdientur.

EXERCISE 12.2: THE EMPEROR CLAUDIUS INVADES BRITAIN

The fourth emperor of Rome was Claudius. To many at the time, Claudius must have been a surprising choice: he had been kept away from the public eye by Augustus and the rest of his family because he was physically disabled and suffered from frequent illness. According to the historian Suetonius, even Claudius' own mother Antonia despised him, referring to him as a 'monster; a man whom Nature had not finished but had merely begun'.

Claudius, however, proved that his family had been wrong to treat him with such undeserved contempt: when the third emperor, Caligula, was assassinated, Claudius was greeted by the soldiers of the imperial bodyguard as the new emperor. He ordered the invasion of Britain in AD 43 and won control of significantly more territory than Julius Caesar had managed nearly 100 years previously.

inter <u>nepōtēs</u> Augustī erat Claudius. ubi puer et deinde iuvenis erat, Claudius saepe <u>aeger</u> erat. māter Claudiī, <u>Antōnia</u> nōmine, saepe īrāta erat: 'hic fīlius saepius aeger est,' sibi inquit; 'neque corpore neque <u>mente</u> validus est. numquam fīlius meus ā cīvibus Rōmānīs laudābitur, numquam mīlitēs in
5 proelium ā fīliō meō dūcentur, numquam hostēs superābuntur.' etiam Augustus nōlēbat Claudium esse nōtissimum: 'nōlī in forum īre,' iubēbat. 'nōlī ad lūdōs adesse. tū es aeger nec validus es. in forō ā cīvibus vidēberis; ā cēterīs cīvibus rīdēberis, nec laudāberis.'

post multōs annōs Caligula, quī eō tempore <u>imperātor</u> erat, saevē interfectus
10 est. mīlitēs, quī imperātōrem custōdiēbant, perterritī erant: 'quis nunc imperātor erit?' rogāvērunt. subitō Claudium, quī post <u>columnam</u> stābat, cōnspexērunt: 'ecce!' inquiunt clāmantēs, 'hīc est Claudius! Claudius est nepōs Augustī! Claudius nunc imperātor erit!'

prīmō Claudius miser erat: 'nēmō mē laudābat,' sibi inquit; 'omnēs mē rīdēbant.
15 <u>quōmodo</u> laudābor? quōmodo imperātor erō?' deinde Claudius mīlitēs in Britanniam dūcere cōnstituit. 'mīlitēs in Britanniam ā mē dūcentur!' nūntiāvit Claudius. 'multī Britannī superābuntur! tum omnēs mē laudābunt!'

nepōs, nepōtis, m	descendant
aeger, aegra, aegrum	sick
Antōnia, Antōniae, f	Antonia
mēns, mentis, f	mind
imperātor, imperātōris, m	emperor
columna, columnae, f	column
quōmodo	how?

eō tempore in Britanniā multae gentēs cum aliīs gentibus pugnābant. aliī rēgēs
sociī Rōmānōrum esse volēbant; aliī rēgēs omnem Britanniam līberātam esse
volēbant. 'rēgibus, quī sociī Rōmānōrum esse volunt, auxilium dabō,' Claudius   20
cōnstituit; 'deinde, ubi cēterī rēgēs ab hīs rēgibus nōbisque superātī erunt, in
Britanniā plūs <u>potestātis</u> habēbimus.'

Claudius plūrimōs mīlitēs et ducem, <u>Aulum Plautium</u> nōmine, in Britanniam
mīsit. Aulus Plautius erat dux clārissimus et fortissimus quī suōs optimē dūxit;
hī mīlitēs fortiter contrā Britannōs pugnāvērunt. tandem Claudius advēnit.   25
'ecce!' clāmāvit, 'nunc adsum! et nunc hī mīlitēs ā mē dūcentur!' rēgēs autem
<u>ūndecim</u> nōn diūtius pugnāre iam cōnstituerant: 'nunc, ō Claudī,' inquiunt,
'sociī Rōmānōrum esse volumus. nōn diūtius contrā Rōmānōs pugnābimus.'

Claudius laetissimus erat: 'nunc clārissimus sum,' inquit, 'quod nunc in Britanniā
Rōmānī plūs potestātis habent. nunc hī rēgēs auxiliō nostrō regent; hī rēgēs   30
gentēs suās regent sed nōbis <u>sīcut</u> servī erunt.'

potestās, potestātis, f	power
Aulus Plautius, Aulī Plautiī, m	Aulus Plautius
ūndecim	eleven
sīcut	just like

Idiom: *nec / neque*

Latin does not follow *et* with a **negative** word; instead *nec / neque* is used.

English idiom	We stayed for a long time **and** we did **not** flee.
Latin idiom	diū manēbāmus **neque** effūgimus.

Idiom: *nihil, nūllus, nēmō*

You have met various **negative** words so far, and several of these are used in an **idiomatic** way in Latin. Details of this idiom are listed below.

- *nihil* – this neuter word is usually met only in the nominative or accusative cases.

  in illā urbe **nihil** est bonum.   In that city **nothing** is good.
  nōbis **nihil** nārrāvit.   He told **nothing** to us.

- *nūllus, nūlla, nūllum* (*not any, no*) – this word looks like a 2-1-2 adjective, but its endings for the genitive and dative singular are different.

	masculine	femine	neuter
genitive sg	nūllīus	nūllīus	nūllīus
dative sg	nūllī	nūllī	nūllī

- *nēmō* (*no one, nobody*) – this word also has unusual endings, and it does not have any plural forms.

nominative sg	nēmō
accusative sg	nēminem
genitive sg	nūllīus
dative sg	nēminī
ablative sg	nūllō

> **Note that** these genitive and dative endings are also used for the number *ūnus*, and are very similar to some of the genitive and dative sg pronoun endings. For a full table of these endings, see the Reference Grammar p251.

EXERCISE 12.3

1. cūr mīlitēs nēminem ducī trādidērunt?
2. ego nūllam aquam bibī sed tū omnem vīnum bibistī.
3. quamquam per noctem nūntium exspectāvērunt, nihil dē proeliō audīvērunt.
4. cūr dominus illum servum nēminī vēndidit? servus validus est et multa portāre potest.
5. hic equus nūllīus est; eum igitur in agrōs meōs traham.
6. parentēs, postquam in vīllīs nūllōs līberōs invēnērunt, dēspērābant.
7. trēs hōrās in illō locō sedēbam quamquam nēminem exspectābam.
8. quod diū per mare nāvigābam, nihil dē morte parentium audīvī.
9. ad urbem contendērunt nec tamen senātōrēs cōnspexērunt.
10. nūllī virō amōrem meum dabō; nam marītum habēre nōlō.

Consolidation: participles

You have met two different categories of participles.

present participle	ruling	**regēns, regentis**
perfect passive participle (PPP)	having been ruled	**rēctus, rēcta, rēctum**

Look it up! For the full table of participle endings, see the Reference Grammar, pp242–243.

Each of these participles behaves like an **adjective** and has to **agree** with the noun it describes.

Latin uses participles much more often than English does; this means that it is often best to move away from a very literal translation and use a **subordinate clause** instead.

incolās **effugientēs** cōnspexī.

I saw the **fleeing** inhabitants.

→ I saw the inhabitants **who were fleeing**.

soror frātrem **necātum** cōnspexit.

The sister saw her **having been killed** brother.

→ The sister saw her brother **who had been killed**.

The sister saw her brother **after he had been killed**.

EXERCISE 12.4

1. cūr senex omnia dē vestrīs patribus dēspērantibus vōbis nārrāvit?

2. vīllam incēnsam cōnspeximus et lacrimāvimus.

3. ō mīlitēs, contendite et hostēs effugientēs capite!

4. hic servus, ā tē vēnditus, pessimus est.

5. herī mulier mea, prope templum sedēns, amīcōs novōs salūtābat.

6. omnēs amīcī cēnam ab hīs fēlīcibus servīs parātam laudābant.

7. hodiē epistulam ā tē scrīptam accēpī.

8. hī incolae, gladiōs tenentēs, nōs terrent.

9. crās sociī, ā duce vocātī, aderunt.

10. fortasse in hāc īnsulā, ab incolīs audācibus defēnsā, multum aurum invenīre volēbant.

EXERCISE 12.5: BOUDICCA LEADS A REBELLION

During the reign of Rome's fifth emperor, Nero, the king of the Iceni tribe was Prasutagus. He made a gift of his kingdom to the Romans in his will, in the hope that the Romans would respect his wishes that his daughters should maintain control of his kingdom. The Romans, however, chose to keep the kingdom for themselves, and the Iceni were most shamefully treated by the Roman soldiers stationed in Britain. Boudicca was Prasutagus' wife: in AD 60, outraged at the wrongs inflicted upon her people by the Romans, she led a revolt against them.

To begin with, Boudicca achieved significant success: the majority of the Roman legions stationed in Britain were fighting far away on the north coast of Wales. Boudicca marched south and ransacked the city of Camulodunum (Colchester). The small number of troops stationed there were no match for her and the city was destroyed, including the temple built in honour of the deified emperor Claudius.

inter gentēs, quī sociī Rōmānōrum esse cōnstituerant, erant Icēnī. rēx Icēnōrum, Prāsutāgus nōmine, fīliās duās habēbat. 'aliquandō perībō,' putābat Prāsutāgus, 'et, quod sociī Rōmānōrum sumus, rēgnum Rōmānīs dabō. sed Rōmānī, quod amīcī sunt, rēgnum meum fīliīs meīs dabunt.' ubi tamen
5   Prāsutāgus periit, Rōmānī rēgnum fīliīs Prāsutāgī dare nōlēbant. 'hoc rēgnum est nostrum!' inquiunt Rōmānī rīdentēs, 'et nunc Icēnōs regere possumus.' mīlitēs, quī prope Icēnōs collēctī erant, erant crūdēlissimī. ex Icēnīs pecūniam rapuērunt, multōs virōs fēmināsque interfēcērunt et uxōrem fīliāsque Prāsutāgī violāvērunt.

10 uxor Prāsutāgī, Boudicca nōmine, erat fēmina audācissima. 'Rōmānī putant nōs servōs esse,' clāmōre īrātō inquit Boudicca. 'Rōmānī putant sē validōs esse. Rōmānī putant sē omnia nostra rapere posse. nōn sōlum Rōmānī validī sunt: ego validissima sum! ego fortissima sum! ego audācissima sum! rēgnum meum ab Rōmānīs captum rapiam; deinde alia rēgna ab Rōmānīs rapiam et Britannīs
15 trādam. tum Rōmānī intellegent sē nōn validōs esse sed miserrimōs.'

aliquandō	one day
violō, violāre, violāvī, violātum	violate
sōlum	only

deinde Boudicca, postquam multōs Britannōs collēgit, magnās cōpiās
<u>Camulodūnum</u> celeriter contendentēs dūxit. ubi in oppidum advēnērunt, mīlitēs
Rōmānōs ibi habitantēs saevissimē necāvērunt. 'ecce!' clāmāvit Boudicca, 'hoc
est templum <u>dīvī</u> Claudiī. hoc templum ā nōbis dēlēbitur! Claudius deus nōn
est; Claudius erat dominus servōrum Britannōrum. herī servī erāmus; hodiē   20
hoc templum et hoc oppidum dēlēmus! crās et omnem Britanniam et nōs
līberābimus!'

Camulodūnum, Camulodūnī, n	Camulodunum (modern-day Colchester)
dīvus, dīva, dīvum	divine

The ablative absolute

Participles **agree** with the nouns that they describe, and the case of those nouns depends upon their **role** in the sentence.

cibum ā servīs **portātum** cōnsūmpsit.   He ate the **food** which had been carried by the slaves.

Here, *cibum* is accusative because it is the object of *cōnsūmpsit.* This means that its participle, *portātum*, needs to be accusative too.

It is very common, however, for a noun and participle phrase to be used at the start of a sentence, even if that noun does not appear in the rest of the sentence. This construction is known as the **ablative absolute**: *absolute* means that it is grammatically cut off from the rest of the sentence because the label *absolute* derives from the Latin verb *absolvō – I separate from.*

For this sort of noun and participle phrase the **ablative** case is always used. It is often helpful to use the word ***with*** to translate this phrase literally, before recasting it into better English as a **subordinate clause** starting with ***when / while / after / since***.

vīllīs incēnsīs, incolae effūgērunt.   **(With)** their houses having been **burned**, the inhabitants fled.

→   The inhabitants fled **when their houses had been burned.**

EXERCISE 12.6

1. duce necātō, mīlitēs magnopere errāvērunt.

2. equō vēnditō, Rōmam contendere nōn possum.

3. uxōre frūstrā quaesītā, vir līberīque dēspērābant.

4. cīvibus territīs, senātōrēs nūntium in forum vocāvērunt.

5. viīs novīs aedificātīs, nunc celerius in urbem iter faciēmus.

6. incolīs collēctīs, rēx novus nūntiātus est.

7. aurō deīs datō, cīvēs ā templō abiērunt.

8. morte ducis audītō, mīlitēs lacrimābant.

9. hostibus effugientibus, mīlitēs corpora mortuōrum collēgērunt.

10. hōc librō lectō, vīsne in hortum exīre?

EXERCISE 12.7: BOUDICCA IS DEFEATED

Boudicca's success continued: she marched to London and destroyed the city. Meanwhile, Suetonius, the Roman governor of Britain, was marching his troops back towards the south. The two armies met at the Battle of Watling Street. Jubilant and over-confident at her previous success, Boudicca encouraged her troops to bring their families to watch the battle. This was a devastating mistake: Suetonius' troops won an easy victory, and the escape routes for the Britons were blocked by the crowds of spectators. Trapped in the battle plain, the Britons were massacred by the Romans.

eō tempore in Britanniā <u>praefectus</u> Rōmānus erat Suētōnius Paulīnus. mox Suētōniō nūntiātum est Boudiccam magnās cōpiās contrā Rōmānōs dūcere: 'Camulodūnō dēlētō,' nūntius inquit, 'Boudicca nunc omnem Britanniam līberāre vult.' Suētōnius igitur mīlitēs suōs movēre cōnstituit: 'celerrimē contendite!' inquit. 'dēbēmus contrā Boudiccam quam celerrimē contendere.'   5

Boudicca, tamen, cōpiās Londīnium – nunc caput huius īnsulae sed tum oppidum parvum – celerrimē dūcēbat. 'herī Camulodūnum dēlētum vīdimus; mox Londīnium <u>ārdēns</u> vidēbimus! nōs Britannī fortissimī sumus! nōs Britannī Rōmānōs docēbimus Britannōs ferōciōrēs quam Rōmānōs esse.'

10 ubi Boudicca et cōpiae Londīnium advēnērunt, celerrimē hanc urbem
occupāvērunt: vīllās incendērunt et omnēs, quī nōn effūgerant, interfēcērunt.
'hodiē, multīs vīllīs incēnsīs et multīs hominibus interfectīs, Londīnium dēlētum
est,' laetissima clāmāvit Boudicca, 'et Rōmānīs ostendimus nōs validōs esse.
mox contrā Suētōnium pugnābimus. mox ā nōbis, quī <u>tam</u> ferōcēs sumus,
15 cōpiae Suētōniī superābuntur.'

Boudicca, tamen, magnopere errāvit. iūssit plūrimōs Britannōs proelium
spectāre: 'uxōrēs līberōsque colligite!' inquit. 'fīliās sorōrēsque colligite!
<u>plaustra</u> trahite! in plaustrīs sedentēs uxōrēs līberīque hoc proelium spectābunt;
optimum erit spectāre nōs Rōmānōs superantēs.' Boudicca nōn intellēxit
20 Suētōnium esse ducem optimum et mīlitēs <u>perītōs</u> habēre. ubi tempus proeliī
aderat, plaustrīs tractīs, multae uxōrēs, līberī, fīliae et sorōrēs convēnērunt et
proelium spectābant.

Rōmānī fortiter contrā Britannōs pugnāvērunt; multī Britannī vulnerātī
cadēbant. 'effugite!' clāmāvit Boudicca. 'quam celerrimē effugite! hodiē nōn
25 vīcimus; effugite et fortasse posteā iterum pugnābimus.' uxōrēs autem plūrimae
et līberī prope proelium collēctī erant; in tractīs plaustrīs sedēbant. tum
Boudicca dēspērābat: 'quō effugere possumus?' magnō cum clāmōre inquit.
'viae plaustrīs nostrīs <u>clausae sunt</u>; audācior eram; nōn intellēxī Rōmānōs
mīlitēs optimōs esse. nunc superātī sumus.' deinde Boudicca et multī Britannī
30 sē interfēcērunt: 'superātī sumus,' dēspērantēs inquiunt, 'nec tamen erimus
servī Rōmānōrum.'

praefectus, praefectī, m	prefect; governor
Camulodūnum, Camulodūnī, n	Camulodunum (modern-day Colchester)
ārdeō, ārdēre, ārsī	burn; be on fire
tam	so
plaustrum, plaustrī, n	wagon
perītus, perīta, perītum	skilled; experienced
claudō, claudere, clausī, clausum	block

Consolidation: accusative case

You have met the following uses of the **accusative case**.

- the **object** of an **active verb**

  frāter **sorōrem** portābat.   The brother was carrying his **sister**.

- the **subject** or **object** of an infinitive

  tē comitēs colligere volō.   I want **you** to gather your **companions**.
  dīxit **sorōrem** dēspērāre.   He said that his **sister** was despairing.

- in **time phrases** to show **how long** something lasted

  multōs annōs   **For many years**
     Britannī dēspērābant.   the Britons despaired.

- after **prepositions**

  per **silvās**   Through the **woods**,
     incolae effūgērunt.   the inhabitants escaped.

- with the **names of towns** to show **motion towards** that town

  nunc **Rōmam**   Now **to Rome**
     celeriter contendēmus.   we shall march quickly.

Consolidation: genitive case

You have met the following uses of the **genitive case**.

- to connect one noun with another: it is often best to translate the genitive case with the word *of* because it regularly shows that one noun belongs to another.

  cūr in oppidum **huius gentis**   Why to the town **of this tribe**
     effūgistī?   did you flee?

- after the words **satis** (*enough*) and **plus** (*more*)

  satis cibī cōnsūmpsī.   I have eaten **enough food**.

Consolidation: dative case

You have met the following uses of the **dative case**.

- as the **indirect object**: in this use the dative is often best translated as **to** or **for**

  servus cibum **dominō** dedit. The slave gave food to his master.

- after **verbs** such as **persuādeō** or **crēdō**

  frāter **sorōrī** persuāsit. The brother persuaded his **sister**.

- to show **possession**

  hīs parentibus **These parents**
  līberī optimī sunt. **have** excellent children.

1. duās hōrās sorōrēs lacrimābant et nunc frātrēs quoque lacrimant; nam herī dē morte fīliae meae audīvērunt.

2. cūr magister hīs puerīs nōn persuāsit? etiam nunc hunc librum legere nōlunt.

3. mihī multī servī ancillaeque sunt, sed tibī paucī.

4. mihī plūs cibī ferte! diū in agrīs labōrābam et nunc multa cōnsūmere volō.

5. soror frātrem ad templum contendere iūssit, quod dōna deīs portāre cupiēbat.

6. crās Rōmam festīnābimus, sed hodiē in vīllā huius cīvis manēmus.

7. intellēxistisne, cīvēs, mīlitēs omnēs ab hostibus effugere?

8. numquam in rēgnum illīus rēgis crūdēlis redībimus.

9. fīlius ducis in illō proeliō occīsus est.

10. ubi amīcus meus quaerēbātur, eius soror dēspērābat.

EXERCISE 12.9: CALGACUS ROUSES THE SCOTS

Agricola was governor of Britain from AD 77 to 84. He extended the reach of Roman territory considerably, taking his troops far into Scotland. His son-in-law, the historian Tacitus, wrote a biography about him. One of the most dramatic moments in this biography is the battle of Mount Graupius in the summer of AD 83: Tacitus vividly imagined the speech of the Caledonian leader Calgacus, as he urged his men to make one final stand for freedom against the might of the Roman army.

Calgacus, postquam cōpiae convēnērunt et tacentēs stābant, sīc suōs iūssit: 'Britannī ā Rōmānīs saepe superātī sunt. hīs Britannīs superātīs, nautae Rōmānī per mare circum īnsulam nostram nāvigant. <u>ubique</u> sunt gentēs ā Rōmānīs victae. multa rēgna Rōmānīs vēndita sunt ā rēgibus quī pecūniam magis quam <u>lībertātem</u> amābant. nunc nōs – nūllī aliī – ad proelium parātī 5 sumus.

Rōmānī nōbis sunt dominī crūdēlissimī saevissimīque: uxōrēs nostrās rapuērunt; līberōs nostrōs servōs fēcērunt; ex vīllīs pecūniam capiunt et etiam ex agrīs cibum. iubent nōs viās per silvās magnās et trāns montēs altōs aedificāre; iubent nōs semper labōrāre, numquam laetōs esse. quid nunc 10 habēmus? pāxne et <u>imperium</u> nōbis data sunt? <u>immō</u>, Rōmānī nōbis nihil aliud relīquērunt quam <u>servitūdinem</u> et <u>sōlitūdinem</u>.

nunc nōbis necesse est prō lībertāte pugnāre. hodiē patrēs, frātrēs, fīliī adsunt: omnēs nunc prō līberīs, prō sorōribus, prō mātribus pugnābimus. nōs, quī terram nostram amāmus, nunc prō hāc īnsulā nostrā ferōciter pugnābimus. ō 15 Britannī, nōlīte Rōmānōs timēre: multī mīlitum nōn Rōmānī sunt, sed hominēs quī ex aliīs locīs convēnērunt. multī hōrum mīlitum nōn prō patriā pugnābunt; nōn prō uxōribus, sorōribus līberīsque pugnābunt. mīlitēs Rōmānī propter pecūniam pugnant, nōn propter amōrem. multī hōrum mīlitum nōn fortēs sunt: ducibus <u>pārent</u> quod putant hōs ducēs validōs esse. mox ducēs suōs in proeliō 20 cadentes vidēbunt; mox hī mīlitēs līberābuntur! deinde multī hōrum mīlitum auxilium nōbis, nōn Rōmānīs, dabunt; deinde prō nōbis lībertāteque pugnābunt!'

hīs verbīs audītīs, cōpiae Calgacī ferōcissimē pugnāvērunt, nec tamen vīcērunt. postquam ē proeliō effūgērunt, agrōs suōs dēlēvērunt; uxōrēs suās, fīliās sorōrēsque necāvērunt; etiam sē interfēcērunt. 'nihil Rōmānīs relinquēmus,' 25 īrātissimī clāmāvērunt. 'numquam erimus servī Rōmānōrum.'

ubique	everywhere
lībertās, lībertātis, f	freedom
imperium, imperiī, n	empire; government
immō	indeed no!
servitūdō, servitūdinis, f	servitude
sōlitūdō, sōlitūdinis, f	desolation
pāreō, pārēre, pāruī (+ dative)	obey

Consolidation: ablative case

The **ablative** case is often best translated with the words **by / with / from / than / in**.

The **ablative** case is also used in the following ways.

- after **prepositions**

prō patriā   On behalf of his country,
  ferōcissimē pugnābat.   he was fighting very fiercely.

- in **time phrases** to show **when** an action took place

prīmō annō   In the first year,
  coniūnx laeta erat.   the wife was happy.

prīmō mīlitēs   At first, the soldiers
  incolās terrēbant.   terrified the inhabitants.

- with the **names of towns** to show **motion away** from a place

Rōmā effugiēbant.   They were fleeing **away from Rome**.

- to show **instrument** (i.e. the thing with which an action is done).

dux rēgem **gladiō** interfēcit.   The leader killed the king **with a sword**.

- with **ā / ab** to show **agent** (i.e. the person by whom the action of a **passive** verb is done)

rēx **ā duce** interfectus est.   The king was killed **by the leader**.

- after a **comparative** adjective or adverb to mean **than**

hī incolae laetiōrēs sunt   These inhabitants are happier
  illīs mīlitibus.   **than those soldiers**.

- to show **extent**

sorōrēs **multō** saeviōrēs   The sisters were **much** more savage
  erant quam frātrēs.   than their brothers.

- in an **ablative absolute**

duce vulnerātō,   **Because their general had been
  mīlitēs dēspērābant.   wounded**, the soldiers despaired.

EXERCISE 12.10

1. haec gēns multō ferōcior est quam illī incolae.

2. Rōmā nūntius ad ducem quam celerrimē contendit.

3. equus novus, quamquam celer erat, ab agricolā vēnditus est.

4. prīmō frāter sorōrem vulnerātam portābat; posteā, quod illa gravis erat et ille fessus, eam tenēre nōn poterat.

5. multīs vīllīs incēnsīs, ex urbe multī cīvēs effugiēbant quod multī hostēs aderant.

6. tertiō annō īnsula, quamquam incolae fortiter eam dēfenderant, occupāta est.

7. putāsne hoc oppidum maius illō esse?

8. multae nāvēs celerēs ventō dēlētae sunt.

9. ō sorōrēs, herī nēmō celerius contendit quam frāter vester.

10. saepe mīlitēs Graecī, prō patriā pugnantēs, hostēs sagittīs vulnerāvērunt.

GRAMMAR QUIZ

Identify the way in which each of the following ablative nouns has been used in Exercise 12.10.

1. multō (from Q1)

2. Rōmā (from Q2)

3. agricolā (from Q3)

4. prīmō (from Q4)

5. vīllīs (from Q5)

6. annō (from Q6)

7. illō (from Q7)

8. ventō (from Q8)

9. patriā (from Q10)

10. sagittīs (from Q10)

In AD 122 the Roman army started to build a vast wall stretching across the north of England from east to west. It is hard to know for sure why the Romans decided to build this wall, but it must have stood as a visible reminder of the scale of the Romans' power.

Writing tablets and letters have been found amongst the Roman remains of the wall, most notably at Vindolanda. Some of these tablets predate the Roman wall, but they suggest that for many soldiers, life in this area of the empire was fairly miserable. You can read the text of one of the Vindolanda tablets in Source 12.4.

ubi Rōmae Hadriānus <u>imperātor</u> erat, annōs sex in Britannia mīlitēs Rōmānī mūrum longissimum altissimumque aedificābant. prope hunc mūrum multa <u>castra</u> aedificāvērunt. 'Britannī <u>Calēdoniīque</u> hunc mūrum vidēbunt,' Hadriānus putābat, 'et intellegent Rōmānōs <u>potentissimōs</u> esse.'

hōc mūrō aedificātō, multī mīlitēs prope mūrum habitābant. saepe hī mīlitēs   5
nōn laetī erant: 'miserum est prope hunc mūrum habitāre,' lacrimantēs inquiunt; 'miserrimī sumus. in Britanniā semper ventus est et <u>frīgus</u> et <u>pluvia</u> gravis. nox longissima est. herī <u>sōlem</u> vidēre nōn poterāmus, hodiē sōlem vidēre nōn possumus, crās sōlem vidēre nōn poterimus. numquam sōlem vidēmus. semper <u>frīgidī</u> sumus, semper fessī, nam <u>cotīdiē</u> labōrāmus: <u>sarcinās</u>   10
gravēs portāmus et multa aedificāmus. hunc mūrum aedificāvimus; mūrō aedificātō, tum viās fēcimus; illīs viīs factīs, nunc <u>fossās</u> <u>fodimus</u>. omnēs incolae, quī prope mūrum habitant, saevissimī sunt. uxōrēs nostrae absunt; necesse est nōbis in oppida īre et invenīre fēminās saevās quās amāre <u>possīmus</u>. in hīs oppidīs tabernae sunt malae et incolae vīnum pessimum vēndunt. ducēs   15
nostrī <u>mendācēs</u> sunt: iterum et iterum <u>idem</u> dīcunt: 'pecūniam vōbis dabimus!' saepius tamen pecūnia minima nōbis data est. omnī pecūniā nostrā cōnsūmptā, nūllum vīnum, nūllās fēminās emere possumus. hīc, prope hunc mūrum habitantēs et nūllam pecūniam habentēs, miserrimī sumus.'

aliī hōrum mīlitum epistulās scrīpsērunt: 'frīgidī sumus,' in hīs epistulīs   20
scrīpsērunt. 'mittite igitur ad nōs plūrēs <u>vestēs</u>! necesse est nōbis <u>subligācula</u> nova habēre. semper sunt ventī, semper pluvia; semper frīgidī et miserrimī sumus.'

aliī tamen mīlitum alia putābant: quamquam propter frīgus pluviamque aliī mīlitum miserrimī erant, aliī erant laetiōrēs quod putābant mūrum optimum   25
esse. 'hic mūrus,' inquiunt, 'ā plūrimīs vidēbitur. hic mūrus est longior meliorque quam aliī mūrī. fortasse plūrimōs annōs hic mūrus in hōc locō manēbit. fortasse hic mūrus in hōc locō manēbit diūtius quam Rōmānī. fortasse, ubi omnēs Rōmānī mortuī erunt, aliae gentēs hunc mūrum vidēbunt et propter hunc mūrum poterunt intellegere multa dē Rōmānīs.'   30

imperātor, imperātōris, m	emperor
castra, castrōrum, n pl	camp
Calēdoniī, Calēdoniōrum, m pl	Scots
potēns, potentis	powerful
frīgus, frīgoris, n	cold
pluvia, pluviae, f	rain
sōl, sōlis, m	sun
frīgidus, frīgida, frīgidum	cold
cotīdiē	every day
sarcina, sarcinae, f	baggage; bag
fossa, fossae, f	ditch
fodiō, fodere, fōdī, fossum	dig
possīmus	'we might be able'
mendāx, mendācis	deceitful, a liar
idem	'the same thing'
vestis, vestis, f	clothes
subligāculum, subligāculī, n	underwear

Chapter 12: Additional Language

SECTION A12: CHAPTER 12 VOCABULARY

Exercise A12.1: Derivations

The following sentences contain derivations from Latin vocabulary for Chapter 12. Explain the meaning of the word in **purple** and give the Latin word that it comes from.

1. The existence of **capital** punishment is a very controversial issue.
2. Owls and bats are **nocturnal** creatures.
3. **Portable** devices are very useful for long journeys.
4. Perhaps a **sedentary** lifestyle is bad for our health.
5. The USA has a written **constitution** which begins with the words, 'We the people'.
6. The museum has an impressive **collection** of Roman artefacts.
7. The waterfall **cascades** over the steep rocks.
8. This **tractor** pulls agricultural machinery on the farm.
9. The ice-cream **vendor** displayed an impressive variety of flavours.
10. We **insulate** our homes to stay warm in winter and cool in summer.

Exercise A12.2: Case endings

Circle the stem, give the meaning, and identify the declension of the following nouns and adjectives from Chapter 12. Then give the new form requested. Remember that **nēmō** and **nūllus** are irregular; you can see their forms on p251 in the Reference Grammar.

	Latin	meaning	declension	
1	**nēmō**, nūllīus			accusative sg =
2	**nūllus**, nūlla, nūllum			accusative feminine sg =
3	gravis, grave			nominative masculine pl =
4	nox, noctis, f			ablative sg =
5	caput, capitis, n			nominative pl =
6	ventus, ventī, m			accusative pl =
7	rēgnum, rēgnī, n			ablative pl =

	Latin	meaning	declension	
8	soror, sorōris, f			accusative pl =
9	gēns, gentis, f			dative pl =
10	frāter, frātris, m			dative sg =

Exercise A12.3: Verbs

Identify the tense of the Chapter 12 verbs in the table below and translate each one. Then change the form from singular to plural, or plural to singular, keeping the tense and person the same.

Remember that you need to look at the stem as well as the ending. Here are the principal parts for each verb so that you can see their different stems.

> contendō, contendere, contendī, contentum
> effugiō, effugere, effūgī
> portō, portāre, portāvī, portātum
> vēndō, vēndere, vēndidī, vēnditum
> cadō, cadere, cecidī, cāsum
> nārrō, nārrāre, nārrāvī, nārrātum
> dēspērō, dēspērāre, dēspērāvī, dēspērātum
> sedeō, sedēre, sēdī, sessum
> colligō, colligere, collēgī, collēctum

	Latin	tense	translation	new form
1	contendit			
2	effūgimus			
3	portat			
4	vēndidit			
5	cecidistī			
6	nārrāveram			
7	dēspērant			
8	cadēbant			
9	sedēs			
10	colligēs			

SECTION B12: GRAMMAR

Exercise B12.1: Future passive

This exercise practises verbs from the vocabulary lists for Chapter 11 and Chapter 12.

Translate these future passive verbs into English.

	Latin	translation
1	portābuntur	
2	cōnstituētur	
3	colligentur	
4	trahar	
5	vēndēmur	
6	nūntiābitur	
7	servāberis	
8	relinquēminī	
9	accipiēris	
10	reducentur	

Exercise B12.2: Conjugations and the future passive

This exercise practises verbs from the vocabulary lists for Chapters 10–12.

Here is a reminder of the future passive in all four conjugations.

	1st conjugation	2nd conjugation	3rd conjugation	4th conjugation
I	am**ābor**	terr**ēbor**	reg**ar**	aud**iar**
you (sg)	am**āberis**	terr**ēberis**	reg**ēris**	aud**iēris**
he / she / it	am**ābitur**	terr**ēbitur**	reg**ētur**	aud**iētur**
we	am**ābimur**	terr**ēbimur**	reg**ēmur**	aud**iēmur**
you (pl)	am**ābiminī**	terr**ēbiminī**	reg**ēminī**	aud**iēminī**
they	am**ābuntur**	terr**ēbuntur**	reg**entur**	aud**ientur**

Look it up! For the future passive endings for the mixed conjugation, see p240.

Identify the conjugation of each of the following and then give the future passive form requested.

	Latin verb	conjugation	
1	portō, portāre, portāvī, portātum		we shall be carried =
2	accipiō, accipere, accēpī, acceptum		you (sg) will be received =
3	trahō, trahere, trāxī, tractum		they will be dragged =
4	doceō, docēre, docuī, doctum		she will be taught =
5	inveniō, invenīre, invēnī, inventum		I shall be found =

Exercise B12.3: Cases: noun and adjective agreement

This exercise practises nouns and adjectives from the vocabulary lists for Chapters 10–12.

Make each adjective agree with its noun and then translate each noun and adjective phrase.

Remember that **alius** and **nūllus** have irregular endings: you can see these on pp250–251 in the Reference Grammar.

	adjective	noun	adjective form	translation
1	celer, celeris, celere	ventum		
2	**alius**, alia, aliud	rēgnum		
3	validus, valida, validum	capita		
4	cārus, cāra, cārum	sorōrem		
5	**nūllus**, nūlla, nūllum	gentēs		
6	cārus, cāra, cārum	frātrī		
7	mīrābilis, mīrābile	nocte		
8	tūtus, tūta, tūtum	īnsulīs		
9	gravis, grave	poētam		
10	celer, celeris, celere	sociōs		

Exercise B12.4: Present participles

This exercises focuses on present participles from the verbs in the vocabulary list for Chapter 12.

Complete the sentence with the correct present participle to agree with the noun in **purple**. You will need to think about the case of the noun it describes. Then translate the whole sentence into English.

1. **mīles** (dēspērāns / dēspērantēs) socium vulnerātum tenēbat.
2. **servus** cibum (portāns / portantem) ā dominō laudātus est.
3. servī plūs vīnī **frātrī** (sedentī / sedēns) dedērunt.
4. gēns perterrita ā **mīlitibus** (contendentēs / contendentibus) effūgit.
5. **nautae** ē nāvibus (effugiēns / effugientēs) dēspērābant.
6. **dux** (sedentem / sedēns) prope equum vulnerātum lacrimābat.
7. **sagittās** dē caelō (cadentēs / cadentem) timēbāmus.
8. invēnistīne in forō, ō puellae, **hominem** servōs (vēndentem / vēndentēs)?
9. **ancillae** līberōs (colligēns / colligentēs) ā dominā laudābantur.
10. **frātrēs** per silvam (errantēs / errāns) locum bonum quaerēbant.

Exercise B12.5: Perfect passive participles

This exercises focuses on PPPs from the verbs in the vocabulary lists for Chapter 11 and Chapter 12.

Choose the correct Latin perfect passive participle to agree with the noun in **purple** in each of the following sentences. Then translate the whole sentence into English.

1. nōs **dōnum** in templum (portātus / portātum) deīs dedimus.
2. **incolae** ā sociīs (servātae / servātī) laetissimī erant.
3. **equus** in agrum (tractus / tracta) laetē currēbat.
4. servum laudāvistī propter **epistulās** (acceptās / accepta).
5. **cōnsilium** ā senātōribus (nūntiātum / nūntiātīs) erat difficile et grave.
6. saepissimē **corpora** ā proeliō (tracta / tractī) mortua erant.
7. **hasta** ā frātre (vēnditae / vēndita) ducem mīlitum graviter vulnerāvit.
8. domina **ancillās** (collēcta / collēctās) pūniēbat.
9. tandem **hostēs** (reductī / reductōs) periērunt.
10. **iuvenis** ā patre (relictus / relictōs) librōs legēbat.

SECTION C12: ENGLISH TO LATIN SENTENCES

Exercise C12.1: Ablative absolutes

The following sentences contain a literal English equivalent of a Latin ablative absolute phrase.

Write the Latin for each of the ablative absolute phrases in **purple**. Then, rewrite each sentence in more natural English.

1. **(With) the book having been read**, the boy was no longer stupid.
2. **(With) the citizens walking into the forum**, suddenly the senator died.
3. **(With) the town having been defended**, the inhabitants were not overpowered.
4. **(With) the children sleeping**, the parents drank the wine.
5. **(With) the men having been punished**, the gods smiled.
6. **(With) food having been prepared**, they began to eat dinner.

Exercise C12.2: Sentences to translate into Latin

1. No young men will die today because the city is being defended by our allies.
2. I thought that no one was saving the temple of the gods.
3. No one will be killed because our men always fight most fiercely.
4. O son, do not stray! It is much safer for you to stay on the road.
5. Because he had conquered more tribes, this leader was much more famous than that one.
6. The enemy, who had gathered together at first light, were being guarded. When night came, they were killed.
7. Despairing, the sailors, who were the first to escape, guarded their ships and asked for help.
8. The women could neither read nor write, but they were very often praised on account of their children.
9. The sad sailor, sitting near the sea, was weeping for many hours. He was despairing because he could not return to his own homeland.
10. The sailor said that the sea was very cruel and there was great danger in the waves.

SECTION D: CONSOLIDATION

Exercises for Additional Language Section D are available on the companion website. Exercises are structured by grammatical category, and cover all Core Vocabulary met so far within each category. For Chapter 12, these exercises are as follows:

- Exercise D12.1: Chapter 7 and Chapter 8 accusative nouns
- Exercise D12.2: Chapter 9 and Chapter 10 genitive nouns
- Exercise D12.3: Chapter 11 and Chapter 12 dative nouns

REFERENCE GRAMMAR

NOUNS

Cases

Latin uses different case endings to show a noun's role in a sentence. The main roles are as follows:

nominative	• the subject of the sentence, e.g. The **father** loves his daughter. / The **general** is killed by the soldier.
vocative	• a noun which is directly addressed, e.g. O **king**, do not punish us!
accusative	• the object of an active verb, e.g. The father loves his **daughter**. • after certain prepositions • in time phrases to show how long, e.g. **for three hours** • for the subject of an infinitive • for the names of towns to show motion towards that town
genitive	• used to show that one noun is connected to another: most typically it shows possession, e.g. the **father's** daughter • often best translated as *of*
dative	• the indirect object, used to mean *to* or *for* • after certain verbs such as *persuādeō* • to show possession
ablative	• used without a preposition to mean *by, with* or *from* • after certain prepositions • in time phrases to show when, e.g. **in the second year** • with the names of towns to show motion away from that town • within a comparison to mean *than*

Latin has one more case – the **locative** case – which is used mainly for the names of towns and small islands. The locative case shows that someone or something is in or at that place. The locative case looks identical to the ablative case, with the exception of singular 1st and 2nd declension nouns; for these, the locative looks the same as the genitive.

e.g. Rōmae senātōrem clārissimum cōnspexī. – At Rome I saw a very famous senator.

Declensions

There are three main groups of Latin nouns; nouns in each group (declension) share the same endings.

You can identify the declension of a noun by looking at how it is listed in a dictionary or word list. The nominative and genitive singular forms are given, together with the gender.

The genitive singular allows us to work out the declension of the noun and its stem.

fēmina, **fēminae**, f	1st declension feminine	stem = fēmin-
deus, **deī**, m	2nd declension masculine	stem = de-
bellum, **bellī**, n	2nd declension neuter	stem = bell-
rēx, **rēgis**, m	3rd declension masculine	stem = rēg-
flūmen, **flūminis**, n	3rd declension neuter	stem = flūmin-

N.B. Neuter nouns have slightly different endings from masculine / feminine nouns in the same declension.

1st declension	
nominative sg	fēmin-a
accusative sg	fēmin-am
genitive sg	fēmin-ae
dative sg	fēmin-ae
ablative sg	fēmin-ā
nominative pl	fēmin-ae
accusative pl	fēmin-ās
genitive pl	fēmin-ārum
dative pl	fēmin-īs
ablative pl	fēmin-īs

- *fēmina* is a feminine noun; masculine first declension nouns (e.g. *agricola*) have exactly the same endings. There are no neuter nouns in the 1st declension.
- in the 1st declension, vocative endings are the same as the nominative

2nd declension		neuter nouns
nominative sg	de-us	bell-um
accusative sg	de-um	bell-um
genitive sg	de-ī	bell-ī
dative sg	de-ō	bell-ō
ablative sg	de-ō	bell-ō
nominative pl	de-ī	bell-a
accusative pl	de-ōs	bell-a
genitive pl	de-ōrum	bell-ōrum
dative pl	de-īs	bell-īs
ablative pl	de-īs	bell-īs

- *deus* is a masculine noun; feminine second declension nouns are extremely rare and have exactly the same endings
- second declension nouns have a separate vocative singular ending as follows:
  - for nouns such as *servus, servī, m* the vocative is *serve*
  - for nouns such as *fīlius, fīliī, m* the vocative is *fīlī*
  - *deus* has an irregular vocative singular form *deus*
- for the vocative plural, the ending is the same as the nominative plural
- some second declension masculine nouns have a nominative sg ending in *-er* e.g. *puer, puerī* and *ager, agrī*

3rd declension		neuter nouns
nominative sg	(rēx)	(flūmen)
accusative sg	rēg-em	(flūmen)
genitive sg	rēg-is	flūmin-is
dative sg	rēg-ī	flūmin-ī
ablative sg	rēg-e	flūmin-e
nominative pl	rēg-ēs	flūmin-a
accusative pl	rēg-ēs	flūmin-a
genitive pl	rēg-um	flūmin-um
dative pl	rēg-ibus	flūmin-ibus
ablative pl	rēg-ibus	flūmin-ibus

- *rēx* is a masculine noun; feminine and masculine 3rd declension nouns have the same endings
- there is no uniform ending for the nominative singular (or for neuter nouns the nominative and accusative singular). This is why *rēx* and *flūmen* are written in brackets: they cannot serve as a template for another 3rd declension nominative singular.
- vocative endings in the 3rd declension are the same as the nominative
- some nouns in the 3rd declension have *-ium* as their genitive plural ending: typically these are nouns such as *hostis* (where the genitive singular and the nominative singular are the same) or nouns such as *mōns* (where the nominative singular ends in two consonants). The nouns you have met of this type in *de Romanis* are as follows: *mōns, urbs, cīvis, hostis, mors, nāvis, pars, gēns*. In addition, *mare* has unusual endings; these are listed in full on p250.

ADJECTIVES

There are two main types of adjectives: those with a mixture of 2nd and 1st declension endings, and those with 3rd declension endings.

Adjectives must agree with the noun they describe in case, gender and number.

It is fairly common for an adjective to be used without a noun: in these circumstances the gender of the adjective should guide its translation.

e.g. *īrātī rēgem interfēcērunt.* – The angry men killed the king.

For further notes on the use of adjectives, see Chapter 10, pp128–129.

2-1-2 adjectives

	masculine	feminine	neuter
nominative sg	īrāt-us	īrāt-a	īrāt-um
accusative sg	īrāt-um	īrāt-am	īrāt-um
genitive sg	īrāt-ī	īrāt-ae	īrāt-ī
dative sg	īrāt-ō	īrāt-ae	īrāt-ō
ablative sg	īrāt-ō	īrāt-ā	īrāt-ō
nominative pl	īrāt-ī	īrāt-ae	īrāt-a
accusative pl	īrāt-ōs	īrāt-ās	īrāt-a
genitive pl	īrāt-ōrum	īrāt-ārum	īrāt-ōrum
dative pl	īrāt-īs	īrāt-īs	īrāt-īs
ablative pl	īrāt-īs	īrāt-īs	īrāt-īs

N.B. As with some 2nd declension nouns, some 2-1-2 adjectives have a nominative masculine sg ending in *-er,* for example *pulcher, pulchra, pulchrum* and *miser, misera, miserum.*

3rd declension adjectives

There are two main types of 3rd declension adjectives: those with a separate neuter nominative sg ending, and those without. Each type is listed slightly differently in a word list, and the stem can be found as follows:

fortis, **fort**e   – brave; strong   (nominative forms only given)

ingens, **ingent**is – huge   (nominative and genitive given)

	masculine / feminine	neuter	masculine / feminine	neuter
nominative sg	fort-is	fort-e	(ingēns)	(ingēns)
accusative sg	fort-em	fort-e	ingent-em	(ingēns)
genitive sg	fort-is	fort-is	ingent-is	ingent-is
dative sg	fort-ī	fort-ī	ingent-ī	ingent-ī
ablative sg	fort-ī	fort-ī	ingent-ī	ingent-ī
nominative pl	fort-ēs	fort-ia	ingent-ēs	ingent-ia
accusative pl	fort-ēs	fort-ia	ingent-ēs	ingent-ia
genitive pl	fort-ium	fort-ium	ingent-ium	ingent-ium
dative pl	fort-ibus	fort-ibus	ingent-ibus	ingent-ibus
ablative pl	fort-ibus	fort-ibus	ingent-ibus	ingent-ibus

N.B. *celer, celeris, celere* is an exception. It has three different nominative sg forms: *celer* (nominative masculine sg), *celeris* (nominative feminine sg) and *celere* (nominative neuter sg). For all other cases it has the same endings as *fortis*.

Comparative adjectives

Comparative adjectives are formed by adding the following endings to a noun's stem. These endings are used for all types of adjectives. They are very similar to the usual 3rd declension adjective endings.

A comparative adjective means *more . . . / rather. . . / too . . . .*

	masculine / feminine	neuter
nominative sg	laet-ior	laet-ius
accusative sg	laet-iōrem	laet-ius
genitive sg	laet-iōris	laet-iōris
dative sg	laet-iōrī	laet-iōrī
ablative sg	laet-iōre	laet-iōre
nominative pl	laet-iōrēs	laet-iōra
accusative pl	laet-iōrēs	laet-iōra
genitive pl	laet-iōrum	laet-iōrum
dative pl	laet-iōribus	laet-iōribus
ablative pl	laet-iōribus	laet-iōribus

Latin has two ways of comparing nouns:

- the ablative of comparison: e.g. *rēx cīvibus laetior erat.* – The king was happier than the citizens.
- using *quam* to mean *than*: e.g. *rēx laetior quam cīvēs erat.* – The king was happier than the citizens.

For further notes on comparison, see Chapter 8, p61.

Superlative adjectives

A superlative adjective means *very . . . / the most . . .*

Superlative adjectives are easy to recognize. The different types of adjectives you have met form their superlative in the following ways:

fortis, forte – strong	fortissimus, fortissima, fortissimum – very strong
audāx, audācis – bold	audācissimus, audācissima, audācissimum – very bold
celer, celeris, celere – quick	celerrimus, celerrima, celerrimum – very quick
pulcher, pulchra, pulchrum – beautiful	pulcherrimus, pulcherrima, pulcherrimum – very beautiful
facilis, facile – easy	facillimus, facillima, facillimum – very easy
difficilis, difficile – difficult	difficillimus, difficillima, difficillimum – very difficult

Superlative adjectives have 2-1-2 endings.

	masculine	feminine	neuter
nominative sg	īrātissim-us	īrātissim-a	īrātissim-um
accusative sg	īrātissim-um	īrātissim-am	īrātissim-um
for the other 2-1-2 case endings see p229			

Common irregular comparative and superlative adjectives

Some of Latin's most common adjectives have irregular comparative and superlative stems; the case endings used with these stems, however, are the same as for any other comparative or superlative adjective.

bonus, bona, bonum – good	melior, melius – better	optimus, optima, optimum – best
malus, mala, malum – bad	peior, peius – worse	pessimus, pessima, pessimum – worst
magnus, magna, magnum – big	maior, maius – bigger	maximus, maxima, maximum – largest
parvus, parva, parvum – small	minor, minus – smaller	minimus, minima, minimum – smallest; least
multus, multa, multum – much; many	plūs – more *	plūrimus, plūrima, plūrimum – most; very many

*N.B. *plūs* is unusual in the way it is used: for more details see Appendix 1 p252.

PRONOUNS

Pronouns are words that can be used instead of nouns. Pronouns change their endings according to the gender and number of the noun they represent, and they take the case that is right for their role in the sentence.

is, ea, id

is, ea, id usually means *he, she, it, they*; used with a noun (rather than on its own) it can mean *that, those*.

e.g. *eum rēgem timēbam.* – I feared that king.

he / she / it	masculine	feminine	neuter		masculine	feminine	neuter
nominative sg	is	ea	id	nominative pl	eī	eae	ea
accusative sg	eum	eam	id	accusative pl	eōs	eās	ea
genitive sg	eius	eius	eius	genitive pl	eōrum	eārum	eōrum
dative sg	eī	eī	eī	dative pl	eīs	eīs	eīs
ablative sg	eō	eā	eō	ablative pl	eīs	eīs	eīs

hic, haec, hoc and *ille, illa, illud*

hic, haec, hoc usually means *this* or *these*. *ille, illa, illud* usually means *that* or *those*.

Sometimes *ille, illa, illud* is used to mean *he, she, it*, especially when there is a change in subject.

e.g. *pater fīlium pūnīvit: ille trīstis erat.* – The father punished the son: he was sad.

Both these pronouns are often used on their own to mean *that man*, or *those women*, or *these things* etc.

e.g. *haec audīvit.* – He heard these things.

this / these	masculine	feminine	neuter		masculine	feminine	neuter
nominative sg	hic	haec	hoc	nominative pl	hī	hae	haec
accusative sg	hunc	hanc	hoc	accusative pl	hōs	hās	haec
genitive sg	huius	huius	huius	genitive pl	hōrum	hārum	hōrum
dative sg	huic	huic	huic	dative pl	hīs	hīs	hīs
ablative sg	hōc	hāc	hōc	ablative pl	hīs	hīs	hīs

that / those	masculine	feminine	neuter		masculine	feminine	neuter
nominative sg	ille	illa	illud	nominative pl	illī	illae	illa
accusative sg	illum	illam	illud	accusative pl	illōs	illās	illa
genitive sg	illīus	illīus	illīus	genitive pl	illōrum	illārum	illōrum
dative sg	illī	illī	illī	dative pl	illīs	illīs	illīs
ablative sg	illō	illā	illō	ablative pl	illīs	illīs	illīs

quī, quae, quod

quī, quae, quod means *who* or *which*. It is known as the relative pronoun, because it introduces a clause that relates to a noun in the sentence.

Like any other pronoun it takes its gender and number from the noun it represents, and its case from its role in the sentence. Because the relative pronoun is used in a different clause from the noun it relates to, it may have a different role in its own clause and so it may need a different case.

who / which	masculine	feminine	neuter		masculine	feminine	neuter
nominative sg	quī	quae	quod	nominative pl	quī	quae	quae
accusative sg	quem	quam	quod	accusative pl	quōs	quās	quae
genitive sg	cuius	cuius	cuius	genitive pl	quōrum	quārum	quōrum
dative sg	cui	cui	cui	dative pl	quibus	quibus	quibus
ablative sg	quō	quā	quō	ablative pl	quibus	quibus	quibus

quis, quis, quid

The question word *quis, quis, quid* – *who? what? which?* looks very similar to the relative pronoun; it only has different endings for its nominative sg (and neuter accusative sg) forms.

who? / what? / which?	masculine	feminine	neuter		masculine	feminine	neuter
nominative sg	quis	quis	quid	nominative pl	qui	quae	quae
accusative sg	quem	quam	quid	accusative pl	quōs	quās	quae
genitive sg	cuius	cuius	cuius	genitive pl	quōrum	quārum	quōrum
dative sg	cui	cui	cui	dative pl	quibus	quibus	quibus
ablative sg	quō	quā	quō	ablative pl	quibus	quibus	quibus

Personal pronouns

Like other pronouns, personal pronouns have different case endings, and like other pronouns their case depends upon their role in their clause.

	I	you (sg)	we	you (pl)	himself, herself, itself	themselves
nominative	ego	tū	nōs	vōs		
accusative	mē	tē	nōs	vōs	sē	sē
genitive	meī	tuī	nostrum	vestrum	suī	suī
dative	mihī	tibī	nōbis	vōbis	sibi	sibi
ablative	mē	tē	nōbis	vōbis	sē	sē

Unlike other pronouns, they do not have different forms for different genders.

sē is known as the reflexive pronoun; this means that it has to refer to the subject of the sentence. This is why it has no nominative form: it has to refer to the subject and so can never be used as the subject. Unlike all other pronouns, *sē* does not have different singular and plural forms.

e.g. *rēx sē interfēcit.* – The king killed himself.
cīvēs sē interfēcērunt. – The citizens killed themselves.
rēx eum interfēcit. – The king killed him.

ADVERBS

Like English, Latin can turn adjectives into adverbs by changing their endings.

The two main adverb endings are *-ē* and *-ter*.

laetus, laeta, laetum – happy → laetē – happily
fortis, forte – brave; strong → fortiter – bravely; strongly

Latin also has lots of adverbs which do not use these endings; examples of these are:

etiam	also; even	celeriter	quickly
saepe	often	diū	for a long time
tum	then	ōlim	once; some time ago
fortiter	bravely; strongly	subitō	suddenly
nōn	not	tandem	at last; finally

semper	always	hīc	here
iterum	again	iam	now; already
magnopere	greatly; very much	ibi	there
mox	soon	numquam	never
nunc	now	sīc	thus; in this way

Sometimes adjectives are used instead of adverbs.

e.g. *līberī prīmī fūgērunt.* – The children were the first to flee.

māter īrāta fīliōs pūnīvit. – The mother punished her sons angrily.

For further notes on adverbs, see Chapter 11 pp166–167.

Comparative and superlative adverbs

Adverbs also have comparative and superlative forms: as for normal adverbs, the endings for each of these do not change.

Here are some examples:

adverb	comparative adverb	superlative adverb
fortiter – bravely	fortius – more bravely	fortissimē – most bravely
celeriter – quickly	celerius – more quickly	celerrimē – most quickly
ferōciter – fiercely	ferōcius – more fiercely	ferōcissimē – most fiercely
saepe – often	saepius – more often	saepissimē – most often
diū – for a long time	diūtius – for rather a long time	diūtissimē – for a very long time
magnopere – greatly	magis – more	maximē – very greatly

If *quam* is used with a superlative adverb, it means *as . . . as possible.*

e.g. *quam celerrimē cucurrī.* – I ran as quickly as possible.

PREPOSITIONS

A preposition is a word that is positioned before a noun and shows its relationship to something else in the sentence.

In Latin, each preposition has to be followed by a particular case: this is usually the accusative or the ablative. The case required by a preposition is listed in a dictionary or word list, for example:

ad	+ accusative	to; towards; at
contrā	+ accusative	against
in	+ accusative	into
ā, ab	+ ablative	from; away from; by
ē, ex	+ ablative	from; out of; out from
in	+ ablative	in; on

QUESTION WORDS

Like English, Latin has several words which are used to ask a question. It is usual for the question word to be the first word in the sentence.

There are three different words used to introduce questions which have *yes* or *no* as their answer.

-ne	invites the answer *yes* or *no*
nōnne . . .?	invites the answer *yes*
num . . . ?	invites the answer *no*

-ne is used at the end of the first word in the question, which typically will be a verb.

e.g. *tulistīne ad templum dōna?* – Did you bring gifts to the temple?

There are different question words for questions that do not have *yes* or *no* as their answers. These include:

cūr?	why?	quis / quis / quid?	who? what?
quandō?	when?	quō?	to where?
ubi?	where?	unde?	from where?

quis / quis / quid is a pronoun and so it changes its endings: it takes the number and gender of the noun it represents and the case needed for its own role in the sentence (see p233).

VERBS

Principal parts

The principal parts of a verb show the verb's conjugation and stems

amō	amāre	**amāv**ī	**amāt**um
I love	to love	I loved	
present tense	infinitive	perfect tense	supine
present stem		**perfect stem**	**supine stem**

The present stem is used for the present, imperfect and future tenses; the perfect stem is used for the perfect and pluperfect tenses; the supine stem is used for the perfect passive participle (PPP).

Conjugations

There are four main groups of Latin verbs. Verbs in each group (conjugation) share the same endings.

The first two principal parts show which conjugation a verb is in:

am**ō**	am**āre**	amāvī	amātum	1st conjugation
terr**eō**	terr**ēre**	terruī	territum	2nd conjugation
reg**ō**	reg**ere**	rēxī	rēctum	3rd conjugation
aud**iō**	aud**īre**	audīvī	audītum	4th conjugation

Some verbs are a mixture of the 3rd and 4th conjugations.

| cap**iō** | cap**ere** | cēpī | captum | mixed conjugation |

Infinitives

An infinitive is listed as the second principal part of a Latin verb. It can be translated as follows: *amāre – to love*.

The vowel used for the infinitive ending depends on the verb's conjugation.

conjugation	infinitive	meaning	conjugation	infinitive	meaning
1st	am**ā**re	to love	4th	aud**ī**re	to hear
2nd	terr**ē**re	to frighten	mixed	cap**e**re	to capture
3rd	reg**e**re	to rule			

Infinitives are often used in Latin just like in English, e.g. *Rōmulus Rōmānōs pugnāre iūssit. –* Romulus ordered the Romans to fight.

If an adjective is used with an infinitive it will be neuter in gender, e.g. *difficile erat pugnāre. –* It was difficult to fight.

Sometimes an infinitive is used with a noun, e.g. *tempus erat fugere. –* It was time to flee.

If the infinitive has a subject, it will be in the accusative case, e.g. *volō puellās audīre. –* I want the girls to listen.

It is very common for an infinitive and its accusative subject to follow a verb of saying / thinking / knowing. e.g. *dīxī Rōmānōs pugnāre. –* I said that the Romans were fighting.

This is known as indirect statement; for further notes, see Chapter 11, p172.

Active and passive

A verb form is either active or passive.

- The subject of an active verb does the action: e.g. The senator heard the citizens.
- The subject of a passive verb suffers or experiences the action: e.g. The citizens were heard by the senator.
- Remember, the subject of a verb will be nominative, whether or not the verb is active or passive.

Present tense (active)

Verbs in the present tense use the present stem and the following endings; the vowel depends on a verb's conjugation.

The present active can be translated as follows: *amō – I love* or *I am loving*.

present active	1st conjugation	2nd conjugation	3rd conjugation	4th conjugation	mixed conjugation
I	am**ō**	terr**eō**	reg**ō**	aud**iō**	cap**iō**
you (sg)	am**ā**s	terr**ē**s	reg**is**	aud**ī**s	cap**is**
he / she / it	am**a**t	terr**e**t	reg**it**	aud**i**t	cap**i**t
we	am**ā**mus	terr**ē**mus	reg**imus**	aud**ī**mus	cap**imus**
you (pl)	am**ā**tis	terr**ē**tis	reg**itis**	aud**ī**tis	cap**itis**
they	am**a**nt	terr**e**nt	reg**unt**	aud**iunt**	cap**iunt**

Present tense (passive)

Verbs in the present tense use the present stem and the following endings; the vowel used depends on a verb's conjugation:

The present passive can be translated as follows: *amor* – *I am loved* or *I am being loved*.

present passive	1st conjugation	2nd conjugation	3rd conjugation	4th conjugation	mixed conjugation
I	am**or**	terr**eor**	reg**or**	aud**ior**	cap**ior**
you (sg)	am**āris**	terr**ēris**	reg**eris**	aud**īris**	cap**eris**
he / she / it	am**ātur**	terr**ētur**	reg**itur**	aud**ītur**	cap**itur**
we	am**āmur**	terr**ēmur**	reg**imur**	aud**īmur**	cap**imur**
you (pl)	am**āminī**	terr**ēminī**	reg**iminī**	aud**īminī**	cap**iminī**
they	am**antur**	terr**entur**	reg**untur**	aud**iuntur**	cap**iuntur**

Imperfect tense (active)

Verbs in the imperfect tense use the present stem; the vowel used depends on the verb's conjugation.

The imperfect tense is used in Latin for past actions that are viewed as ongoing, or lasting quite a long time.

The imperfect active can be translated in three main ways:

regēbam – I was ruling / I used to rule / I began to rule

N.B. Although in Latin the imperfect is used for actions which typically last for some time, in English we are often more likely to use the perfect tense. This means that sometimes the best translation for a Latin imperfect tense is an English perfect tense.

e.g. *diū rēx regēbat.* – The king ruled for a long time.

imperfect active	1st conjugation	2nd conjugation	3rd conjugation	4th conjugation	mixed conjugation
I	am**ābam**	terr**ēbam**	reg**ēbam**	aud**iēbam**	cap**iēbam**
you (sg)	am**ābās**	terr**ēbās**	reg**ēbās**	aud**iēbās**	cap**iēbās**
he / she / it	am**ābat**	terr**ēbat**	reg**ēbat**	aud**iēbat**	cap**iēbat**
we	am**ābāmus**	terr**ēbāmus**	reg**ēbāmus**	aud**iēbāmus**	cap**iēbāmus**
you (pl)	am**ābātis**	terr**ēbātis**	reg**ēbātis**	aud**iēbātis**	cap**iēbātis**
they	am**ābant**	terr**ēbant**	reg**ēbant**	aud**iēbant**	cap**iēbant**

Imperfect tense (passive)

Verbs in the imperfect passive use the present stem; the vowel used depends on the verb's conjugation.

The imperfect passive can be translated as follows: *amābar – I was being loved* or *I used to be loved* or *I began to be loved.*

N.B. Although in Latin the imperfect is used for actions that typically last for some time, in English we are often more likely to use the perfect tense. This means that sometimes the best translation for a Latin imperfect tense is an English perfect tense.

e.g. *diū cīvēs regēbantur.* – The citizens were ruled for a long time.

imperfect passive	1st conjugation	2nd conjugation	3rd conjugation	4th conjugation	mixed conjugation
I	am**ā**b**ar**	terr**ē**b**ar**	reg**ē**b**ar**	aud**iē**b**ar**	cap**iē**b**ar**
you (sg)	am**ā**b**āris**	terr**ē**b**āris**	reg**ē**b**āris**	aud**iē**b**āris**	cap**iē**b**āris**
he / she / it	am**ā**b**ātur**	terr**ē**b**ātur**	reg**ē**b**ātur**	aud**iē**b**ātur**	cap**iē**b**ātur**
we	am**ā**b**āmur**	terr**ē**b**āmur**	reg**ē**b**āmur**	aud**iē**b**āmur**	cap**iē**b**āmur**
you (pl)	am**ā**b**āminī**	terr**ē**b**āminī**	reg**ē**b**āminī**	aud**iē**b**āminī**	cap**iē**b**āminī**
they	am**ā**b**antur**	terr**ē**b**antur**	reg**ē**b**antur**	aud**iē**b**antur**	cap**iē**b**antur**

Future tense (active)

Verbs in the future tense use the present stem and the following endings.

There are two sets of endings depending on the verb's conjugation. The 1st and 2nd conjugations share the same endings, and the 3rd and 4th conjugations share a different set of endings. The vowel used before the endings depends on the verb's conjugation.

The future active can be translated as follows: *amābō – I shall love.*

future active	1st conjugation	2nd conjugation	3rd conjugation	4th conjugation	mixed conjugation
I	am**ā**b**ō**	terr**ē**b**ō**	reg**am**	aud**iam**	cap**iam**
you (sg)	am**ā**b**is**	terr**ē**b**is**	reg**ēs**	aud**iēs**	cap**iēs**
he / she / it	am**ā**b**it**	terr**ē**b**it**	reg**et**	aud**iet**	cap**iet**
we	am**ā**b**imus**	terr**ē**b**imus**	reg**ēmus**	aud**iēmus**	cap**iēmus**
you (pl)	am**ā**b**itis**	terr**ē**b**itis**	reg**ētis**	aud**iētis**	cap**iētis**
they	am**ā**b**unt**	terr**ē**b**unt**	reg**ent**	aud**ient**	cap**ient**

Future tense (passive)

Verbs in the future passive use the present stem and the following endings.

There are two sets of endings depending on the verb's conjugation. The 1st and 2nd conjugations share the same endings, and the 3rd and 4th conjugations share a different set of endings. The vowel used before the endings depends on the verb's conjugation.

The future passive can be translated as follows: *amābor – I shall be loved.*

future passive	1st conjugation	2nd conjugation	3rd conjugation	4th conjugation	mixed conjugation
I	am**ā**bor	terr**ē**bor	reg**ar**	aud**i**ar	cap**i**ar
you (sg)	am**ā**beris	terr**ē**beris	reg**ē**ris	aud**i**ēris	cap**i**ēris
he / she / it	am**ā**bitur	terr**ē**bitur	reg**ē**tur	aud**i**ētur	cap**i**ētur
we	am**ā**bimur	terr**ē**bimur	reg**ē**mur	aud**i**ēmur	cap**i**ēmur
you (pl)	am**ā**biminī	terr**ē**biminī	reg**ē**minī	aud**i**ēminī	cap**i**ēminī
they	am**ā**buntur	terr**ē**buntur	reg**entur**	aud**i**entur	cap**i**entur

Perfect tense (active)

All verbs in Latin use the same set of endings for the perfect tense; these endings are added to the perfect stem.

The perfect active can be translated as follows: *amāvī – I loved* or *I have loved.*

perfect active	1st conjugation	2nd conjugation	3rd conjugation	4th conjugation	mixed conjugation
I	amāv**ī**	terru**ī**	rēx**ī**	audīv**ī**	cēp**ī**
you (sg)	amāv**istī**	terru**istī**	rēx**istī**	audīv**istī**	cēp**istī**
he / she / it	amāv**it**	terru**it**	rēx**it**	audīv**it**	cēp**it**
we	amāv**imus**	terru**imus**	rēx**imus**	audīv**imus**	cēp**imus**
you (pl)	amāv**istis**	terru**istis**	rēx**istis**	audīv**istis**	cēp**istis**
they	amāv**ērunt**	terru**ērunt**	rēx**ērunt**	audīv**ērunt**	cēp**ērunt**

Perfect tense (passive)

The perfect passive uses two words: the perfect passive participle + *sum, es, est, sumus, estis, sunt.*

The perfect passive can be translated as follows: *amātus sum – I was loved* or *I have been loved.*

perfect passive	1st conjugation	2nd conjugation	3rd conjugation	4th conjugation	mixed conjugation
I	amātus sum	territus sum	rēctus sum	audītus sum	captus sum
you (sg)	amātus es	territus es	rēctus es	audītus es	captus es
he / she / it	amātus est	territus est	rēctus est	audītus est	captus est
we	amātī sumus	territī sumus	rēctī sumus	audītī sumus	captī sumus
you (pl)	amātī estis	territī estis	rēctī estis	audītī estis	captī estis
they	amātī sunt	territī sunt	rēctī sunt	audītī sunt	captī sunt

Remember that the PPP changes its endings to agree with the noun it describes. For the perfect passive, this will be its nominative subject:

e.g. The boy was loved. – puer am**ātus** est.   The gold was seized.   – aurum rapt**um** est.

The girl was loved. – puella am**āta** est.   The citizens were captured. – cīvēs capt**ī** sunt.

Pluperfect tense (active)

All verbs in Latin use the same set of endings for the pluperfect tense; these endings are added to the perfect stem.

The pluperfect active can be translated as follows: *amāveram – I had loved.*

pluperfect active	1st conjugation	2nd conjugation	3rd conjugation	4th conjugation	mixed conjugation
I	amāv**eram**	terru**eram**	rēx**eram**	audīv**eram**	cēp**eram**
you (sg)	amāv**erās**	terru**erās**	rēx**erās**	audīv**erās**	cēp**erās**
he / she / it	amāv**erat**	terru**erat**	rēx**erat**	audīv**erat**	cēp**erat**
we	amāv**erāmus**	terru**erāmus**	rēx**erāmus**	audīv**erāmus**	cēp**erāmus**
you (pl)	amāv**erātis**	terru**erātis**	rēx**erātis**	audīv**erātis**	cēp**erātis**
they	amāv**erant**	terru**erant**	rēx**erant**	audīv**erant**	cēp**erant**

Pluperfect tense (passive)

The pluperfect passive uses two words: the perfect passive participle + *eram, erās, erat, erāmus, erātis, erant.*

The pluperfect passive can be translated as follows: *amātus eram – I had been loved.*

pluperfect passive	1st conjugation	2nd conjugation	3rd conjugation	4th conjugation	mixed conjugation
I	amātus eram	territus eram	rēctus eram	audītus eram	captus eram
you (sg)	amātus erās	territus erās	rēctus erās	audītus erās	captus erās
he / she / it	amātus erat	territus erat	rēctus erat	audītus erat	captus erat
we	amātī erāmus	territī erāmus	rēctī erāmus	audītī erāmus	captī erāmus
you (pl)	amātī erātis	territī erātis	rēctī erātis	audītī erātis	captī erātis
they	amātī erant	territī erant	rēctī erant	audītī erant	captī erant

Remember that the PPP changes its endings to agree with the noun it describes. For the perfect passive, this will be its nominative subject:

e.g. The boy had been loved. – puer am**ātus** erat.   The gold had been seized.   – aurum rapt**um** erat.

The girl had been loved. – puella am**āta** erat.   The citizens had been captured. – cīvēs capt**ī** erant.

Imperatives

An imperative is the part of the verb used to give a command or an order directly to someone.

The imperative can be translated as follows: *amā – love!*

Imperatives use the present stem of the verb, and so the endings are slightly different in each of the conjugations.

	1st conjugation	2nd conjugation	3rd conjugation	4th conjugation	mixed conjugation
imperative (sg)	am**ā**	terr**ē**	reg**e**	aud**ī**	cap**e**
imperative (pl)	am**āte**	terr**ēte**	reg**ite**	aud**īte**	cap**ite**

To tell someone not to do something, *nōlī* (sg), *nōlīte* (pl) is used with the infinitive:

e.g. *ō rēx, nōlī rēgīnam interficere!* – O king, do not kill the queen!

ō līberī, nōlīte clāmāre!   – Children, do not shout!

nōlī / nōlīte are the imperatives of *nōlō*.

PARTICIPLES

Present participles

A participle behaves like an adjective: the present participle describes a noun as *doing* an action. Like any adjective, the present participle must agree with the noun it describes.

e.g. *puerōs rīdēntēs videō. –* I see the laughing boys.

1st conjugation	am**āns**, am**antis** – loving	4th conjugation	aud**iēns**, aud**ientis** – listening
2nd conjugation	terr**ēns**, terr**entis** – terrifying	mixed conjugation	cap**iēns**, cap**ientis** – taking
3rd conjugation	reg**ēns**, reg**entis** – ruling		

All present participles use 3rd declension adjective endings, and decline like *ingēns, ingēntis*.

	masculine / feminine	neuter
nominative sg	regēns	regēns
accusative sg	regent-em	regēns
genitive sg	regent-is	regent-is
dative sg	regent-ī	regent-ī
ablative sg	regent-ī	regent-ī
nominative pl	regent-ēs	regent-ia
accusative pl	regent-ēs	regent-ia
genitive pl	regent-ium	regent-ium
dative pl	regent-ibus	regent-ibus
ablative pl	regent-ibus	regent-ibus

In some circumstances (e.g. an ablative absolute), present participles use *-e* for their ablative sg ending, e.g. *regēnte*.

Perfect passive participles

The PPP is formed from the fourth principal part of the verb. It declines like a 2-1-2 adjective, such as *īrātus*.

rēct-us, rēct-a, rēct-um – having been ruled

The literal translation is often unwieldy, and it can be better to translate the participle phrase with a clause.

e.g. *dux vulnerātus mortuus est.* – The having been wounded commander is dead.
→ The commander, who has been wounded, is dead.

epistulam scrīptam lēgī. – I read the having been written letter
→ I read the letter, which had been written.

1st conjugation	amātus, amāta, amātum – having been loved
2nd conjugation	territus, territa, territum – having been frightened
3rd conjugation	rēctus, rēcta, rēctum – having been ruled
4th conjugation	audītus, audīta, audītum – having been heard
mixed conjugation	captus, capta, captum – having been captured

Ablative absolute

It is very common for a participle to be used to describe a noun that is grammatically unconnected to the rest of the sentence. In this circumstance the ablative case is used and the construction is known as the ablative absolute.

e.g. *vīllīs incēnsīs, incolae effūgērunt.* – (With) their houses having been burned, the inhabitants fled.

In an ablative absolute, it is usual for an ablative singular participle to use the alternative ablative ending *-e*, e.g. *regēnte*.

For further notes on the ablative absolute and how best to translate it, see Chapter 12, p209.

IRREGULAR VERBS

sum, esse, fuī – *be*

	present – *I am, etc.*	imperfect – *I was, etc.*	future – *I shall be, etc.*
I	sum	eram	erō
you (sg)	es	erās	eris
he / she / it	est	erat	erit
we	sumus	erāmus	erimus
you (pl)	estis	erātis	eritis
they	sunt	erant	erunt

As for all Latin verbs, the perfect tense is formed from the perfect stem with the usual perfect endings: *fuī* (*I have been*) etc.

The pluperfect tense is formed from the perfect stem with the usual pluperfect endings: *fueram* (*I had been*) etc.

It is unusual, however, to meet the perfect and pluperfect tenses of *sum*. This is because Latin typically uses the imperfect tense for the past tense of verbs referring to actions that naturally last for some time.

possum, posse, potuī – *can, be able*

	present – *I am able, etc.*	imperfect – *I was able, etc.*	future – *I shall be able, etc.*
I	possum	poteram	poterō
you (sg)	potes	poterās	poteris
he / she / it	potest	poterat	poterit
we	possumus	poterāmus	poterimus
you (pl)	potestis	poterātis	poteritis
they	possunt	poterant	poterunt

As for all Latin verbs, the perfect tense is formed from the perfect stem with the usual perfect endings: *potuī* (*I have been able*) etc.

The pluperfect tense is formed from the perfect stem with the usual pluperfect endings: *potueram* (*I had been able*) etc.

It is unusual, however, to meet the perfect and pluperfect tenses of *possum*. This is because Latin typically uses the imperfect tense for the past tense of verbs referring to actions that naturally last for some time.

eō, īre, īvī (or iī) – *go*

	present – *I go, etc.*	imperfect – *I was going, etc.*	future – *I shall go, etc.*
I	eō	ībam	ībō
you (sg)	īs	ībās	ībis
he / she / it	it	ībat	ībit
we	īmus	ībāmus	ībimus
you (pl)	ītis	ībātis	ībitis
they	eunt	ībant	ībunt

As for all Latin verbs, the perfect tense is formed from the perfect stem with the usual perfect endings: *īvī* (*I have gone*) etc.

The pluperfect tense is formed from the perfect stem with the usual pluperfect endings: *īveram* (*I had gone*) etc.

In compound verbs (e.g. *abeō*) it is more usual for the alternative perfect stem to be used: *abiī* (*I have gone away*) etc.

present participle	iēns, euntis – going

imperative sg	ī – go!
imperative pl	īte

volō, velle, voluī – *want*

	present – *I want, etc.*	imperfect – *I wanted, etc.*	future – *I shall want, etc.*
I	volō	volēbam	volam
you (sg)	vīs	volēbās	volēs
he / she / it	vult	volēbat	volet
we	volumus	volēbāmus	volēmus
you (pl)	vultis	volēbātis	volētis
they	volunt	volēbant	volent

As for all Latin verbs, the perfect tense is formed from the perfect stem with the usual perfect endings: *voluī* (*I wanted*) etc.

The pluperfect tense is formed from the perfect stem with the usual pluperfect endings: *volueram* (*I had wanted*) etc.

It is unusual, however, to meet the perfect and pluperfect tenses of *volō*. This is because Latin typically uses the imperfect tense for the past tense of verbs refering to actions that naturally last for some time.

present participle	volēns, volentis – wanting

nōlō, nolle, nōluī – *not want; refuse*

	present – *I do not want, etc.*	imperfect – *I did not want, etc.*	future – *I shall not want, etc.*
I	nōlō	nōlebam	nōlam
you (sg)	nōn vīs	nōlebās	nōlēs
he / she / it	nōn vult	nōlebat	nōlet
we	nōlumus	nōlebāmus	nōlēmus
you (pl)	nōn vultis	nōlebātis	nōlētis
they	nōlunt	nōlebant	nōlent

As for all Latin verbs, the perfect tense is formed from the perfect stem with the usual perfect endings: *nōluī* (*I did not want*) etc.

The pluperfect tense is formed from the perfect stem with the usual pluperfect endings: *nōlueram* (*I had not wanted*) etc.

It is unusual, however, to meet the perfect and pluperfect tenses of *nōlō*. This is because Latin typically uses the imperfect tense for the past tense of verbs refering to actions that naturally last for some time.

present participle	nōlēns, nōlentis – not wanting

imperative sg	nōlī – do not want!
imperative pl	nōlīte

ferō, ferre, tulī, lātum – *carry; bear*

	present active *I carry, etc.*	imperfect active *I was carrying, etc.*	future active *I shall carry, etc.*	perfect active *I carried, etc.*	pluperfect active *I had carried, etc.*
I	ferō	ferēbam	feram	tulī	tuleram
you (sg)	fers	ferēbās	ferēs	tulistī	tulerās
he / she / it	fert	ferēbat	feret	tulit	tulerat
we	ferimus	ferēbāmus	ferēmus	tulimus	tulerāmus
you (pl)	fertis	ferēbātis	ferētis	tulistis	tulerātis
they	ferunt	ferēbant	ferent	tulērunt	tulerant

	present passive *I am carried, etc.*	imperfect passive *I was being carried, etc.*	future passive *I shall be carried, etc.*	perfect passive *I was carried, etc.*	pluperfect passive *I had been carried, etc.*
I	feror	ferēbar	ferar	lātus sum	lātus eram
you (sg)	ferris	ferēbāris	ferēris	lātus es	lātus erās
he / she / it	fertur	ferēbātur	ferētur	lātus est	lātus erat
we	ferimur	ferēbāmur	ferēmur	lātī sumus	lātī erāmus
you (pl)	feriminī	ferēbāminī	ferēminī	lātī estis	lātī erātis
they	feruntur	ferēbantur	ferentur	lātī sunt	lātī erant

present participle	ferēns, ferentis – carrying
perfect passive participle	lātus, lāta, lātum – having been carried

imperative sg	fer – bring!
imperative pl	ferte

NUMBERS

ūnus, ūna, ūnum	1	octō	8
duo, duae, duo	2	novem	9
trēs, tria	3	decem	10
quattuor	4	centum	100
quīnque	5	mīlle	1000
sex	6	mīlia, mīlium	1000s
septem	7		

In Latin, *ūnus, duo* and *trēs* change their endings, but the Latin words for 4–100 do not change.

mīlle is an exception: it does not change in the singular (1000), but its plural form (*mīlia* – 1000s) does change its endings and behaves like a 3rd declension neuter noun. *mīlia* is often followed by a genitive noun: e.g. *Rōmānī duo mīlia hostium interfēcērunt.* – The Romans killed 2000 enemy.

one	masculine	feminine	neuter	two	masculine	feminine	neuter
nominative	ūnus	ūna	ūnum	nominative	duo	duae	duo
accusative	ūnum	ūnam	ūnum	accusative	duōs	duās	duo
genitive	ūnīus	ūnīus	ūnīus	genitive	duōrum	duārum	duōrum
dative	ūnī	ūnī	ūnī	dative	duōbus	duābus	duōbus
ablative	ūnō	ūnā	ūnō	ablative	duōbus	duābus	duōbus

three	masculine	feminine	neuter
nominative	trēs	trēs	tria
accusative	trēs	trēs	tria
genitive	trium	trium	trium
dative	tribus	tribus	tribus
ablative	tribus	tribus	tribus

Latin also has adjectives for *first, second, third* etc.

prīmus, prīma, prīmum	first	sextus, sexta, sextum	sixth
secundus, secunda, secundum	second	septimus, septima, septimum	seventh
tertius, tertia, tertium	third	octāvus, octāva, octāvum	eighth
quārtus, quārta, quārtum	fourth	nōnus, nōna, nōnum	ninth
quīntus, quīnta, quīntum	fifth	decimus, decima, decimum	tenth

NEGATIVES

Latin has several negative words. These include:

nōn	not	nōlō, nōlle, nōluī	not want; refuse
nihil	nothing	nūllus, nūlla, nūllum	not any; no
nēmō, nūllius	no one; nobody	num . . . ?	surely not . . .? (expects the answer *no*)
neque, nec	and not; nor; neither	numquam	never

nihil, nēmō, nōlō and *nūllus* all have unusual forms. The endings for *nōlō* are listed above on p246; details of *nihil, nēmō* and *nūllus* are in Appendix 1 below (p251).

Further notes on the use of negatives are in Chapter 12, pp204–205.

REFERENCE GRAMMAR APPENDIX 1: WORDS WITH UNUSUAL FORMS

You have learned the following words in the vocabulary checklists, but each has slightly unusual forms or is used in a slightly unusual way:

- alius
- inquit
- mare
- nēmō
- necesse
- nihil
- nūllus
- plūs
- satis

alius, alia, aliud – *other; another*

alius is very like a 2-1-2 adjective, but for the nominative and accusative neuter sg and all genders of the genitive and dative sg different endings are used.

	masculine	feminine	neuter		masculine	feminine	neuter
nominative sg	alius	alia	aliud	nominative pl	aliī	aliae	alia
accusative sg	alium	aliam	aliud	accusative pl	aliōs	aliās	alia
genitive sg	alīus	alīus	alīus	genitive pl	aliōrum	aliārum	aliōrum
dative sg	aliī	aliī	aliī	dative pl	aliīs	aliīs	aliīs
ablative sg	aliō	aliā	aliō	ablative pl	aliīs	aliīs	aliīs

In the plural, *aliī. . .aliī* is often used to mean *some . . . others*, e.g. *aliī pugnābant sed aliī fugiēbant.* – Some men were fighting, but others were fleeing.

Notice also the following idiom: *aliī alia faciunt.* – Different men do different things.

inquit – *he / she / it / said*

inquit is known as a defective verb, i.e. not all its forms remain. In this course you have met only two of its forms:

inquit – he / she / it / said
inquiunt – they / said

It is the verb most often used after direct speech and, although technically present tense in form, it is usually best translated into English as a past tense.

e.g. *'omnēs līberōs amāmus,' inquiunt parentēs laetī.* – 'We love all our children,' said the happy parents.

mare – *sea*

A small number of 3rd declension nouns have endings that resemble 3rd declension adjective endings; *mare* is one of these nouns.

nominative sg	mare	nominative pl	mar-ia
accusative sg	mare	accusative pl	mar-ia
genitive sg	mar-is	genitive pl	mar-(i)um
dative sg	mar-ī	dative pl	mar-ibus
ablative sg	mar-ī	ablative pl	mar-ibus

nēmō – *no one*

nēmō is extremely irregular. Naturally enough, it has no plural forms.

nominative sg	nēmō
accusative sg	nēminem
genitive sg	nūllīus
dative sg	nēminī
ablative sg	nūllō

necesse – *necessary*

necesse is indeclinable; this means that it never changes its endings.

It is often used with a dative noun and an infinitive.

    e.g. *necesse est līberīs audīre.* – It is necessary for the children to listen.

nihil – *nothing*

nihil is usually met only in the nominative and accusative case. Since it is neuter, it has the same form for each of these cases.

nūllus, nūlla, nūllum – *not any; none*

nūllus is very similar to a 2-1-2 adjective, but it has different genitive and dative singular endings.

	masculine	feminine	neuter		masculine	feminine	neuter
nominative sg	nūll-us	nūll-a	nūll-um	nominative pl	nūll-ī	nūll-ae	nūll-a
accusative sg	nūll-um	nūll-am	nūll-um	accusative pl	nūll-ōs	nūll-ās	nūll-a
genitive sg	nūll-īus	nūll-īus	nūll-īus	genitive pl	nūll-ōrum	nūll-ārum	nūll-ōrum
dative sg	nūll-ī	nūll-ī	nūll-ī	dative pl	nūll-īs	nūll-īs	nūll-īs
ablative sg	nūll-ō	nūll-ā	nūll-ō	ablative pl	nūll-īs	nūll-īs	nūll-īs

plūs – *more*

plūs in the singular is a neuter noun and it is often followed by a genitive.

e.g. *plūs cibī mihī dā!* – Give me more food!

In the plural it is a 3rd declension adjective.

e.g. *plūrēs Rōmānī pugnābant quam incolae.* – More Romans were fighting than inhabitants.

				masculine / feminine	neuter
nominative sg	plūs	nominative pl		plūr-ēs	plūr-a
accusative sg	plūs	accusative pl		plūr-ēs	plūr-a
genitive sg	plūr-is	genitive pl		plūr-ium	plūr-ium
dative sg	plūr-ī	dative pl		plūr-ibus	plūr-ibus
ablative sg	plūr-e	ablative pl		plūr-ibus	plūr-ibus

satis – *enough*

satis is often used as an indeclinable noun, i.e. it does not change its form.

Like *plūs*, it is often followed by a genitive, e.g. *satis pecūniae habeō.* – I have enough money.

REFERENCE GRAMMAR APPENDIX 2: LATIN WORD ORDER

Latin word order is more flexible than English word order, but the following key principles apply:

- the subject is often the first word in the sentence and the verb is often the last word. This means that it is very common for the object to be written before the verb.
- adjectives are typically next to their nouns: it is common for adjectives of size / quantity to be written before their nouns, and for other adjectives to be after their nouns.
- adverbs are typically before the word they describe, which is often the verb. If the adverb applies to the whole sentence then it is usual for it to be at the very start of the sentence.
- prepositions are positioned before their nouns.
- clauses often follow temporal order, i.e. the first event comes first in the sentence, then the second, and so on.

It is common, however, for Latin to break from these principles in order to emphasize important words within a sentence. Key words can be placed at the start or end of a sentence for emphasis, or they can be arranged in patterns. Latin's most famous pattern is known as a chiasmus: in a chiasmus Latin uses word order which creates a mirror image.

e.g. *audāx   dux   laudāvit   mīlitēs   fortēs.*
   adjective   noun   verb   noun   adjective

For certain words stricter rules apply: *enim, igitur* and *tamen* are typically the second word in their sentence.

GLOSSARY OF NAMES

This glossary contains the names that are introduced at the start of each chapter and therefore not glossed elsewhere in the relevant chapter. All other names are glossed separately at the end of each Latin story.

Romans typically had three names, but they are usually referred to by only one or two of these names.

Name	Chapter	
Actium, Actiī, n	11	**Actium**, a town on the west coast of Greece, and famous for the sea battle fought there between Octavian and Antony (1st century BC)
Aegyptiī, Aegyptiōrum, m pl	10	**Egyptians**, one of the wealthiest and oldest communities in the ancient world
Aegyptus, Aegyptī, f	10	**Egypt** became a Roman province in 30 BC
Alexander, Alexandrī, m	10	**Alexander the Great**, king of Macedonia and possibly the world's most successful military leader (4th century BC)
Alexandrīa, Alexandrīae, f	10	**Alexandria**, one of ancient Egypt's most important cities, named after its founder, Alexander the Great
Augustus, Augustī, m	11	**Augustus**, the name given to Octavian when he became Rome's first emperor (1st century BC)
Boudicca, Boudiccae, f	12	**Boudicca**, queen of the Iceni and the leader of a British revolt against the Romans (1st century AD)
Britannī, Britannōrum, m pl	9,12	**Britons**, the Celtic inhabitants of Britain
Britannia, Britanniae, f	9,12	**Britannia**, the Roman province of Britain
Caesar, Caesaris, m	9,10,11	**Julius Caesar**, possibly Rome's most famous general; he was appointed dictator at Rome but murdered because some thought he wanted to be king (1st century BC)
Calgacus, Calgacī, m	12	**Calgacus**, the leader of the Caledonian tribes who fought against the Roman governor Agricola at the battle of Mount Graupius (1st century AD)
Carthāgo, Carthāginis, f	7	**Carthage**, a North African city and a leading power in the Mediterranean, finally conquered by Rome in the 2nd century BC

Name	Chapter	
Catilīna, Catilīnae, m	8	**Catiline**, the member of a distinguished but impoverished family who led a violent uprising against the consuls of Rome (1st century BC) and was put to death by Cicero
Catō, Catōnis, m	8	**Cato the Elder**, a conservative and distinguished Roman senator (2nd / 1st century BC)
Cicerō, Cicerōnis, m	8	**Cicero**, Rome's most famous orator (1st century BC) and one of the consuls during Catiline's conspiracy
Cincinnātus, Cincinnātī, m	7	**Cincinnatus**, a famous Roman citizen who was appointed dictator to deal with a military crisis (5th century BC)
Claudius, Claudiī, m	12	**Claudius**, the fourth emperor of Rome (1st century AD)
Cleopātra, Cleopātrae, f	10,11	**Cleopatra**, queen of Egypt (1st century BC)
Gallī, Gallōrum, m pl	9	**Gauls**, the Celtic inhabitants of France and the surrounding areas
Gallia, Galliae, f	9	**Gaul**, a huge area of land including France, Luxembourg, Belgium and parts of Switzerland, Italy, the Netherlands and Germany
Hadriānus, Hadriānī, m	12	**Hadrian**, the fourteenth emperor of Rome who ordered a wall to be built from east to west across the north of Britain (2nd century AD)
Hannibal, Hannibalis, m	7	**Hannibal**, a Carthaginian noble and Rome's greatest enemy (3rd century BC)
Hērodotus, Hērodotī, m	10	**Herodotus**, the Greek writer known as the father of history (5th century BC)
Horātius, Horātiī, m	7	**Publius Horatius**, a famous Roman soldier who killed his sister because she loved one of the enemy soldiers he had just killed (7th century BC)
Icēnī, Icēnōrum, m pl	12	**Iceni**, a Celtic tribe based in Norfolk
Lepidus, Lepidī, m	11	**Lepidus**, one of the major power holders in the collapse of the Roman Republic, and a member of the powerful alliance with Octavian and Antony known as the triumvirate (1st century BC)
Lucrētia, Lucrētiae, f	7	**Lucretia**, a chaste and noble Roman who was brutally raped by the son of the last king of Rome (6th century BC)
Lūcullus, Lūcullī, m	9	**Lucullus**, an extraordinarily wealthy Roman general (1st century BC)

Name	Chapter	
Marcus Antōnius, Marcī Antōniī, m	8, 10, 11	**Mark Antony**, Julius Caesar's right-hand man and one of the leading generals in the civil wars at the end of the Roman Republic (1st century BC)
Marius, Mariī, m	9	**Marius**, a Roman noble who became consul seven times and instituted major reforms to the Roman army (2nd century BC)
Numa, Numae, m	7	**Numa**, the second king of Rome (8/7th century BC)
Octāviānus, Octāviānī, m	10, 11	**Octavian**, the Roman noble who later became known as Augustus, the first emperor of Rome (1st century BC–1st century AD)
Plīnius, Plīniī, m	8	**Pliny the Younger**, a famous statesmen and writer of letters, and nephew of Pliny the Elder, who was a military commander and natural historian (1st century AD)
Pompēius, Pompēiī, m	9	**Pompey**, a brilliant and exceptional Roman general who lost against Julius Caesar in a civil war (1st century BC)
Prāsutāgus, Prāsutāgī, m	12	**Prasutagus**, king of the Iceni and husband of Boudicca (1st century AD)
Quīntus Fabius Maximus, Quīntī Fabiī Maximī, m	7	**Quintus Fabius Maximus**, one of the most distinguished members of the noble Fabian family, famous for his role as dictator in the wars against Hannibal (3rd century BC)
Rōmulus, Rōmulī, m	7	**Romulus**, the founder and first king of Rome (8th century BC)
Scīpiō, Scīpiōnis, m	7	**Scipio**, the Roman general who, after years of war, conquered Hannibal and the Carthaginians (3rd / 2nd century BC)
Sextus Tarquinius, Sextī Tarquiniī, m	7	**Sextus Tarquinius**, the wanton son of the last king of Rome (6th century BC)
Suētōnius Paulīnus, Suētōniī Paulīnī, m	12	**Suetonius Paulinus**, the Roman governor of Britain at the time of Boudicca's revolt (1st century AD)
Vercingetorīx, Vercingetorīgis, m	9	**Vercingetorix**, a Gallic chieftain who led a united force of Gallic tribes against Julius Caesar (1st century BC)
Vergilius, Vergiliī, m	11	**Virgil**, an Augustan poet and the author of Rome's most famous epic poem, the *Aeneid* (1st century BC)

LATIN-TO-ENGLISH VOCABULARY LIST

		Chapter	
ā, ab	+ ablative	3	from, away from, by
abeō	abīre, abiī, abitum	8	go away
absum	abesse, āfuī	5	be absent, be away, be distant from
accipiō	accipere, accēpī, acceptum	11	receive, accept, take in
ad	+ accusative	2	to, towards, at
adeō	adīre, adiī, aditum	8	go to, approach
adsum	adesse, adfuī	5	be here, be present
adveniō	advenīre, advēnī, adventum	11	arrive
aedificō	aedificāre, aedificāvī, aedificātum	4	build
ager	agrī, m	4	field
agricola	agricolae, m	5	farmer
alius	alia, aliud	10	other, another
aliī. . . .aliī.		10	some . . . others
altus	alta, altum	6	high, deep
ambulō	ambulāre, ambulāvī, ambulātum	7	walk
amīcus	amīcī, m	6	friend
amō	amāre, amāvī, amātum	1	love, like
amor	amōris, m	10	love
ancilla	ancillae, f	5	slave-girl, slave-woman
annus	annī, m	6	year
antequam		7	before
appropinquō	appropinquāre, appropinquāvī, appropinquātum + dative	8	approach, come near to
aqua	aquae, f	5	water
arma	armōrum, n pl	2	arms, weapons
ascendō	ascendere, ascendī, ascēnsum	3	climb
audāx	audācis	2	bold, daring
audiō	audīre, audīvī, audītum	3	hear, listen to
aurum	aurī, n	4	gold
autem		11	but, however
auxilium	auxiliī, n	3	help
bellum	bellī, n	2	war
bene		9	well
bibō	bibere, bibī	5	drink
bonus	bona, bonum	3	good
cadō	cadere, cecidī, cāsum	12	fall
caelum	caelī, n	3	sky, heaven
capiō	capere, cēpī, captum	2	take, catch, capture, make (a plan)
caput	capitis, n	12	head

		Chapter	
cārus	cāra, cārum	11	dear, beloved
celer	celeris, celere	12	quick, fast
celeriter		3	quickly
cēna	cēnae, f	5	dinner, meal
centum		6	100
cēterī	cēterae, cētera	5	the rest, the others
cibus	cibī, m	5	food
circum	+ accusative	10	around
cīvis	cīvis, m / f	7	citizen
clāmō	clāmāre, clāmāvī, clāmātum	5	shout
clāmor	clāmōris, m	8	shout, shouting, noise
clārus	clāra, clārum	7	famous, clear
colligō	colligere, collēgī, collēctum	12	gather together, collect
comes	comitis, m / f	9	comrade, companion
coniūnx	coniugis, m / f	10	husband / wife
cōnsilium	cōnsiliī, n	11	plan, idea, advice
cōnspiciō	cōnspicere, cōnspexī, cōnspectum	3	catch sight of, notice
cōnstituō	cōnstituere, cōnstituī, cōnstitūtum	12	decide
cōnsūmō	cōnsūmere, cōnsūmpsī, cōnsūmptum	5	eat
contendō	contendere, contendī, contentum	12	hasten, march, compete
contrā	+ accusative	2	against
conveniō	convenīre, convēnī, conventum	8	come together, gather, meet
cōpiae	cōpiārum, f pl	9	forces, troops
corpus	corporis, n	2	body
crās		12	tomorrow
crēdō	crēdere, crēdidī, crēditum + dative	4	believe, trust
crūdēlis	crūdēle	4	cruel
cum	+ ablative	3	with
cupiō	cupere, cupīvī, cupītum	8	want, desire
cūr?		4	why?
currō	currere, cucurrī, cursum	2	run
custōdiō	custōdīre, custōdīvī, custōdītum	9	guard
dē	+ ablative	3	from, down from, about
dea	deae, f	1	goddess
dēbeō	dēbēre, dēbuī, dēbitum	11	owe, ought, should, must
decem		6	10
decimus	decima, decimum	6	tenth
dēfendō	dēfendere, dēfendī, dēfēnsum	9	defend
deinde		9	then
dēleō	dēlēre, dēlēvī, dēlētum	9	destroy
dēscendō	dēscendere, dēscendī, dēscēnsum	3	go down, come down
dēspērō	dēspērāre, dēspērāvī, dēspērātum	12	despair
deus	deī, m	1	god
dīcō	dīcere, dīxī, dictum	7	say, speak, tell
difficilis	difficile	3	difficult
discēdō	discēdere, discessī, discessum	11	depart, leave
diū		3	for a long time

		Chapter	
dō	dare, dedī, datum	4	give
doceō	docēre, docuī, doctum	10	teach
doctus	docta, doctum	10	educated
domina	dominae, f	7	mistress
dominus	dominī, m	7	master
dōnum	dōnī, n	4	gift, present
dormiō	dormīre, dormīvī, dormītum	6	sleep
dūcō	dūcere, dūxī, ductum	9	lead, take
duo	duae, duo	6	2
dux	ducis, m	9	leader
ē, ex	+ ablative	3	from, out of, out from
ecce!		11	look!
effugiō	effugere, effūgī	12	escape
ego	meī	8	I, me
emō	emere, ēmī, ēmptum	6	buy
enim		8	for
eō	īre, iī / īvī, itum	2	go
epistula	epistulae, f	8	letter
equus	equī, m	3	horse
errō	errāre, errāvī, errātum	12	stray, make a mistake
et		1	and, even
et . . . et		7	both . . . and
etiam		1	also, even
exeō	exīre, exiī, exitum	8	go out from, go away
exspectō	exspectāre, exspectāvī, exspectātum	10	wait for, expect
facilis	facile	3	easy
faciō	facere, fēcī, factum	4	make, do
fēlīx	fēlīcis	3	fortunate, happy, lucky
fēmina	fēminae, f	1	woman
ferō	ferre, tulī, lātum	4	bring, carry, bear
ferōx	ferōcis	8	fierce, ferocious
fessus	fessa, fessum	5	tired
festīnō	festīnāre, festīnāvī, festīnātum	5	hurry
fīlia	fīliae, f	1	daughter
fīlius	fīliī, m	1	son
flūmen	flūminis, n	2	river
fortasse		12	perhaps
forte		10	by chance
fortis	forte	2	brave, strong
fortiter		2	bravely, strongly
forum	forī, n	7	forum, market place
frāter	frātris, m	12	brother
frūstrā		8	in vain
fugiō	fugere, fūgī, fugitum	10	run away, flee
gēns	gentis, f	12	family, tribe, people
gerō	gerere, gessī, gestum	9	wear (clothes), wage (war)
gladius	gladiī, m	2	sword
Graecus	Graeca, Graecum	2	Greek

		Chapter	
gravis	grave	12	heavy, serious
habeō	habēre, habuī, habitum	4	have, hold
habitō	habitāre, habitāvī, habitātum	7	live
hasta	hastae, f	2	spear
herī		12	yesterday
hic	haec, hoc	7	this, these
hīc		6	here
hodiē		12	today
homō	hominis, m	1	man, human being
hōra	hōrae, f	6	hour
hortus	hortī, m	7	garden
hostis	hostis, m	9	enemy
iaciō	iacere, iēcī, iactum	2	throw
iam		6	now, already
ibi		6	there
igitur		12	therefore, and so
ille	illa, illud	7	that, those, he, she, it
in	+ accusative	2	into, onto
in	+ ablative	3	in, on
incendō	incendere, incendī, incēnsum	9	burn, set on fire
incola	incolae, m / f	9	inhabitant
ineō	inīre, iniī, initum	8	go into, enter
ingēns	ingentis	2	huge
inquit	inquiunt	2	he / she says / said, they say / said
īnsula	īnsulae, f	12	island
intellegō	intellegere, intellēxī, intellēctum	11	understand, realize
inter	+ accusative	10	among, between
interficiō	interficere, interfēcī, interfectum	2	kill
intrō	intrāre, intrāvī, intrātum	11	enter
inveniō	invenīre, invēnī, inventum	10	find
invītō	invītāre, invītāvī, invītātum	9	invite
īra	īrae, f	4	anger
īrātus	īrāta, īrātum	1	angry
is	ea, id	7	he, she, it, that, those
itaque		6	and so, therefore
iter	itineris, n	10	journey
iterum		5	again
iubeō	iubēre, iūssī, iūssum	3	order
iuvenis	iuvenis, m	6	young man
labōrō	labōrāre, labōrāvī, labōrātum	8	work, toil
lacrimō	lacrimāre, lacrimāvī, lacrimātum	1	weep, cry
laetus	laeta, laetum	1	happy
laudō	laudāre, laudāvī, laudātum	1	praise
legō	legere, lēgī, lēctum	8	read, choose
liber	librī, m	8	book
līberī	līberōrum, m pl	1	children
līberō	līberāre, līberāvī, līberātum	7	set free

		Chapter	
lībertus	lībertī, m	7	freedman, ex-slave
locus	locī, m	6	place
longus	longa, longum	8	long
lūdus	lūdī, m	5	school, game, public games / festival (pl)
lūx	lūcis, f	10	light, daylight
magis		8	more
magister	magistrī, m	8	teacher
magnopere		5	greatly, very much
magnus	magna, magnum	3	big, large, great
maior	maius	8	bigger, larger, greater
malus	mala, malum	3	evil, bad
maneō	manēre, mānsī, mānsum	2	remain, stay
mare	maris, n	3	sea
marītus	marītī, m	10	husband
māter	mātris, f	1	mother
maximē		8	very greatly
maximus	maxima, maximum	8	greatest, largest, biggest
medius	media, medium	8	middle
melior	melius	8	better
meus	mea, meum	6	my
mīles	mīlitis, m	9	soldier
mīlia	mīlium	6	1000s
mīlle		6	1000
minimus	minima, minimum	8	smallest, least
minor	minus	8	smaller, less
mīrābilis	mīrābile	10	wonderful, extraordinary
miser	misera, miserum	4	miserable, wretched, sad
mittō	mittere, mīsī, missum	9	send
moneō	monēre, monuī, monitum	6	warn, advise
mōns	montis, m	3	mountain
mors	mortis, f	9	death
mortuus	mortua, mortuum	5	dead
moveō	movēre, mōvī, mōtum	9	move
mox		5	soon
mulier	mulieris, f	10	woman, wife
multus	multa, multum	1	much, many
mūrus	mūrī, m	7	wall
nam		12	for
nārrō	nārrāre, nārrāvī, nārrātum	12	tell, relate
nauta	nautae, m	10	sailor
nāvigō	nāvigāre, nāvigāvī, nāvigātum	10	sail
nāvis	nāvis, f	10	ship
-ne		4	(introduces question)
necesse		10	necessary
necō	necāre, necāvī, necātum	9	kill
nēmō	nūllīus	12	no one, nobody
neque, nec		11	and not, nor, neither

		Chapter	
nihil		10	nothing
nōbilis	nōbile	8	of noble birth, renowned
nōlī / nōlīte	+ infinitive	6	do not . . .
nōlō	nōlle, nōluī	4	not want, refuse
nōmen	nōminis, n	4	name
nōn		2	not
nōnne . . .?		4	surely . . .?
nōnus	nōna, nōnum	6	ninth
nōs	nostrum	8	we, us
noster	nostra, nostrum	6	our
nōtus	nōta, nōtum	8	famous, well-known
novem		6	9
novus	nova, novum	6	new
nox	noctis, f	12	night
nūllus	nūlla, nūllum	12	not any, no
num . . .?		4	surely . . . not?
numquam		6	never
nunc		5	now
nūntiō	nūntiāre, nūntiāvī, nūntiātum	11	announce, report
nūntius	nūntiī, m	7	messenger
ō	+ vocative	6	O
occīdō	occīdere, occīdī, occīsum	9	kill
occupō	occupāre, occupāvī, occupātum	9	take possession of, occupy
octāvus	octāva, octāvum	6	eighth
octō		6	8
ōlim		3	once, some time ago
omnis	omne	7	all, every
oppidum	oppidī, n	9	town
oppugnō	oppugnāre, oppugnāvī, oppugnātum	9	attack
optimus	optima, optimum	8	best
ostendō	ostendere, ostendī, ostentum	6	show
parēns	parentis, m / f	10	parent
parō	parāre, parāvī, parātum	5	prepare, provide
pars	partis, f	10	part
parvus	parva, parvum	6	small
pater	patris, m	1	father
patria	patriae, f	9	country, homeland
paucī	paucae, pauca	7	few, a few
pāx	pācis, f	11	peace
pecūnia	pecūniae, f	4	money
peior	peius	8	worse
per	+ accusative	2	through, along
pereō	perīre, periī, peritum	8	die, perish
perīculum	perīculī, n	2	danger
persuādeō	persuādēre, persuāsī, persuāsum + dative	4	persuade
perterritus	perterrita, perterritum	4	terrified
pessimus	pessima, pessimum	8	worst

		Chapter	
petō	petere, petīvī, petītum	3	make for, seek, beg / ask for
plūrēs	plūra	8	more
plūrimus	plūrima, plūrimum	8	most, very many
plūs	+ genitive	8	more
poēta	poētae, m	11	poet
pōnō	pōnere, posuī, positum	4	put, place, set up
porta	portae, f	11	gate
portō	portāre, portāvī, portātum	12	carry, bear, take
possum	posse, potuī	3	can, be able
post	+ accusative	10	after, behind
posteā		11	afterwards
postquam		7	after, when
prīmus	prīma, prīmum	6	first
prō	+ ablative	11	in front of, for, on behalf of
proelium	proeliī, n	9	battle
prope	+ accusative	2	near
propter	+ accusative	11	on account of, because of
puella	puellae, f	6	girl
puer	puerī, m	6	boy
pugnō	pugnāre, pugnāvī, pugnātum	3	fight
pulcher	pulchra, pulchrum	1	beautiful, handsome
pūniō	pūnīre, pūnīvī, pūnītum	1	punish
putō	putāre, putāvī, putātum	11	think
quaerō	quaerere, quaesīvī, quaesītum	10	search for, look for, ask
quam		8	than, how
quam	+ superlative	8	as . . . as possible
quamquam		7	although
quandō?		4	when?
quārtus	quārta, quārtum	6	fourth
quattuor		6	4
-que		10	and
quī	quae, quod	7	who, which
quīnque		6	5
quīntus	quīnta, quīntum	6	fifth
quis?	quis? quid?	7	who? what? which?
quō?		11	to where?
quod		4	because
quoque		7	also, too
rapiō	rapere, rapuī, raptum	9	seize, grab
redeō	redīre, rediī, reditum	8	go back, come back, return
redūcō	redūcere, redūxī, reductum	11	lead back, bring back
rēgīna	rēgīnae, f	1	queen
rēgnum	rēgnī, n	12	kingdom
regō	regere, rēxī, rēctum	1	rule
relinquō	relinquere, relīquī, relictum	11	leave, leave behind
respondeō	respondēre, respondī, respōnsum	6	reply
rēx	rēgis, m	1	king

		Chapter	
rīdeō	rīdēre, rīsī, rīsum	5	laugh, smile, laugh at
rogō	rogāre, rogāvī, rogātum	6	ask, ask for
Rōma	Rōmae, f	7	Rome
Rōmae		7	locative: at Rome
Rōmānus	Rōmāna, Rōmānum	1	Roman
sacer	sacra, sacrum	5	sacred
saepe		1	often
saevus	saeva, saevum	1	savage, cruel
sagitta	sagittae, f	2	arrow
salūtō	salūtāre, salūtāvī, salūtātum	7	greet
satis		10	enough
scrībō	scrībere, scrīpsī, scrīptum	8	write
scūtum	scūtī, n	9	shield
sē	suī	8	himself, herself, itself, themselves
secundus	secunda, secundum	6	second
sed		1	but
sedeō	sedēre, sēdī, sessum	12	sit
semper		4	always
senātor	senātōris, m	7	senator
senex	senis, m	8	old man
septem		6	7
septimus	septima, septimum	6	seventh
servō	servāre, servāvī, servātum	11	save, protect, keep
servus	servī, m	5	slave
sex		6	6
sextus	sexta, sextum	6	sixth
sīc		6	thus, in this way
silva	silvae, f	2	wood
socius	sociī, m	11	ally
soror	sorōris, f	12	sister
spectō	spectāre, spectāvī, spectātum	5	look at, watch
statim		10	at once, immediately
stō	stāre, stetī, statum	11	stand
stultus	stulta, stultum	8	stupid, foolish
subitō		3	suddenly
sum	esse, fuī	1	be
superō	superāre, superāvī, superātum	9	overcome, overpower
suus	sua, suum	6	his, her, its, their (own)
taberna	tabernae, f	5	shop, inn
taceō	tacēre, tacuī, tacitum	11	be silent, be quiet
tamen		4	however
tandem		3	at last, finally
templum	templī, n	4	temple
tempus	temporis, n	11	time
teneō	tenēre, tenuī, tentum	10	hold
terra	terrae, f	3	ground, land, country
terreō	terrēre, terruī, territum	1	frighten, terrify

		Chapter	
tertius	tertia, tertium	6	third
timeō	timēre, timuī, timitum	2	fear, be afraid
trādō	trādere, trādidī, trāditum	9	hand over, hand down
trahō	trahere, trāxī, tractum	12	drag
trāns	+ accusative	2	across
trānseō	trānsīre, trānsiī, trānsitum	8	go over, cross
trēs	tria	6	3
trīstis	trīste	4	sad
tū	tuī	8	you (sg)
tum		1	then
turba	turbae, f	10	crowd
tūtus	tūta, tūtum	10	safe
tuus	tua, tuum	6	your (sg), yours
ubi		7	when, where
ubi?		4	where?
unda	undae, f	11	wave
unde?		11	from where?
ūnus	ūna, ūnum	6	1
urbs	urbis, f	5	city
uxor	uxōris, f	1	wife
validus	valida, validum	11	strong
vēndō	vēndere, vēndidī, vēnditum	12	sell
veniō	venīre, vēnī, ventum	5	come
ventus	ventī, m	12	wind
verbum	verbī, n	6	word
vester	vestra, vestrum	6	your (pl), yours
via	viae, f	7	street, road, way
videō	vidēre, vīdī, vīsum	6	see
vīlla	vīllae, f	5	house, country villa
vincō	vincere, vīcī, victum	2	conquer, win, be victorious, defeat
vīnum	vīnī, n	5	wine
vir	virī, m	8	man, husband
vocō	vocāre, vocāvī, vocātum	5	call
volō	velle, voluī	4	want, wish, be willing
vōs	vestrum	8	you (pl)
vulnerō	vulnerāre, vulnerāvī, vulnerātum	9	wound, injure

ENGLISH-TO-LATIN VOCABULARY LIST

	Chapter		
able, be able	3	possum	posse, potuī
about	3	dē	+ ablative
accept	11	accipiō	accipere, accēpī, acceptum
across	2	trāns	+ accusative
advice	11	cōnsilium	cōnsiliī, n
advise	6	moneō	monēre, monuī, monitum
after	10	post	+ accusative
after	7	postquam	
afterwards	11	posteā	
again	5	iterum	
against	2	contrā	+ accusative
all	7	omnis	omne
ally	11	socius	sociī, m
along	2	per	+ accusative
already	6	iam	
also	1	etiam	
also	7	quoque	
although	7	quamquam	
always	4	semper	
among	10	inter	+ accusative
and	10	-que	
and	1	et	
and not	11	neque, nec	
and so	12	igitur	
and so	6	itaque	
anger	4	īra	īrae, f
angry	1	īrātus	īrāta, īrātum
announce	11	nūntiō	nūntiāre, nūntiāvī, nūntiātum
another	10	alius	alia, aliud
approach	8	adeō	adīre, adiī, aditum
approach	8	appropinquō	appropinquāre, appropinquāvī, appropinquātum + dative
arms, armour	2	arma	armōrum, n pl
around	10	circum	+ accusative
arrive	11	adveniō	advenīre, advēnī, adventum
arrow	2	sagitta	sagittae, f
as . . . as possible	8	quam	+ superlative
ask	10	quaerō	quaerere, quaesīvī, quaesītum

	Chapter		
ask, ask for	6	rogō	rogāre, rogāvī, rogātum
ask for	3	petō	petere, petīvī, petītum
at	2	ad	+ accusative
at last	3	tandem	
at once	10	statim	
attack	9	oppugnō	oppugnāre, oppugnāvī, oppugnātum
bad	3	malus	mala, malum
battle	9	proelium	proeliī, n
be	1	sum	esse, fuī
be absent	5	absum	abesse, āfuī
be present	5	adsum	adesse, adfuī
beautiful	1	pulcher	pulchra, pulchrum
because	4	quod	
before	7	antequam	
behind	10	post	+ accusative
believe	4	crēdō	crēdere, crēdidī, crēditum + dative
best	8	optimus	optima, optimum
better	8	melior	melius
between	10	inter	+ accusative
big	3	magnus	magna, magnum
bigger	8	maior	maius
biggest	8	maximus	maxima, maximum
body	2	corpus	corporis, n
bold	2	audāx	audācis
book	8	liber	librī, m
both . . . and	7	et . . . et	
boy	6	puer	puerī, m
brave	2	fortis	forte
bravely	2	fortiter	
bring	4	ferō	ferre, tulī, lātum
brother	12	frāter	frātris, m
build	4	aedificō	aedificāre, aedificāvī, aedificātum
burn	9	incendō	incendere, incendī, incēnsum
but	11	autem	
but	1	sed	
buy	6	emō	emere, ēmī, ēmptum
by	3	ā, ab	+ ablative
by chance	10	forte	
call	5	vocō	vocāre, vocāvī, vocātum
can	3	possum	posse, potuī
capture	2	capiō	capere, cēpī, captum
carry	4	ferō	ferre, tulī, lātum
carry	12	portō	portāre, portāvī, portātum
catch sight of	3	cōnspiciō	cōnspicere, cōnspexī, cōnspectum
children	1	līberī	līberōrum, m pl
choose	8	legō	legere, lēgī, lēctum

	Chapter		
citizen	7	cīvis	cīvis, m / f
city	5	urbs	urbis, f
clan	12	gēns	gentis, f
clear	7	clārus	clāra, clārum
climb	3	ascendō	ascendere, ascendī, ascēnsum
collect	12	colligō	colligere, collēgī, collēctum
come	5	veniō	venīre, vēnī, ventum
come together	8	conveniō	convenīre, convēnī, conventum
compete	12	contendō	contendere, contendī, contentum
comrade, companion	9	comes	comitis, m / f
conquer	2	vincō	vincere, vīcī, victum
country (one's own)	9	patria	patriae, f
cross	8	trānseō	trānsīre, trānsiī, trānsitum
crowd	10	turba	turbae, f
cruel	4	crūdēlis	crūdēle
cruel	1	saevus	saeva, saevum
cry	1	lacrimō	lacrimāre, lacrimāvī, lacrimātum
danger	2	perīculum	perīculī, n
daring	2	audāx	audācis
daughter	1	fīlia	fīliae, f
dead	5	mortuus	mortua, mortuum
dear	11	cārus	cāra, cārum
death	9	mors	mortis, f
decide	12	cōnstituō	cōnstituere, cōnstituī, cōnstitūtum
deep	6	altus	alta, altum
defeat	2	vincō	vincere, vīcī
defend	9	dēfendō	dēfendere, dēfendī, dēfēnsum
depart	11	discēdō	discēdere, discessī, discessum
desire	8	cupiō	cupere, cupīvī, cupītum
despair	12	dēspērō	dēspērāre, dēspērāvī, dēspērātum
destroy	9	dēleō	dēlēre, dēlēvī, dēlētum
die	8	pereō	perīre, periī, peritum
difficult	3	difficilis	difficile
dinner	5	cēna	cēnae, f
do	4	faciō	facere, fēcī, factum
do not . . .	6	nōlī / nōlīte	+ infinitive
drag	12	trahō	trahere, trāxī, tractum
drink	5	bibō	bibere, bibī
easy	3	facilis	facile
eat	5	cōnsūmō	cōnsūmere, cōnsūmpsī, cōnsūmptum
eighth	6	octāvus	octāva, octāvum
enemy	9	hostis	hostis, m
enough	10	satis	
enter	8	ineō	inīre, iniī, initum
enter	11	intrō	intrāre, intrāvī, intrātum
escape	12	effugiō	effugere, effūgī

English	Chapter	Latin	
even	1	et	
even	1	etiam	
every	7	omnis	omne
evil	3	malus	mala, malum
expect	10	exspectō	exspectāre, exspectāvī, exspectātum
extraordinary	10	mīrābilis	mīrābile
fall	12	cadō	cadere, cecidī, cāsum
famous	7	clārus	clāra, clārum
famous	8	nōtus	nōta, nōtum
farmer	5	agricola	agricolae, m
fast	12	celer	celeris, celere
father	1	pater	patris, m
fear, be afraid	2	timeō	timēre, timuī, timitum
ferocious	8	ferōx	ferōcis
festival, public games	5	lūdī	lūdōrum, m pl
few	7	paucī	paucae, pauca
field	4	ager	agrī, m
fierce	8	ferōx	ferōcis
fifth	6	quīntus	quīnta, quīntum
fight	3	pugnō	pugnāre, pugnāvī, pugnātum
finally	3	tandem	
find	10	inveniō	invenīre, invēnī, inventum
first	6	prīmus	prīma, prīmum
flee	10	fugiō	fugere, fūgī, fugitum
food	5	cibus	cibī, m
foolish	8	stultus	stulta, stultum
for	8	enim	
for	12	nam	
for a long time	3	diū	
forces (military)	9	cōpiae	cōpiārum, f pl
fortunate	3	fēlīx	fēlīcis
forum	7	forum	forī, n
fourth	6	quārtus	quārta, quārtum
freedman	7	lībertus	lībertī, m
friend	6	amīcus	amīcī, m
frighten	1	terreō	terrēre, terruī, territum
from, away from	3	ā, ab	+ ablative
from, down from	3	dē	+ ablative
from, out of	3	ē, ex	+ ablative
garden	7	hortus	hortī, m
gate	11	porta	portae, f
gather together	12	colligō	colligere, collēgī, collēctum
gift	4	dōnum	dōnī, n
girl	6	puella	puellae, f
give	4	dō	dare, dedī, datum
go	2	eō	īre, iī / īvī, itum

	Chapter		
go away	8	abeō	abīre, abiī, abitum
go back	8	redeō	redīre, rediī, reditum
go down, come down	3	dēscendō	dēscendere, dēscendī, dēscēnsum
go out, go away	8	exeō	exīre, exiī, exitum
go to	8	adeō	adīre, adiī, aditum
god	1	deus	deī, m
goddess	1	dea	deae, f
gold	4	aurum	aurī, n
good	3	bonus	bona, bonum
great	3	magnus	magna, magnum
greater	8	maior	maius
greatest	8	maximus	maxima, maximum
greatly	5	magnopere	
Greek	2	Graecus	Graeca, Graecum
greet	7	salūtō	salūtāre, salūtāvī, salūtātum
ground	3	terra	terrae, f
guard	9	custōdiō	custōdīre, custōdīvī, custōdītum
hand over	9	trādō	trādere, trādidī, trāditum
handsome	1	pulcher	pulchra, pulchrum
happy	1	laetus	laeta, laetum
hasten	12	contendō	contendere, contendī, contentum
have, hold	4	habeō	habēre, habuī, habitum
he, she, it	7	is	ea, id
head	12	caput	capitis, n
hear	3	audiō	audīre, audīvī, audītum
heaven	3	caelum	caelī, n
heavy	12	gravis	grave
help	3	auxilium	auxiliī, n
here, in this place	6	hīc	
high	6	altus	alta, altum
himself, herself, itself, themselves	8	sē	suī
his, her, its, their (own)	6	suus	sua, suum
hold	10	teneō	tenēre, tenuī, tentum
homeland	9	patria	patriae, f
horse	3	equus	equī, m
hour	6	hōra	hōrae, f
house	5	vīlla	vīllae, f
how, to what extent	8	quam	
however	11	autem	
however	4	tamen	
huge	2	ingēns	ingentis
human being	1	homō	hominis, m
hurry	5	festīnō	festīnāre, festīnāvī, festīnātum
husband	10	marītus	marītī, m
husband	8	vir	virī, m
husband, wife	10	coniūnx	coniugis, m / f

	Chapter		
I, me	8	ego	meī
idea	11	cōnsilium	cōnsiliī, n
immediately	10	statim	
in, on	3	in	+ ablative
in front of	11	prō	+ ablative
in this way	6	sīc	
in vain	8	frūstrā	
inhabitant	9	incola	incolae, m / f
injure	9	vulnerō	vulnerāre, vulnerāvī, vulnerātum
into, onto	2	in	+ accusative
invite	9	invītō	invītāre, invītāvī, invītātum
island	12	īnsula	īnsulae, f
journey	10	iter	itineris, n
kill	2	interficiō	interficere, interfēcī, interfectum
kill	9	necō	necāre, necāvī, necātum
kill	9	occīdō	occīdere, occīdī, occīsum
king	1	rēx	rēgis, m
kingdom	12	rēgnum	rēgnī, n
large	3	magnus	magna, magnum
larger	8	maior	maius
largest	8	maximus	maxima, maximum
laugh, laugh at	5	rīdeō	rīdēre, rīsī, rīsum
lead	9	dūcō	dūcere, dūxī, ductum
lead back	11	redūcō	redūcere, redūxī, reductum
leader	9	dux	ducis, m
least	8	minimus	minima, minimum
leave behind	11	relinquō	relinquere, relīquī, relictum
less	8	minor	minus
letter	8	epistula	epistulae, f
light	10	lūx	lūcis, f
listen to	3	audiō	audīre, audīvī, audītum
live	7	habitō	habitāre, habitāvī, habitātum
long	8	longus	longa, longum
look at	5	spectō	spectāre, spectāvī, spectātum
look!	11	ecce!	
love	1	amō	amāre, amāvī, amātum
love	10	amor	amōris, m
lucky	3	fēlīx	fēlīcis
make, do	4	faciō	facere, fēcī, factum
make a mistake	12	errō	errāre, errāvī, errātum
make for	3	petō	petere, petīvī, petītum
man	8	vir	virī, m
man	1	homō	hominis, m
many	1	multī	multae, multa
march	12	contendō	contendere, contendī, contentum
master	7	dominus	dominī, m

	Chapter		
meal	5	cēna	cēnae, f
meet	8	conveniō	convenīre, convēnī, conventum
messenger	7	nūntius	nūntiī, m
middle	8	medius	media, medium
miserable	4	miser	misera, miserum
mistress	7	domina	dominae, f
money	4	pecūnia	pecūniae, f
more	8	magis	
more	8	plūrēs	plūra
more	8	plūs	+ genitive
most	8	plūrimus	plūrima, plūrimum
mother	1	māter	mātris, f
mountain	3	mōns	montis, m
move	9	moveō	movēre, mōvī, mōtum
much	1	multus	multa, multum
my	6	meus	mea, meum
name	4	nōmen	nōminis, n
near	2	prope	+ accusative
necessary	10	necesse	
never	6	numquam	
new	6	novus	nova, novum
night	12	nox	noctis, f
ninth	6	nōnus	nōna, nōnum
no one, nobody	12	nēmō	nūllīus
noble	8	nōbilis	nōbile
noise	8	clāmor	clāmōris, m
nor, neither	11	neque, nec	
not	2	nōn	
not any, no	12	nūllus	nūlla, nūllum
not want	4	nōlō	nōlle, nōluī
nothing	10	nihil	
notice	3	cōnspiciō	cōnspicere, cōnspexī, cōnspectum
now	6	iam	
now	5	nunc	
o	6	ō	+ vocative
occupy	9	occupō	occupāre, occupāvī, occupātum
often	1	saepe	
old man	8	senex	senis, m
on account of	11	propter	+ accusative
on behalf of	11	prō	+ ablative
once	3	ōlim	
order	3	iubeō	iubēre, iūssī, iūssum
other	10	alius	alia, aliud
others, the rest	5	cēterī	cēterae, cētera
our	6	noster	nostra, nostrum
overcome, overpower	9	superō	superāre, superāvī, superātum

	Chapter		
owe, ought	11	dēbeō	dēbēre, dēbuī, dēbitum
parent	10	parēns	parentis, m / f
part	10	pars	partis, f
peace	11	pāx	pācis, f
people	12	gēns	gentis, f
perhaps	12	fortasse	
persuade	4	persuādeō	persuādēre, persuāsī, persuāsum + dative
place	6	locus	locī, m
place	4	pōnō	pōnere, posuī, positum
plan	11	cōnsilium	cōnsiliī, n
poet	11	poēta	poētae, m
praise	1	laudō	laudāre, laudāvī, laudātum
prepare	5	parō	parāre, parāvī, parātum
present	4	dōnum	dōnī, n
protect	11	servō	servāre, servāvī, servātum
provide	5	parō	parāre, parāvī, parātum
punish	1	pūniō	pūnīre, pūnīvī, pūnītum
put	4	pōnō	pōnere, posuī, positum
queen	1	rēgīna	rēgīnae, f
quick	12	celer	celeris, celere
quickly	3	celeriter	
read	8	legō	legere, lēgī, lēctum
receive	11	accipiō	accipere, accēpī, acceptum
refuse	4	nōlō	nōlle, nōluī
remain	2	maneō	manēre, mānsī, mānsum
reply	6	respondeō	respondēre, respondī, respōnsum
report	11	nūntiō	nūntiāre, nūntiāvī, nūntiātum
return	8	redeō	redīre, rediī, reditum
river	2	flūmen	flūminis, n
road	7	via	viae, f
Roman	1	Rōmānus	Rōmāna, Rōmānum
Rome	7	Rōma	Rōmae, f
rule	1	regō	regere, rēxī, rēctum
run	2	currō	currere, cucurrī, cursum
run away	10	fugiō	fugere, fūgī, fugitum
sacred	5	sacer	sacra, sacrum
sad	4	trīstis	trīste
safe	10	tūtus	tūta, tūtum
sail	10	nāvigō	nāvigāre, nāvigāvī, nāvigātum
sailor	10	nauta	nautae, m
savage	1	saevus	saeva, saevum
save	11	servō	servāre, servāvī, servātum
say	7	dīcō	dīcere, dīxī, dictum
says, said	2	inquit	inquiunt
school	5	lūdus	lūdī, m
sea	3	mare	maris, n

	Chapter		
search for	10	quaerō	quaerere, quaesīvī, quaesītum
second	6	secundus	secunda, secundum
see	6	videō	vidēre, vīdī, vīsum
seize	9	rapiō	rapere, rapuī, raptum
sell	12	vēndō	vēndere, vēndidī, vēnditum
senator	7	senātor	senātōris, m
send	9	mittō	mittere, mīsī, missum
serious	12	gravis	grave
set free	7	līberō	līberāre, līberāvī, līberātum
seventh	6	septimus	septima, septimum
shield	9	scūtum	scūtī, n
ship	10	nāvis	nāvis, f
shop, inn	5	taberna	tabernae, f
shout	5	clāmō	clāmāre, clāmāvī, clāmātum
shout, shouting	8	clāmor	clāmōris, m
show	6	ostendō	ostendere, ostendī, ostentum
silent, be silent	11	taceō	tacēre, tacuī, tacitum
sister	12	soror	sorōris, f
sit	12	sedeō	sedēre, sēdī, sessum
sixth	6	sextus	sexta, sextum
sky	3	caelum	caelī, n
slave	5	servus	servī, m
slave-girl, slave-woman	5	ancilla	ancillae, f
sleep	6	dormiō	dormīre, dormīvī, dormītum
small	6	parvus	parva, parvum
smaller	8	minor	minus
smallest	8	minimus	minima, minimum
smile	5	rīdeō	rīdēre, rīsī, rīsum
soldier	9	mīles	mīlitis, m
some . . . others	10	aliī. . . .aliī.	
son	1	fīlius	fīliī, m
soon	5	mox	
spear	2	hasta	hastae, f
stand	11	stō	stāre, stetī, statum
stay	2	maneō	manēre, mānsī, mānsum
stray	12	errō	errāre, errāvī, errātum
street	7	via	viae, f
strong	2	fortis	forte
strong	11	validus	valida, validum
stupid	8	stultus	stulta, stultum
suddenly	3	subitō	
surely . . .?	4	nōnne . . .?	
surely . . . not?	4	num . . .?	
sword	2	gladius	gladiī, m
take	2	capiō	capere, cēpī, captum
teach	10	doceō	docēre, docuī, doctum

English	Chapter	Latin	
teacher	8	magister	magistrī, m
tell	12	nārrō	nārrāre, nārrāvī, nārrātum
temple	4	templum	templī, n
tenth	6	decimus	decima, decimum
terrified	4	perterritus	perterrita, perterritum
terrify	1	terreō	terrēre, terruī, territum
than	8	quam	
that	7	ille	illa, illud
that, those	7	is	ea, id
then	9	deinde	
then	1	tum	
there, in that place	6	ibi	
therefore	12	igitur	
therefore	6	itaque	
think	11	putō	putāre, putāvī, putātum
third	6	tertius	tertia, tertium
this, these	7	hic	haec, hoc
through	2	per	+ accusative
throw	2	iaciō	iacere, iēcī, iactum
thus	6	sīc	
time	11	tempus	temporis, n
tired	5	fessus	fessa, fessum
to, towards	2	ad	+ accusative
today	12	hodiē	
tomorrow	12	crās	
town	9	oppidum	oppidī, n
tribe	12	gēns	gentis, f
troops	9	cōpiae	cōpiārum, f pl
trust	4	crēdō	crēdere, crēdidī, crēditum + dative
understand	11	intellegō	intellegere, intellēxī, intellēctum
very greatly	8	maximē	
very many	8	plūrimus	plūrima, plūrimum
very much	5	magnopere	
wage (war)	9	gerō	gerere, gessī, gestum
wait for	10	exspectō	exspectāre, exspectāvī, exspectātum
walk	7	ambulō	ambulāre, ambulāvī, ambulātum
wall	7	mūrus	mūrī, m
want, be willing	4	volō	velle, voluī
want, desire	8	cupiō	cupere, cupīvī, cupītum
war	2	bellum	bellī, n
warn	6	moneō	monēre, monuī, monitum
watch	5	spectō	spectāre, spectāvī, spectātum
water	5	aqua	aquae, f
wave	11	unda	undae, f
we, us	8	nōs	nostrum
weapons	2	arma	armōrum, n pl

	Chapter		
weep	1	lacrimō	lacrimāre, lacrimāvī, lacrimātum
well	9	bene	
when, where	7	ubi	
when?	4	quandō?	
where from?	11	unde?	
where to?	11	quō?	
where?	4	ubi?	
who, which	7	quī	quae, quod
who? what? which?	7	quis?	quis? quid?
why?	4	cūr?	
wife	1	uxor	uxōris, f
win	2	vincō	vincere, vīcī, victum
wind	12	ventus	ventī, m
wine	5	vīnum	vīnī, n
with	3	cum	+ ablative
woman	1	fēmina	fēminae, f
woman, wife	10	mulier	mulieris, f
wonderful	10	mīrābilis	mīrābile
wood	2	silva	silvae, f
word	6	verbum	verbī, n
work	8	labōrō	labōrāre, labōrāvī, labōrātum
worse	8	peior	peius
worst	8	pessimus	pessima, pessimum
wound	9	vulnerō	vulnerāre, vulnerāvī, vulnerātum
write	8	scrībō	scrībere, scrīpsī, scrīptum
year	6	annus	annī, m
yesterday	12	herī	
you (pl)	8	vōs	vestrum
you (sg)	8	tū	tuī
young man	6	iuvenis	iuvenis, m
your (pl), yours	6	vester	vestra, vestrum
your (sg), yours	6	tuus	tua, tuum
? (introduces a question)	4	-ne	
1	6	ūnus	ūna, ūnum
2	6	duo	duae, duo
3	6	trēs	tria
4	6	quattuor	
5	6	quīnque	
6	6	sex	
7	6	septem	
8	6	octō	
9	6	novem	
10	6	decem	
100	6	centum	
1000	6	mīlle	
1000s	6	mīlia	mīlium

BIBLIOGRAPHY

Alison E. Cooley (2009), *Res Gestae Divi Augusti, Text, Translation, and Commentary*), Cambridge: Cambridge University Press.

Appian, *The Civil Wars*, trans. John Carter, London: Penguin Books.

Appian (1913), *Historia Romana*, trans. Horace While (1913), Loeb Classical Library, Cambridge, MA: Harvard University Press.

Augustus Caesar (1967), *Res Gestae Divi Augusti*, ed. P.A. Brunt and J.M. Moore (1967), Oxford: Oxford University Press.

Augustus (2011), *Res Gestae Divi Augusti*, trans. Alison Cooley (2011), *Res Gestae Divi Augusti: Text, Translation, and Commentary*, Cambridge: Cambridge University Press.

Aulus Gellius (1946), *Attic Nights*, trans. John C. Rolfe (1946), Loeb Classical Library, Cambridge, MA: Harvard University Press.

Bilows, Richard A. (2009), *Julius Caesar: The Colossus of Rome*, New York: Routledge.

Caesar (1996), *The Gallic War*, trans. Carolyn Hammond (1996), Oxford: Oxford University Press.

Caesar (2016), *Civil War*, trans. Cynthia Damon (2016), Loeb Classical Library, Cambridge, MA: Harvard University Press.

Caesar (2001), *Civil Wars*, trans. A.G. Peskett (2001), Loeb Classical Library, Cambridge, MA: Harvard University Press.

Caesar (1997), *The Gallic War*, trans. H.J. Edwards (1997), Cambridge, MA: Harvard University Press.

Caesar (2012), *Gallic Wars*, 4.23.1—24.4, trans. Yvette Rathbone (2012), LACTOR 11, A2, London: London Association of Classical Teachers.

Carter, Ashley & Phillip Parr (2003), *Cambridge Latin Anthology*, Cambridge: Cambridge University Press.

Cassius Dio (1916), *Roman History*, trans. Earnest Cary (1916), Loeb Classical Library, Cambridge, MA: Harvard University Press.

Cassius Dio (1987), *Roman History, 50.4–5*, trans. Ian Scott-Kilvert (1987), *The Roman History: The Reign of Augustus*, London: Penguin Books.

Cicero (1986), *Selected Letters*, trans. D.R. Shackleton Bailey (1986), London: Penguin Classics.

Cicero (1979), *Selected Works, 2nd Philippic*, trans. Michael Grant (1979), London: Penguin Classics.

Cicero (1908–1909), *The Letters of Cicero*, trans. Evelyn S. Shuckburgh (1908–1909), London: George Bell & Sons.

Ciceronis Orationes Vol I, ed. A.C. Clark (1970), Oxford: Oxford University Press.

Connolly, Peter, *The Roman Fort* (1997), Oxford: Oxford University Press.

Diodorus Siculus (1933), *Bibliotheca Historica*, trans. C.H. Oldfather (1933), Loeb Classical Library, Cambridge, MA: Harvard University Press.

Erdkamp, Paul ed. (2013), *The Cambridge Companion to Ancient Rome*, Cambridge: Cambridge University Press.

Gildersleeve, B., & Lodge, G. (2009). *Gildersleeve's Latin Grammar* (Dover ed.). Mineola, NY: Dover Publications.

Herodotus (2003), *The Histories*, trans. Aubrey de Sélincourt, revised John Marincola (2003), London: Penguin Classics.

Hinds, Kathryn (2005), *Life in the Roman Empire: Religion*, New York: Benchmark Books.

Horace (1995), *Odes*, trans. David West (1995), Oxford: Oxford University Press.

Horace (2004), *The Odes*, ed. Kenneth Quinn (2004), London: Bristol Classical Press.

Hornblower and Spawforth (eds.) (1996), *The Oxford Classical Dictionary – Third Edition*, Oxford: Oxford University Press.

Johns, Catherine, *The Jewellery of Roman Britain: Celtic and Classical Traditions*, London: Routledge.

Kennedy, B., and Mountford, J. (1962), *The Revised Latin Primer*, London.

Kershaw, Stephen P. (2013), *A Brief History of the Roman Empire*, London: Constable & Robinson.

Livy in Seneca the Elder, *Declamations, Suasoria*, trans. John Murrell in LACTOR 7 'Late Republican Rome' (2017), London: London Association of Classical Teachers.

Livy (2002), *The Early History of Rome*, trans. Aubrey de Sélincourt (2002), London: Penguin Classics.

Livy (1972), *The War with Hannibal*, trans. Aubrey de Sélincourt (1972), London: Penguin Classics.

Metcalf, William E., ed. (2012), *The Oxford Handbook of Greek and Roman Coinage*, Oxford: Oxford University Press.

Morwood, J. (1999), *A Latin Grammar*, Oxford: Oxford University Press.

North, M., and Hillard, A. (1978), *Latin Prose Composition for Schools*, London: Paperduck.

Plutarch (1978), *Makers of Rome*, trans. Ian Scott-Kilvert (1978), London: Penguin Classics.

Plutarch (1979), *Fall of the Roman Republic*, trans. Rex Warner, revised Robin Seagar (1979), London: Penguin Classics.

Plutarch (1920), *Life of Antony* trans. Bernadotte Perrin (1920), Loeb Classical Library, Cambridge, MA: Harvard University Press.

Plutarch (1978), *Life of Antony*, trans. Ian Scott-Kilvert (1978), London: Penguin Classics.

Plutarch (1919), *Life of Caesar*, trans. Bernadotte Perrin (1919), Loeb Classical Library, Cambridge, MA: Harvard University Press.

Plutarch (1920), *The Parallel Lives*, trans. Bernadotte Perrin (1920), Loeb Classical Library, Cambridge, MA: Harvard University Press.

Polybius (1962), *Histories*, trans. Evelyn S. Shuckburgh (1962), London, New York: Macmillan.

Polybius (1960), *The Histories*, trans. William Roger Paton (1960), Loeb Classical Library, Cambridge, MA: Harvard University Press.

Quintilian, Institutio Oratoria, trans. Harold Edgeworth Butler (1920), London: William Heinemann.

Radice, Betty (1973), *Who's Who in the Ancient World*, London: Penguin Books.

Roller, Duane W. (2010), *Cleopatra: A Biography*, Oxford: Oxford University Press.

Sallust (1931), *Bellum Catilinae*, trans. John C. Rolfe (1931), Loeb Classical Library, Cambridge, MA: Harvard University Press.

Simpson, D. (1968), *Cassell's Latin Dictionary*: Latin-English, English-Latin (5th ed.), New York: Wiley.

Strabo (1917–33), *Geography*, trans. Horace Leonard Jones (1917–33), London: Heinemann.

Strabo (1960), *Geography*, trans. H.L. Jones (1960), Loeb Classical Library, Cambridge, MA: Harvard University Press.

Suetonius (2007), *The Twelve Caesars*, trans. Michael Grant (2007), London: Penguins Classics.

Suetonius (1970), *The Twelve Caesars*, trans. Robert Graves (1970), London: Penguin Classics.

Taciti Opera Minora, ed. H Furneaux, revised J.G.C. Anderson

Tacitus (2003), *Annals*, trans. Michael Grant (2003), London: Penguin Classics.

Tacitus (1979), *The Agricola and the Germania*, trans. H. Mattingly, revised S.A. Handford (1979), London: Penguin Classics.

Tacitus (2012), *The Annals*, trans. Cynthia Damon (2012), London: Penguin Classics.

The Letters of the Younger Pliny (1969), trans. Betty Radice (1969), London: Penguin Classics.

Titi Livi Ab Urbe Condita Libri I–V (1974), ed. R.M. Ogilvie (1974), Oxford: Oxford University Press.

Virgil (2003), *The Aeneid*, trans. David West (2003), London: Penguin Classics.

P. Vergili Maronis Opera (1985), ed. R.A.B. Mynors, Oxford: Oxford University Press.

Ward, Allen, Fritz M. Heichelheim and Cedric A. Yeo (2014), *History of the Roman People*, 6th ed. London and New York: Routledge.

West, David (1995), *Horace Odes 1 Carpe Diem: Text, Translation and Commentary*, Oxford: Oxford University Press.

Zanker, Paul (1990), trans. Alan Shapiro (1990), *The Power of Images in the Age of Augustus*, Ann Arbor: University of Michigan Press.

SOURCES OF ILLUSTRATIONS

The hand-drawn illustrations on pp. 17, 21, 25, 29, 32, 57, 59, 62, 65, 67, 91, 97, 101, 103, 106, 131, 133, 137, 141, 143, 169, 171, 174, 177, 179, 204, 208, 210, 215 and 219 are © Beatriz Lostalé.

7.1 UIG via Getty Images; **7.2** © Atlantide Phototravel/Corbis/VCG; **7.3** CM Dixon/Alamy Stock Photo; **7.4** Alamy Stock Photo; **7.5** DeAgostini/Getty Images; **7.6** Mr Melvin Cooley; **7.7** Universal History Archive / Contributor; **8.1** De Agostini/Getty Images; **8.2** Alamy Stock Photo; **8.3** Alamy Stock Photo; **8.4** Getty Images; **8.5** Alamy Stock Photo; **8.6** wildwinds.com; **9.1** The Print Collector/Alamy Stock Photo; **9.2** Peter Horree/Alamy Stock Photo; **9.3** Peter D Noyce/ Alamy Stock Photo; **9.4** Ann Ronan Pictures/ Print Collector/Getty Images; **9.5** Heritage Image Partnership Ltd/ Alamy Stock Photo; **9.6** GL Archive/Alamy Stock Photo; **9.7** Bloomsbury Academic; **10.1** Francisco Martinez / Alamy Stock Photo; **10.2** Granger Historical Picture Archive/Alamy Stock Photo; **10.3** Getty Images; **10.4** Peter Horee/Alamy Stock Photo; **10.5** Eden Breitz / Alamy Stock Photo; **10.6** DeAgostini/Getty Images; **11.1** Erin Babnik/Alamy Stock Photo; **11.2** Getty Images; **11.3** Shutterstock; **11.4** The Art Collector/Print Collector/Getty Images; **11.5** PHAS / Contributor; **11.6** Getty Images; **11.7** wildwinds.com; **11.8** © The Trustees of the British Museum.; **12.1** Bloomsbury Academic; **12.2** Alamy Stock Photo; **12.3** Alamy; **12.4** Alamy Stock Photo; **12.5** Print Collector / Contributor; **12.6** Tombstone of Regina (stone), Roman, (2nd century AD) / Arbeia Roman Fort & Museum, Tyne & Wear Archives & Museums / © Tyne & Wear Archives & Museums / Bridgeman Images; **12.7** Lisa Trentin.

SOURCES OF QUOTATIONS

9 "Young and vigorous . . ." Livy, *The History of Rome* 1.48, trans. Aubrey de Selincourt, *Livy, The Early History of Rome* (London: Penguin Classics, 2002); **10** "Then, when the rule . . ." Sallust, *Bellum Catilinae* 6.7–9.3, trans. Katharine Radice (2019); **11** "The father, while . . ." Aulius Gellius, *Attic Nights* 2.2.13, trans. Katharine Radice (2019); **12** "When the day . . ." Cicero, *Letters to Atticus* 1.14, trans. D.R. Shackleton Bailey, *Cicero Selected Letters* (London: Penguin Books, 1986); **46** "For after our . . ." Cicero, *de Oratore* 1.IV.14–V.18, trans. Katharine Radice (2019); **47** "So, criminal . . ." Cicero, *The Second Phillipic Against Antony* 85–87, trans. Michael Grant, *Cicero Selected Works* (London: Penguin Books, 1979) p.139; **48** "I must tell you . . ." Cicero, *Letters to Atticus* 1.18, trans. D.R. Shackleton Bailey, *Cicero Selected Letters* (London: Penguin Books, 1986); **48** "I am most grateful . . ." Cicero, *Letters to his Friends* 16.16, trans. Katharine Radice (2019); **48** "I shall next write . . ." Cicero, *Letters to his Friends* 14.7, trans. D.R. Shackleton Bailey, *Cicero Selected Letters* (London: Penguin Books, 1986); **82** "They choose . . ." Polybius, *The Histories*, trans. William Roger Paton, (Vol. 3) (Cambridge, Mass.: Harvard University Press, 1960); **85** "Caesar himself . . ." Caesar, *Gallic Wars* 4.23.1–24.4, trans. S.A. Handford, revised by Jane Gardner, *Caesar, The Conquest of Gaul* (London: Penguin Books, 1982); **86** "If we compare . . ." Plutarch, *Life of Caesar* 15, trans. Rex Warner, *Plutarch, Fall of the Roman Republic* (London: Penguin Books, 1979); **86** "an amalgamation of . . ." and "his achievements in . . ." both Cicero, *Second Philippic Against Antony* 116, trans. Michael Grant, *Cicero Selected Works* (London: Penguin Books, 1979); **121** "Caesar was . . ." Cassius Dio, *Roman History* Vol. IV 42.34–35, trans. Earnest Cary (Cambridge, Mass.: Harvard University Press, 1916); **122** "She received . . ." Plutarch, *Life of Antony* 26, trans. Ian Scott-Kilvert, *Makers of Rome* (London: Penguin Books, 1978); **123** "The Romans were so . . ." Cassius Dio, *Roman History* 50.4–5, trans. Ian Scott-Kilvert, *The Roman History: The Reign of Augustus* (London: Penguin Books, 1987); **124** "Now we must . . ." Horace, *Odes* 1.37, trans. David West, *Horace, Odes* (Oxford: Oxford University Press, 1995); **158** "The triumvirs posted . . ." Appian, *The Civil Wars* 4.32–4, trans. John Carter, (London: Penguin Books, 1996); **161** "In my sixth . . ." Augustus, *Res Gestae Divi Augusti* 34–35, trans. Alison Cooley, *Res Gestae Divi Augusti: Text, Translation, and Commentary* (Cambridge: Cambridge University Press, 2011); **162** "After Brutus . . ." Tacitus, *Annals* 1.2, trans. Cynthia Damon (London: Penguin Books, 2012); **196** "Most of the island . . ." Strabo, *Geography* 4.5.2, trans. Horace Leonard Jones, *The Geography of Strabo* Vol. 2, (Cambridge, Mass.: Harvard University Press, 1923); **197** "Boudicca drove . . ." Tacitus, *The Annals of Imperial Rome* 14.36–37, trans. Michael Grant (London: Penguin Books, 1986) p.330; **198** "To the spirits . . ." RIB 1065, trans. Robin George Collingwood and R.P. Wright, https://romaninscriptionsofbritain.org/inscriptions/1065; **199** "I have sent . . ." Stephen P. Kershaw *Tab. Vindol.* 346 in *A Brief History of the Roman Empire* (London: Constable & Robinson, 2013).